Darkest Hour

Darkest Hour

*How Churchill Brought Us
Back from the Brink*

ANTHONY MCCARTEN

VIKING
an imprint of
PENGUIN BOOKS

VIKING

UK | USA | Canada | Ireland | Australia
India | New Zealand | South Africa

Viking is part of the Penguin Random House group of companies whose
addresses can be found at global.penguinrandomhouse.com.

First published 2017
001

Copyright © Anthony McCarten, 2017

The moral right of the author has been asserted

Set in 12.5/14.75 pt Garamond MT Std
Typeset by Jouve (UK), Milton Keynes
Printed in Great Britain by Clays Ltd, St Ives plc

A CIP catalogue record for this book is available from the British Library

ISBN: 978-0-241-32710-4

Contents

Introduction

Over the years, my bookshelves have always held a few volumes whose subject could broadly be called 'Great Speeches That Changed the World'. The thesis of these books is that this questionable feat has been achieved multiple times, under the right conditions: timely words, alloyed to a timely idea, spoken by a timely, brilliant person.

In these anthologies I could expect to find at least one speech by Winston Spencer Churchill. Often two or three. They sounded slightly old-fashioned, lofty, with his wordsmithery elevated to near pomposity, yet always they contained a brace of exquisite phrases, superb sound-bites that would have been just as memorable to an audience 1,000 years in the past as 1,000 years in the future.

As I became a minor student of the speeches of Nehru, Lenin, George Washington, Hitler, Martin Luther King and others, I fed my admiration for the art of oratory and these men's rising arrow-showers of words. At their best they had the power to summon into being the unexpressed thoughts of a people, to galvanize disparate emotions into a locus of shared passion capable of making the unthinkable a reality.

What struck me as remarkable about Churchill was that he wrote three of these speeches within just four weeks. For him, May 1940 was a single span of inspired grandiloquence. And he did so all by himself. What was it about that moment that spurred him to such heights? What political and personal pressures compelled him, three times in so few days, to turn coal into such diamonds?

The simple answer? Britain was at war. The horrors of Blitzkrieg saw one European democracy after another fall in rapid succession to the Nazi boot and shell. Facing this horror, with pen in hand and typist-secretary at the ready, Britain's new Prime Minister wondered what words could rouse the country to a heroic resistance when the invasion of the country by a terrible foe seemed mere hours away.

This book, and the screenplay for the film *Darkest Hour*, emerged from these questions and from this fascination. The aim is to look at the working methods, leadership qualities, thinking and psychological states of one man in these critical days – a man who believed, in the core of his rather poetic soul, that words mattered, that they counted, and could intercede to change the world.

My initial research led me to focus on the period from Churchill's unexpected promotion to the prime ministership on 10 May 1940 until the near-complete evacuation of the endangered British army from Dunkirk (which signalled the imminent fall of France) on 4 June – the date, by the way, on which he delivered the last speech in his rhetorical trilogy.

The National Archives provided a vital research tool: access to the actual minutes of the War Cabinet meetings that Winston chaired during those dimming days. These shed light on a rare period of uncertainty in his career, a wobble in his otherwise steady leadership. Pedestals are for statues, not for people, and a close reading of the minutes reveals not only a leader in trouble, under attack from all sides and uncertain at times what direction to take, but also a story I had not heard: of a British War Cabinet that, had it made peace with the enemy, would have reshaped the world for ever. How close did Winston come to entering into a peace deal with Hitler? Dangerously so, I discovered.

The question before that War Cabinet, gathering in 1940 initially at the Admiralty (a short walk up Whitehall from Downing Street) and thereafter in its bunker deep under the Treasury Building, was whether Britain was to fight on alone, perhaps to the destruction of its armed forces and even the nation itself, or play it safe by exploring a peace deal with Hitler. The Italian Ambassador in London, in exchange for some colonial trades in Africa and Malta and Gibraltar, had indicated he was prepared to ask the Italian fascist leader, Benito Mussolini, to act as the go-between for Berlin and London in such a deal. With Winston's rival for the leadership, Lord Halifax, emphatic in his call for this option to be explored, at least until Hitler's terms could be discerned, and with Winston's predecessor as PM, Neville Chamberlain, agreeing that this seemed the only sensible way to escape almost certain annihilation, Winston faced some very lonely hours in which he truly had only his own counsel to draw upon.

Many readers will be astonished to learn that the great Winston Churchill, presented to history as a staunch and unyielding foe of Hitler, told his colleagues in the War Cabinet that he would not object in principle to peace talks with Germany 'if Herr Hitler was prepared to make peace on terms of the restoration of German colonies and the overlordship of Central Europe'. At one point, on 26 May, he went further, and was reported to have stated 'that he would be *thankful* to get out of our present difficulties, provided we retained the essentials of our vital strength, even at the cost of some cession of territory'. What territory? Not only European, but *British* territory. And there was more. Chamberlain's diary for 27 May records that Churchill told the War Cabinet that 'if we could get out of this jam by giving up Malta and Gibraltar and some African colonies he [Winston] would jump at it'.

Was Churchill seriously considering entering into peace talks with a homicidal maniac whom he loathed beyond all others? It would seem so. Such were the pressures upon him that he not only entertained the idea but permitted Halifax to begin drafting a top-secret memorandum to the Italians, laying out Britain's terms and taking the first step in a process to find out how severe Hitler's would be.

For those who might find that any image of a Churchill willing to seriously consider such a deal belittles the great man, doing injury to his reputation, I would argue the opposite: that the public image of a pugnacious battler who never doubted himself does not do him justice; it makes him unreal, a cliché, less a three-dimensional human being than the product of a collective dream. Rather than diminish him, his indecision, his ability to put on a strong face in order to keep morale up while thinking of different solutions, recommends him.

These, then, are the dark hours to which the title refers, but from them – and, moreover, because of them – Churchill emerged with two *coups de théâtre*, magnificent examples of peroration: the first delivered to a group of

**HITLER HAD ALREADY INVADED
CZECHOSLOVAKIA, POLAND,
DENMARK AND NORWAY.**

———

**HE WAS NOW POISED TO CONQUER
THE REST OF EUROPE.**

———

**IN BRITAIN, PARLIAMENT HAD LOST
FAITH IN ITS LEADER, NEVILLE CHAMBERLAIN.
THE SEARCH FOR A REPLACEMENT
HAD ALREADY BEGUN.**

———

1. A House Divided

The Debating Chamber of the British Parliament was in an uproar of condemnation and invective. 'Out, out!' they howled from the upper galleries, where aristocrats and members of the House of Lords craned forward to get a clear view. 'Resign, man! Resign!' British politics had never seen anything quite like it. Members of the Opposition parties were rolling their order papers into daggers and thrusting them in the direction of the collapsed, already failing and secretly ailing figure sitting in front of the despatch box – the Conservative Prime Minister of Great Britain, Neville Chamberlain.

But Chamberlain, for many reasons, was reluctant to stand down as leader – not least because of his deep uncertainty about who could possibly succeed him.

Britain had been at war for eight months, and it was going badly. Both politicians and the public were baying not just for a leader, but, as all great times demand, a *great* leader – one capable of delivering what only great leaders can: words that can move and sway and convince and galvanize and inspire and even forge in the hearts of the public levels of feeling they do not know they have. From these words would come actions and, depending on the wisdom of these actions, either triumph or bloody defeat.

And there was perhaps a more surprising ingredient

that any nation in grave crisis might wish to find in its leader: doubt. The vital ability to doubt his or her own judgements, to possess a mind capable of holding two contrary ideas at the same time and only then to synthesize them; to have a mind not made up, and so remain in conversation with all views. This contrasted with a mind made up which could remain in conversation with only one person: the self. Britain had little use for an ideologue in these days. What it needed was a 360-degree thinker.

As Oliver Cromwell wrote in 1650 to the Church of Scotland: 'I beseech you, in the bowels of Christ, think it possible you may be mistaken.' In these doubtful times, and with the issues faced by the British nation so grave that its very future hung on its next moves, the great question was: where could such a leader be found?

'You have sat too long here for any good you have been doing. Depart, I say, and let us have done with you. In the name of God, go!' Leo Amery, Member of Parliament for Sparkbrook, in Birmingham, resumed his seat to thunderous applause on this, the first night of the now-legendary Norway Debate on Tuesday, 7 May 1940. The House had now been sitting for almost nine hours. It was a warm early summer's evening and darkness had fallen. His words were the knife in fellow-Conservative Chamberlain's side.

Britain was a country divided, and the Government, instead of pulling together, was being torn apart by egos and petty differences which had contributed to catastrophic military failures on both the battlefield and the high seas. The prospect of fascism succeeding and of democracy drawing to a close in Europe was no longer unimaginable.

The seeds of the famous debate happening in the Chamber that night were sown five days earlier, when the news broke that Britain was evacuating her troops from the Norwegian port of Trondheim after coming under heavy Nazi attack for the first time. Leo Amery and members of Lord Salisbury's Watching Committee, made up of Conservative MPs and Lords with the object of holding the Government to account, along with an All-Party Parliamentary Action Group, with a similar objective but led by the Liberal MP Clement Davies and including members of the Labour Party, had agreed to force a debate on the blunders made during this first encounter with Nazi troops, and, with this debate, attempt to finally rid themselves of the leader they felt was failing them and the country.

Chamberlain had first begun to speak to the House on the 'Conduct of the War' at 3.48 p.m. on 7 May, the first of two days of debate. His words, his attempt at a salvage job, did nothing to strengthen his position or to allay fears that Britain was essentially headed for a wreck. Rather, they confirmed him as being tired and defensive, a man who would only speed the nation towards peril. Looking 'heart-broken and shrivelled', as one commentator later put it, he soldiered on, as far more memorable phrases were hurled back at him by his enemies. He knew these phrases well, for he had fashioned them himself: 'Peace in our time!' (his lofty promise of a year earlier) and 'Missed the bus!' (his reference to what he had seen as Hitler's lost opportunity to wreak any havoc at all in Europe). Now they exploded like hand-grenades at his feet.

What muted support Chamberlain received during this speech was described by Labour's Arthur Greenwood as 'synthetic', for the mood of the House had never been graver: 'Its heart is troubled. It is anxious; it is more than anxious; it is apprehensive.'

After Chamberlain retook his seat, the Conservative MP Admiral Sir Roger Keyes, dressed in full military regalia (unheard of in the Commons), made his theatrical entrance and silenced the House. A long-time critic of the PM, Keyes denounced the Government's 'shocking story of ineptitude'. He knew what he was talking about: he had witnessed the blunders first hand.

Next to speak was Clement Attlee, leader of the Opposition Labour Party. He was a man not exactly known for oratorical zingers, but his theme clearly inspired him, and he spoke cuttingly of the Government's 'inept' handling of the situation:

It is not Norway alone. Norway comes as the culmination of many other discontents. People are saying that those mainly responsible for the conduct of affairs are men who have had an almost uninterrupted career of failure. Norway follows Czecho-Slovakia [sic] and Poland. Everywhere the story is 'Too late.' The Prime Minister talked about missing the buses. What about all the buses which he and his associates have missed since 1931? They all missed the peace buses but caught the war bus. The people find that these men who have been consistently wrong in their judgment of events, the same people who thought that Hitler would not attack Czecho-Slovakia, who thought that Hitler could be appeased, seem not to have realised that Hitler would attack Norway.

Just before midnight on 7 May, Chamberlain's fate was sealed, but it seemed to many that the Prime Minister himself was unable to recognize it. This blindness was nothing new. John 'Jock' Colville, his Principal Private Secretary (PPS), had written in his diary on Monday, 6 May 1940: 'The P.M. is very depressed about the press attacks on him . . . I think he suffers from a curious vanity and self-esteem which were born at Munich [referring to September 1938, when Chamberlain was judged to have acquiesced to all of Hitler's demands but maintained he had negotiated peace] and have flourished, in spite of a good many wounds, ever since.'

So it was that on the morning of 8 May, before the second and most decisive day of the debate, and in light of Chamberlain's clear reluctance to stand down as leader, members from both the Watching Committee and the All-Party Parliamentary Action Group convened once more in Parliament. They decided to force a division of the House where the Members would be asked to vote on what the Labour MP Herbert Morrison explained would 'indicate whether they are *content* with the conduct of affairs or whether they are *apprehensive* about the conduct of affairs': in other words, deliver the knock-out punch by draining Chamberlain of the number of supporters he needed to effectively go on as leader.

Word went out to the party Whips, who began frantically to strike deals of support among members of the various voting blocs. Colville wrote in his diary how senior Conservatives were 'all talking about reconstituting the Government and seriously discussing schemes such as a bargain (to be put by [Lord] Halifax to [Herbert] Morrison) whereby the Opposition Labour Party should be asked to come into the Government in return for the dropping of key government bigwigs – Sam Hoare, Kingsley Wood, [Sir John] Simon etc., but only on the stipulation that Chamberlain retained the leadership'.

The knives were out and were particularly sharp then when the House met at 2.45 p.m. to resume debating the Conduct of the War.

Pleas to the Labour MP Herbert Morrison not to divide the House had fallen on deaf ears. Labour members had made up their minds: they would not serve in a National Government led by 'that man' Chamberlain. Morrison spoke passionately for twenty minutes, urging the members of the House to vote with their conscience and to think deeply about whether Great Britain could continue with the current state of affairs given the pitiful captaincy of a war only eight months old. The message was simple and clear: not only had Chamberlain to go, but with him all those who had supported the policy of appeasement, the flawed belief that had dominated British policy towards Germany during the 1930s – namely, that a dictator, if well fed, would retire, sated, to his cave.

Out then must also go Sir Samuel Hoare (Minister for Air) and Sir John Simon (Chancellor of the Exchequer).

The decision to resign belonged to Chamberlain. Surely, weakened by attacks from all sides, he would yield. But still he resisted, remaining on his bench and only occasionally looking up into the harsh glare of detraction and calumny. When he did finally rise to his feet – as the memoirs of the Labour MP Hugh Dalton record – he furiously 'jumped up, showing his teeth like a rat in a corner, and cried: "I accept the challenge and I ask my friends, and I still have some friends in this House, to support the Government tonight in the Lobby."'

Chamberlain's failure to grasp the magnitude of the situation facing the nation only deepened the fury of his opponents in the House, and soon members from both sides were leaping to their feet, attempting to catch the Speaker's eye for their turn to speak. Shouts of 'Go!' and 'Resign!' echoed around the Chamber, but still Chamberlain was unmoved. Clearly, one last devastating attack was required, and the perfect man to deliver it rose to his feet. The raucous Chamber fell silent. David Lloyd George, the former Liberal wartime Prime Minister himself, slowly at first but then in a more and more visceral fashion, set about chastising Chamberlain for exposing Britain to 'the worst strategic position in which this country has ever been placed'. The climax came with a call directly to Chamberlain's conscience: 'Give an example of sacrifice, because there is nothing that can contribute more to victory in this war than that he should sacrifice the seals of office.'

Watching from the gallery above, nodding in approval,

was the speaker's wife, Dame Margaret Lloyd George, who would later write:

> I am so glad my husband had a hand in turning Chamberlain out. I have never seen such a *scene*, the House was determined to get rid of him & Sir John Simon & Sam Hoare . . . The howl that followed him out was awful & the shouts of 'Go, go'. I have *never* seen a P.M. retiring with such a send off. He has brought a plight, & the Tory party always said after Munich, 'He has saved us from War'. Poor things, they must have had an eye opener.

The debate raged on into the night. Chamberlain would not go gently. He was just weeks away from admitting for the first time in his diary that he was in 'considerable pain' from the bowel cancer that would lead to his death in just a few short months. Perhaps, in his heart, he knew that this moment was his last chance to avoid being blamed for the collapse of Europe, democracy and the British way of life. And perhaps there was another, more recondite reason for his reluctance to go.

A few seats down the front bench from him sat a man who, in reality, was far more culpable in respect of the previous month's Norway campaign, which had seen the loss of 1,800 men, one aircraft carrier, two cruisers, seven destroyers and a submarine.

Winston Spencer Churchill, as First Lord of the Admiralty, had been the principal architect of the country's disastrous naval strategy. But with attentions diverted entirely onto the PM, and his own turn to speak yet to come, Churchill remained out of the firing line, biding his time, keeping his fingerprints off the murder weapon.

Winston was not popular. Indeed, he was something of a joke figure at this time, an egotist, a 'half-breed American' who, in the words of one Conservative MP, Sir Henry ('Chips') Channon, stood for only one thing: himself. Hard to imagine, now, with Britain having a reported 3,500 pubs and hotels, over 1,500 halls and establishments, and twenty-five streets bearing his name, and with his face emblazoned on everything from beer coasters to door-mats – not to mention his bust sporadically appearing in the Oval Office of the President of the United States – but in May 1940 his was the furthest thing in most people's minds from a safe pair of hands.

Still labelled a turncoat by many in the party for 'crossing the floor' – switching political allegiance from Conservative to Liberal in 1904, and then back to Conservative again in 1924 – Churchill had nonetheless proven himself startlingly loyal to Chamberlain. So he was on this day too, when, in the midst of Lloyd George's speech, he offered himself for punishment in the PM's stead: 'I take complete responsibility for everything that has been done by the Admiralty, and I take my full share of the burden.'

Lloyd George, whose flow Churchill had interrupted, deftly replied, 'The right hon. Gentleman must not allow himself to be converted into an air-raid shelter to keep the splinters from hitting his colleagues.'

Churchill's *mea culpa* was but the first instalment of a

faux rescue mission, one calculated to fail but also to win over his colleagues with a moving display of loyalty – a golden opportunity then to show how 'prime ministerial' he could be when he tried, and to thereby pencil his own name in as a dark horse in the race.

When his turn finally came to speak, and speak at length, the rebels leaned forward, expectant, hopeful for immortal phrases of condemnation, but he uttered nothing immortal, nothing indeed that Chamberlain couldn't have inscribed himself upon his own headstone. Instead Churchill offered praise so exquisitely faint that it delivered just what he wanted: too little, too late. The rescuing verbiage Winston might have uncorked was clearly being saved for another day, another hour. For he had speeches already fermenting, phrases being silently rehearsed that would serve another, more spectacular, purpose in the days to come, and they would not be wasted here.

When Winston sat again, he had achieved perhaps one thing with his speech: his own star, if not yet shining bright, had lost a little of its tarnish at a critical moment when all the others' stars had gone out.

Thus, when the Speaker called for the House to divide and vote, most minds were in no doubt. Chips Channon recalled:

We watched the insurgents file out of the Opposition Lobby . . . 'Quislings', we shouted at them, 'Rats'. 'Yes-men', they replied . . . '281 to 200' . . . There were shouts of 'Resign – Resign' . . . and that old ape Josh Wedgwood began to wave his arms about and sing 'Rule Britannia'.

Harold Macmillan, next to him, joined in, but they were howled down. Neville appeared bowled over by the ominous figures, and was the first to rise. He looked grave and thoughtful and sad . . . No crowds tonight to cheer him, as there were before Munich – only a solitary little man, who had done his best for England.

Despite this narrow win, Chamberlain had lost the confidence of his party as a total of forty-one Conservative MPs had voted against the Government. The youngest of these was John Profumo, who, at just twenty-five, had sneaked away from his barracks to attend the vote and was later castigated by the fearsome Tory Chief Whip, David Margesson: 'you utterly contemptible little shit . . . for the rest of your life you will be ashamed of what you did last night'. With the Conservative majority slashed to just eighty-one, there could be no more debate. What was needed was a public crusade akin to the private thoughts of Chamberlain's PPS, Jock Colville, who noted how 'disgusting' it was 'that everybody is concentrating their energies on an internal political crisis (*à la française*) instead of taking thought for the morrow about Hitler's next move'. A new leader must be found. But who? Who was worthy? And who was ready?

Political infighting had clouded the desperate situation that Britain found herself in. She needed someone not just to unite the Conservative Party but also to bring together the Opposition parties and Armed Forces, the latter having failed to work together in this first military defeat that so abruptly ended the so-called 'Phoney War' of the last eight months initiated by Germany's invasion of Poland.

Channon noted in his diary that 'rumour and intrigue, plot and counter-plot' were now rife among leading politicians. But it was not Churchill, whom so many had defended and praised in the previous days' debates, who was garnering the support of the Conservative Party. One name, above all, was emerging as the only natural successor to Chamberlain. It was that of a man who was not even permitted to sit on either side of the Commons. This was Lord Halifax, the current Foreign Secretary and member of the House of Lords, who had been quietly watching the proceedings from the Peers' Gallery, alongside fellow Lords, ambassadors and leading dignitaries from among Britain's allies.

A major roadblock to Halifax taking over from Chamberlain lay in the constitution itself. The unique nature of the British parliamentary system stipulates that anyone with a seat in the House of Lords cannot *also* stand for or serve as an elected Member of Parliament in the House of Commons. A serious constitutional hurdle would thus arise should Lord Halifax wish to serve as the Prime Minister and parliamentary leader when he was not a parliamentarian himself.

Halifax's biographer, Andrew Roberts, describes how the Foreign Secretary and the Prime Minister had briefly discussed the previously unthinkable outcome of a Halifax leadership during the second day's debate, on 8 May. Chamberlain had 'made it clear that should he be forced to resign he wanted Halifax to take over', but when business resumed on Thursday, 9 May, Lord Halifax's response was not as expected. In his diary, he wrote that the Prime Minister asked him to come to No. 10 Downing Street at 10.15 a.m., where Chamberlain told Halifax that 'he thought the position could not be left as it was by the House of Commons Division, and that it was essential to restore confidence in the Government'. Again, Chamberlain returned to the subject of his replacement, to which Halifax replied (as noted in his diary), 'if it were myself he [Chamberlain] might continue to serve in the Government. I put all the arguments that I could think of against myself, laying considerable emphasis on the difficult position of a Prime Minister unable to make contact with the centre of gravity in the House of Commons.'

One could be forgiven for suspecting false modesty here, as Halifax, by his subsequent actions, would show that he wished very much to keep his hands on the levers of power. In his diary, he remarked that 'The conversation and the evident drift of his [Chamberlain's] mind left me with a bad stomach ache. I told him again, as I had told him the day before, that if the Labour people said that they would only serve under me I should tell them that I was not prepared to do it.'

A stomach ache? The Conservative MP R. A. 'Rab' Butler recorded a rather different recollection of a conversation he had with the wily Halifax after his meeting with Chamberlain:

He [Halifax] told me that he felt he could do the job. He also felt that Churchill needed a restraining influence.

Could that restraint be better exercised as Prime Minister or as a Minister in Churchill's government? Even if he chose the former role, Churchill's qualities and experience would surely mean that he would be 'running the war anyway' and Halifax's own position would speedily turn into a sort of honorary Prime Minister.

Despite Halifax's protestations, this seems a more credible reason for declining the one role that defines the culmination of success in British politics. Halifax's reservations were fundamentally caused by his position in the Lords preventing him from sitting as Prime Minister in the House of Commons. So where would that leave Halifax as leader of the nation?

To be handed the title of leader of Great Britain but to wield no real power, in addition to being consistently undermined by Churchill, whom he knew to be a better strategist and war leader than himself, was hardly an attractive prospect for a man of Halifax's stature and ego. But how could his fellow politicians have so misjudged his intentions? The Lords wanted Halifax, King George VI wanted Halifax, even Labour wanted Halifax. It seemed they were mustering their support for a man who all of a sudden had little interest in taking the job, at least within the current framework.

And so it was that Churchill's name, incredibly, worked itself to the top of the list.

What a turnaround this was. The unthinkable, just days before, was now being considered as a viable option. But none were easy about the choice, for what a conundrum he was, an amalgam of irreconcilable parts: showman, show-off, blow-hard, poet, journalist, historian, adventurer, melancholic, arguably an alcoholic, inarguably of pensionable age, at sixty-five a man whose primary distinction was as a consistent failure, reliably misreading the writing on the wall, getting things badly wrong too often, and too often when he needed to get them very, very right. Considered a dangerous warmonger for his mistakes as First Lord of the Admiralty during the Great War (principally for the human disaster that was the Gallipoli campaign against the Ottomans in the Eastern Mediterranean, in which 45,000 Commonwealth men lost their lives), he had spent most of the last ten years in a self-described 'wilderness' after a catalogue of other mistakes, among them his opposition to Indian Home Rule, and his rough handling of a miners' strike in Wales.

It can only be natural that Churchill, after so many mistakes, harboured doubts about his *own* suitability. Indeed, given the enormity of his mistakes, it would be the more extraordinary claim – and be psychologically untenable – to conclude otherwise. He knew he was flawed. He knew that at this point in his career he was the butt of many jokes and the delight of cartoonists: something that many people today who only know what he *became* might find startling. While his own ambition to assume the role was not in question – he had desired the role of Prime Minister since childhood, so as to complete a family narrative left unfinished by his late father, Randolph – he knew how poorly he had handled these past crises, and how high the human cost had been. But if he himself deemed self-doubt a negative – speaking often of leadership as the decisive application of an informed vision – there is no reason we should agree with him, for as long as self-doubt is not paralysing, it also allows for alternative points of view to be given their proper weight and consideration and so can be considered a vital step in any sound decision-making process.

Typical of the general view of Winston at this time was that of Sir Edmund Ironside, Commander of the Imperial General Staff, who noted his ambivalence in his diary: 'Naturally the only man who can succeed [Chamberlain] is Winston but he is too unstable, though he has the genius to bring the war to an end.'

And so, while elevation to the top job was far from a certainty, one thing Winston clearly had over Halifax was his first-hand experience of war. His military credentials – he had served in both the Boer War and the First World War, and observed several other skirmishes as a journalist – were, for all his missteps, superior in every respect to those of the Foreign Secretary, who knew little of battle or even military strategy, and had only a month before revealed his ignorance of matters military: Roberts writes how when Halifax was asked if 'an attack on Trondheim might have been more effective than one on Narvik, he was forced to admit that he was not competent to answer the question'.

Another minus in Halifax's column, blemishing his standing with the public, was his backing for the policy of appeasement. Even when Hitler proved insatiable, Halifax had persisted in his belief in peace, and peace at almost any price.

The field, then, was unusually empty of other viable contenders. Even Anthony Eden's popularity had fallen by the wayside. In March 1939, Eden had the support of 38 per cent of the public in an opinion poll of who they would like to see as the next Prime Minister, compared to Churchill and Halifax's paltry 7 per cent. Having resigned as Foreign Secretary over Chamberlain's policy of appeasement, he had rejoined the Government as Secretary of State for Dominion Affairs, but this lower-ranking position eliminated him from any potential leadership bid at this juncture.

Thus, with Halifax shrinking for now from the task, Churchill assumed the strut and mien and talk – above all the talk – of a leader.

To subtly advance his cause without appearing to do so, Churchill met several of his close allies on the morning of 9 May. Eden joined him at the Admiralty, and while Churchill shaved he 'rehearsed to me [Eden] the events of the previous evening. He thought that Neville would not be able to bring in Labour and that a national Government must be formed.'

Next Churchill saw his old friend Lord Beaverbrook, the powerful newspaper baron, who tried to elicit a clear answer on the question of leadership. Again, Churchill gave nothing away, saying, 'I will serve under any Minister capable of prosecuting the War.'

Churchill had lunch with Eden and the Lord Privy Seal, Sir Kingsley Wood, that day. There, Wood made it clear he supported the First Lord of the Admiralty for leader and urged him 'that if asked he should make plain his willingness [to succeed]'. As Eden recalled, he had been 'surprised to find Kingsley Wood there giving a warning that Chamberlain would want Halifax to succeed him and would want Churchill to agree. Wood advised: "Don't agree, and don't say anything." I was shocked that Wood should talk in this way, for he had been so much Chamberlain's man, but it was good counsel and I seconded it.'

Chamberlain, with his mind made up to step down, summoned Halifax and Churchill to Downing Street at 4.30 that afternoon.

The contradictory accounts of this history-altering meeting have become something of a legend. What we do know is that in attendance were Neville Chamberlain, Lord Halifax, Winston Churchill and the Chief Whip, David Margesson. The PM had gathered them all together to inform them of his decision to step down and to decide upon whom the task of leading the country should fall. The most immediate account of events comes from Halifax's diary. He recalls how Chamberlain affirmed his decision to step down but did not indicate a preferred replacement, only that 'he would happily do service under either man'. As the leaders of the Labour Party – who held the whip-hand in any talks about the composition of a unity government – were due to travel to Bournemouth that night for their conference, the Government's concession that any new administration must feature them in prominent positions meant any decision had to be made swiftly.

The tension was unbearable for Halifax. Recalling that

his 'stomach ache continued', it seems that his body was physically rejecting the idea of leadership. His thoughts were not just of Winston's 'qualities compared to [his] own', but they also returned to the question of what exactly his position would be were he to assume the leadership: 'Winston would be running Defence . . . and I [as a Peer] should have no access to the House of Commons. The inevitable result would be that being outside both these points of vital contact I should speedily become a more or less honorary Prime Minister, living in a kind of twilight just outside the things that really mattered.' This poignant assessment of the situation was followed by a somewhat scathing opinion of Winston's 'suitable expression of regard and humility, [he] said he could not but feel the force of what I had said, and the P.M. reluctantly, and Winston evidently with much less reluctance, finished by accepting my view'. This account is corroborated by the diary entry made the same day by the Permanent Under-Secretary to the Foreign Office and Halifax's right-hand man, Sir Alexander Cadogan.

Churchill's account of events is perhaps the least reliable of all. He incorrectly identified the meeting as occurring on the following day, 10 May, in his memoir *The Gathering Storm*. With true Churchillian verve, he wrote of the moments following Chamberlain's charged question – 'Can you see any reason, Winston, why in these days a Peer should not be prime minister?' – after which Winston 'remained silent [and] a very long pause ensued. It certainly seemed longer than the two minutes which one observes in the commemorations of Armistice Day.'

What he wished history to record was that it was a silence so uncomfortable that it prompted Lord Halifax to break it and, with his nerves shredded, speak at length about why he could not become Prime Minister. According to David Margesson, the silence was broken almost immediately by Halifax urging Churchill's greater fitness for leadership in war.

Silence or no, they had come to an agreement. Sir Alexander Cadogan noted in his diary that by this stage 'Chief Whip [Margesson] and others think feeling in the House has been veering towards him [Churchill]. If N.C. [Chamberlain] remains [in the Cabinet] – as he is ready to do – his advice and judgement would steady Winston.' And, with that, they were ready to let the lion out of his cage. When the talks ended, Chamberlain met Labour's Clement Attlee and Arthur Greenwood at 6.15 p.m. The two men confirmed that they were willing to enter into a National Government but suspected the Labour Party would not serve under Chamberlain, and so would have to consult the Executive when they reached the party conference in Bournemouth the following day.

Meanwhile, Halifax and Churchill retired to the garden of No. 10 Downing Street for tea. Churchill recalled in his memoirs that they talked about 'nothing in particular' before he returned to the Admiralty to prepare for the task ahead. He dined with Anthony Eden again that evening, recounting to him the drama of the day's events. Churchill said he 'hoped NC [Chamberlain] would stay, would lead House of Commons and continue as leader of [the] party'. It was expected that Chamberlain would tender his resignation to the King the following afternoon and advise him to send for Churchill. What was more interesting was that Winston would become not only Prime Minister but also give himself the newly created role of Minister of Defence.

Whatever the outcome of these long and intense meetings on 9 May might yet be, one thing was certain: Winston Churchill would be running the war. And Churchill's hour was coming not a moment too soon. Even then Hitler was quietly lining up his tanks on the borders of Holland, Belgium and France, ready to execute a *Blitzkrieg* or lightning war so terrifying that talk in the corridors of power would soon turn to the potential surrender of the entirety of Europe to the brutal Nazi hordes.

Churchill later recalled, 'I felt as if I were walking with destiny, and that all my past life had been but a preparation for this hour and for this trial . . . I thought I knew a good deal about it all, I was sure I should not fail.' The fate of the nation was now in his hands, and what he did with it was nothing short of extraordinary.

2. The Social Wastrel

So who was this man about to lead Britain into one of the greatest conflicts in her history?

Trying to 'nutshell' Winston Leonard Spencer-Churchill is a task so elusive, we have seen more ink expended on him than on any other figure in history. Books on him dwarf in number those about Washington, Caesar or Napoleon, and render insipid the collective attempts to describe his great enemy Adolf Hitler. This is for the simple reason that seldom in history has a figure done so much, both good and bad, and made such a difference in the course of a long and packed lifetime, let alone the sixty-five years before this story begins in the House of Commons on those tense May days in 1940.

Titanic orator. Drunk. Wit. Patriot. Imperialist. Visionary. Tank designer. Blunderer. Swashbuckler. Aristocrat. Prisoner. War hero. War criminal. Conqueror. Laughing stock. Bricklayer. Racehorse-owner. Soldier. Painter. Politician. Journalist. Nobel Prize-winning author. The list goes on and on, but each label, when taken alone, fails to do him justice; when taken together, they offer a challenge on a par with tossing twenty jigsaw puzzles together and expecting a single unified picture.

So where can we begin if we are to see him whole, view

him cleanly, free of myth, from a modern perspective and employing today's familiar psychological language?

Imagine the following: Winston sitting in a chair before a modern psychiatrist. What category of person would he be deemed? Would he, after speaking of his mood swings, emerge with a diagnosis of being bi-polar, of manic depression, and find himself gulping lithium? Or would he, after confessing all his oddities, his eccentric non-conformism, his impulsiveness and risk-taking and love of red or green velvet one-piece romper suits, be told he's repressing childhood trauma and abandonment issues? What shrink would be brave enough to tell Winston Churchill that he had a serious yet manageable narcissistic personality with a histrionic accentuation? A simple list of what the man *drank* each day would most likely see him written up as a self-medicating alcoholic under today's definitions.

So let us begin on the outside, and work our way inwards: looking first at the forces that shaped him, during those early years that hint at the man he most certainly became – one as capable of fear as confidence, of self-doubt as much as conviction, of self-shame as much as self-esteem, of bull-dog pugnacity as much as harrowing indecision.

Winston was foremost a Victorian. He spent the first twenty-seven years of his life under the Queen's reign, when the empire was at flood tide; his world view was sculpted by the supposed dominance of British superiority across the globe.

He was also an aristocrat. Born at Blenheim Palace, Oxfordshire, on 30 November 1874, he was the first child of Lord Randolph Churchill, son of the 7th Duke of Marlborough, and his wife, Lady Randolph Churchill (née Jennie Jerome) – supposedly two months premature but most likely conceived out of wedlock.

Randolph and Jennie had been introduced by the Prince of Wales, later King Edward VII, at the Cowes Regatta on the Isle of Wight in August 1873. Winston writes in his book *My Early Life* how Randolph 'fell in love with her at first sight', and, impetuously, the pair became engaged just three days later. They were married in a small ceremony in the British Embassy in Paris on 15 April 1874, two months after the groom had won his first seat in the House of Commons for the Conservative Party at just twenty-five years of age.

Jennie was twenty when Winston was born. She adopted the typical upper-class-Victorian approach to childcare, and left her son and his younger brother, Jack, to be largely raised by their devoted nanny, Mrs Elizabeth Everest, whom Winston affectionately nicknamed 'Old Woom'; she called him 'Winny'. Jennie was a glamorous young society woman and the daughter of a wealthy American tycoon from New York known as 'The King of Wall Street'. Interrupting a life of parties, travel and love affairs to look after her children was not Jennie's style. Winston later wrote, 'My mother made the same brilliant impression upon my childhood's eye. She shone for me like the Evening Star. I loved her dearly – but at a distance.'

It was an even worse situation with his father. Winston idolized him, but Lord Randolph's life was consumed by his political career. Recognized as a great orator, Randolph was a champion of progressive Conservatism and a respected Chancellor of the Exchequer and Leader of the House of Commons. However, this meteoric rise as a shining new light in the Tory party did not last long. His star faded, and after less than a year in Cabinet he resigned on 20 December 1886 over problems with the unpopular Budget he had submitted. Randolph remained an MP but the health problems that had plagued him for years advanced rapidly.

The condition from which he was reportedly suffering was syphilis. Speculation remains about when and how exactly he contracted it, but it was possibly as early as 1875. Over the twenty years until his early death, at just forty-five, he suffered an aggressive deterioration of his mental capacities caused by the disease's 'dementia paralytica' – a general paralysis of the insane. This left no opportunity for father and son to grow close and understand each other – a loss which weighed heavily on Winston for the rest of his life. In *My Early Life* he wrote:

My father died on January 24 in the early morning. Summoned from a neighbouring house where I was sleeping, I ran in the darkness across Grosvenor Square, then lapped in snow. His end was quite painless. Indeed, he had long been in stupor. All my dreams of comradeship with him, of entering Parliament at his side and in his support, were ended. There remained for me only to pursue his aims and vindicate his memory.

Winston, like many boys of his class at this time, had been packed off to boarding school at the age of seven and found the experience utterly miserable: 'After all ... I had been so happy in my nursery with all my toys ... Now it was to be all lessons.' Flogging of pupils was commonplace, and this precocious young boy, reading *Treasure Island* and other books far beyond his years, was a frequent recipient of the switch. After attending preparatory schools around the country, Winston eventually started at the prestigious Harrow in April 1888. Since the eighteenth century, Churchills had attended the rival leading boys' school, Eton College, but Harrow, sited on a hill and enjoying a superior air quality, was judged better for Winston's somewhat sickly constitution.

Winston was not an academic pupil and was consequently placed in the bottom class. He loathed Classics but discovered an affinity for English and History, subjects which would serve him well. He described his teacher, Mr Somervell, as 'a most delightful man, to whom my debt is great'. This passionate master was 'charged with the duty of teaching the stupidest boys the most disregarded thing – namely, to write mere English'. Words, sentences, structure and grammar got 'into [his] bones' and never left him.

At Harrow, Winston discovered other pursuits that he both enjoyed and was successful at. He joined the Cadets, took part in fencing championships, won prizes for learning great swathes of poetry by heart, and had several articles published in the *Harrovian*.

When Winston was coming towards the end of his time

at Harrow, he set upon a career in the military and so began preparing to take the entrance exam for the Royal Military Academy at Sandhurst. His first attempt in July 1892 did not go well: he achieved only 5,100 of the minimum 6,457 marks required. He needed a further two attempts before he eventually gained a place in August 1893. The deterioration of Randolph Churchill's mental state, however, meant that the eighteen-year-old Winston, perhaps expecting a letter of warm congratulation from his father, received a shattering rebuke instead. It is worth quoting, to show how his father's great gifts with prose were employed brutally to cut his son down – and to cut him down for good:

9 August 1893

My dear Winston,

I am rather surprised at your tone of exultation over your inclusion in the Sandhurst list. There are two ways of winning in an examination, one creditable the other the reverse. You have unfortunately chosen the latter method, and appear to be much pleased with your success . . .

With all the advantages you had, with all the abilities which you foolishly think yourself to possess & which some of your relations claim for you, with all the efforts that have been made to make your life easy & agreeable & your work neither oppressive or distasteful, this is the grand result that you come up among the 2nd rate & 3rd rate class who are only good for commissions in a cavalry regiment . . . Now it is a good thing to put this business vy plainly before you. Do not think I am going to take the trouble of writing to you long letters after every folly & failure you

commit & undergo. I shall not write again on these matters &
you need not trouble to write any answer to this part of my of my
letter [sic], because I no longer attach the slightest weight to
anything you may say about your own acquirements & exploits.
Make this position indelibly impressed on your mind, that if your
conduct and action at Sandhurst is similar to what it has been in
the other establishments . . . slovenly happy-go-lucky harum
scarum . . . then my responsibility for you is over. I shall leave you
to depend on yourself giving you merely such assistance as may be
necessary to permit of a respectable life. Because I am certain that
if you cannot prevent yourself from leading the idle useless
unprofitable life you have had during your schooldays & later
months, you will become a mere social wastrel one of the hundreds
of the public school failures, and you will degenerate into a
shabby unhappy & futile existence. If that is so you will have to
bear all the blame for such misfortunes yourself. Your own
conscience will enable you to recall and enumerate all the efforts
that have been made to give you the best of chances which you were
entitled to by your position & how you have practically neglected
them all.

I hope you will be the better for your trip. You must apply to
Capt James for advice for us to your Sandhurst equipment. Your
mother sends her love.

Your affte father
Randolph S.C.

The devastating effect of such a letter on a young man
desperate for his father's approval can only be imagined.
Nonetheless, this 'social wastrel' performed well during

his time at Sandhurst, and a month before Lord Randolph died, Winston graduated, placing a distinguished eighth out of 150. After what many considered to be a rather shaky beginning in school, this was a highly respectable end to his education. Churchill later wrote, 'I am all for the Public Schools but I do not want to go there again.'

In March 1895 he joined the 4th Queen's Own Hussars cavalry regiment as a Second Lieutenant. The six-month training course for new recruits was intensive, and Churchill wrote that it 'exceeded in severity anything I had previously experienced in military equitation'. Despite this he took to it quickly and embraced his new-found freedom. He joined a London gentlemen's club, kept abreast of political goings-on, mixed with high society at parties and balls, played polo and raced horses in the Cavalry Brigade steeplechase, but still took his training seriously.

After the death of his father in 1895, life seemed to be looking up for Winston until a telegram arrived on 2 July bringing more shattering news. His former nanny, Mrs Everest, was gravely ill. He raced to North London to be by her side, arriving at the house soaked through after getting caught in a rainstorm. In *My Early Life* he recalled:

> She still knew me, but she gradually became unconscious. Death came very easily to her. She had lived such an innocent and loving life of service to others and held such a simple faith that she had no fears at all . . . She had been my dearest and most intimate friend during the whole twenty years I had lived.

Mrs Everest had no children of her own, but she died peacefully with a young man as devoted as a child by her side. Throughout his life, Winston was known to be a highly emotional man and expressed his feelings publicly. Countless stories of him weeping openly are told not just by close friends but also by politicians and soldiers he served with. For a sensitive child, the emotional strain of parents such as his should not be underestimated; had it not been for the love he'd received from the steadfast Mrs Everest, he would have been an altogether different man with perhaps an altogether different future.

Winston felt increasingly restless in his career, and while continuing his military duties he noted that in:

> the closing decade of the Victorian era the Empire had enjoyed so long a spell of almost unbroken peace, that medals and all they represented in experience and adventure were becoming extremely scarce in the British Army . . . The want of a sufficient supply of active service was therefore acutely felt by my contemporaries in the circles in which I was now called upon to live my life.

This desire for combat would be answered all too soon and all too brutally, but until that terrifying war was laid at their mud-drenched feet in the trenches of Europe, Winston and his fellow officers yearned for action.

Scouring the globe for conflict, he stumbled upon the Cuban War of Independence against the Spanish, which had begun in the early months of 1895.

In late October, a few weeks before Winston's twenty-first birthday, his ship approached its final destination. Winston's excitement was palpable: 'When first in the dim light of early morning I saw the shores of Cuba rise and define themselves from dark-blue horizons, I felt as if I had sailed with Long John Silver and first gazed on Treasure Island.' He sent five despatches back to the *Daily Graphic in London*. In these he honed the skills Mr Somervell had taught him at Harrow, and naturally mixed in a good dose of boys' own tales about dodging bullets and the thrill of guerrilla warfare. After just over a month in Cuba, having offered his services to the Spanish, Winston departed for home with a new-found taste for front-line journalism . . . and as many Cuban cigars as he could possibly carry.

In England, Churchill moved back in with his mother, untill, on 11 September, he and 1,200 other men of the 4th Hussars set sail for India, the 'jewel in the crown' of the British Empire, arriving in Bombay at the beginning of October.

Their regiment was based in the southern city of Bangalore. Winston quickly settled into his new life, enjoying Bangalore's congenial climate, marvelling at the country's beauty and taking pride in the 'keenest realization of the great work which England was doing in India and of her high mission to rule these primitive but agreeable races for their welfare and our own'. These opinions would stay with him throughout his political career, pitting him against his future Conservative colleagues when it came to the topic of independence for this prized colony.

During Winston's time in India, latent feelings of his

distinct inferiority of education bubbled to the surface and spurred him to further his own education. He 'resolved to read history, philosophy, economics, and things like that'. He asked his mother 'for such books as I had heard of on these topics. She responded with alacrity, and every month the mail brought me a substantial package of what I thought were standard works.' In *My Early Life* he described how he then 'embarked on that splendid romance [his lifelong adoration of literature], and . . . voyaged with full sail in a strong wind'.

Over the course of November to May 1897, he read for four or five hours every day, devouring volumes of history, philosophy, poetry, essays, biographies and classic texts such as Gibbons's *Decline and Fall of the Roman Empire*; Macaulay's *The History of England*; Plato's *Republic*; Socrates; the *Politics* of Aristotle; Schopenhauer on pessimism; Malthus on population; Darwin's *Origin of Species*. Name it, he read it, steeping himself even in the twenty-seven-volume record of British parliamentary debate and legislative developments, the *Annual Register*. It was a marathon of self-education: an intellectual boot camp, and a conscious readying for the great role he was now beginning to imagine for himself: as a leader, a *wise* leader, steeped in the ideas of the greatest minds, intimate in his knowledge of the human species and its torments. In order to be influential – in other words – one must be willing to be influenced.

It was now the spring of 1897, and after two years in India Winston was restless once more. In letters to his mother he frequently referred to the possibility of becoming a Member of Parliament. He returned to London and to thoughts of politics, contacting the Conservative Party with a request to organize a few quick speaking engagements. On 26 June the 22-year-old Winston Leonard Spencer-Churchill finally followed in the footsteps of his father, as he had wanted to for so many years, and gave his first political speech.

His performance was well received, but almost as soon as he had finished speaking, he was hotfooting it back to India, where a conflict had broken out between Afghan Pathan tribesmen and British and Indian forces. Winston secured commissions with the *Daily Telegraph* and *Pioneer*, and filed a number of reports.

At the end of 1897, after an exhausting few months on the front line of this very bloody conflict, Winston was able to take some much-needed rest. In typical Churchill fashion, he was not content with idleness and used this time to write not just his first book, a detailed account of the conflict entitled *The Story of the Malakand Field Force*, but also his first and only work of fiction, *Savrola*, a coolly received parody of London society set in a fictional capital run by a dictator, where the leading lady runs away from the dictator, her husband, into the arms of the story's titular character, Savrola – surely a Winston self-portrait – who is tellingly described as someone who could 'know rest only in action, contentment only in danger, and in confusion find their only peace . . . Ambition was the motive force, and he was powerless to resist it.'

The spectre of Lord Randolph's early death at forty-five was always present. His father had been described as 'a man in a hurry', and his son was proving no different.

In 1898 Winston travelled to the Sudan to join Lord Kitchener's regiment, which was fighting in the Mahdist War. There he continued his work as a war correspondent and took part in one of the last great cavalry charges in English history, personally boasting of having killed at least three 'savages'.

He had already decided to enter into politics when he returned to England in March 1899. The death of the MP for Oldham, which forced a by-election in June that year, gave him his first opportunity. He fought a vigorous campaign but was unsuccessful. Not one to let a disappointment such as this hinder him in any way, Winston returned to front-line journalism and travelled to South Africa to report on a new conflict: the Boer War.

Churchill threw himself into the thick of the action and his bravery was widely reported. When the news broke in England that after just a few weeks he had been captured by the Boer, there was a public outcry. Though armed with his trusty Mauser pistol, he claimed 'non-combatant' status, but the Boers were having none of it. Rather than leaving his fate to be negotiated through diplomatic channels, our young adventurer pulled off a daring escape from his POW camp in Pretoria and walked for hours in the beating South African heat until he finally stumbled upon a railway line and hopped on a train to the Transvaal Highveld and freedom. With each one of the near-300 miles that Churchill travelled to safety, his legend grew; he would stay on for a further six months in South Africa, dining out on his fame, before returning to England in July 1900. He immediately set about reigniting his political career. His efforts, and fame, paid off and on 1 October 1900 Winston Churchill was finally elected a Member of Parliament for the Conservative Party. He was two months shy of his twenty-sixth birthday.

One could argue his election was an early example of celebrity politics, but as the eminent Churchill biographer Roy Jenkins described it in *Churchill: A Life*, Winston 'believed in his "star". And his star hovered over Oldham.' As ever with Winston, one career wasn't enough. He continued writing, and embarked on a speaking tour of the UK, United States and Canada, where he was paid vast sums of money to regale audiences with his tales of derring-do in South Africa. On 22 January 1901, however, he received news that Queen Victoria had died; the dawn of a new era was upon the nation. On the day of her funeral, he returned to England and finally took his seat in the House of Commons. Jenkins, again, wrote in his biography that Churchill, 'who was for much of his later career regarded as the last Victorian left in British politics, had by his eagerness for lecture fees forgone the opportunity to take the parliamentary oath of allegiance to the Queen. When he was first admitted, on 14 February, it was to King Edward VII that he swore his fealty.' But admitted he was, and he made his maiden speech to the House on 18 February.

Perhaps sensibly considering his somewhat vainglorious reputation, Winston's first four years in Parliament were on the whole quiet. As he did during his period in India, he took this time to observe and analyse what he heard from his fellow Conservatives and from the Opposition parties, and began to conclude that his seat on the

Government back benches was not where he wanted to be. He wanted to be deciding the fate of the nation. It would be nearly forty more years before he would get the chance to do so.

He would not be quiet for long. Soon he was making speeches that challenged the views of his own party on the matter of increased government spending on the armed forces. In *My Early Life* he recalled:

> I was all for fighting the [Boer] war, which had now flared up again in a desultory manner, to a victorious conclusion; and for that purpose I would have used far larger numbers, and also have organized troops of a higher quality than were actually employed. I would have used Indian troops . . . I thought we should finish the war by force and generosity, and then make haste to return to paths of peace, retrenchment and reform.

The end of the Boer War in 1902 did nothing to align Churchill's opinions with those of senior Tories, and his support of Free Trade, in opposition to his own party, would see him, on 31 May 1904, defect to the Liberal party, shocking the House. His close friend Violet Bonham-Carter described how Winston 'put in an appearance. Standing at the bar, he glanced at his accustomed place below the Ministerial gangway, made a rapid survey of the corresponding bench on the Opposition side, marched a few paces up the floor, bowed to the [Speaker's] Chair, swerved suddenly to the right, and took his seat among the Liberals.' He deliberately placed himself next to fellow Joseph Chamberlain antagonist David Lloyd George.

Churchill's political displays in his first four years in Parliament ensured he was now leading the Liberal efforts to discredit the Conservatives, and to proclaim the glories of Liberalism. Thanks in part to the powerhouse combination of the young turncoat and his dogged Welsh mentor, Lloyd George, the Liberals eventually took office in December 1905 when Arthur Balfour resigned as Prime Minister. Churchill was offered the role of Under-Secretary of State for the Colonies. It was an unremarkable position which suited him well thanks to his first-hand experience of India and South Africa, and he navigated it proficiently. By April 1908 he was able to achieve his next ambition: a position in the Cabinet as the President of the Board of Trade.

As significant as taking a seat at the Cabinet table was, this would dim in cosmic significance compared to the seat he was about to take at the dinner table of one Lady St Helier.

As 'lucky fourteenth' to avoid seating thirteen, Churchill turned to the young guest next to him and found the eyes of a pretty woman who would, in six short months, become the wife he would spend the rest of his life with. She was Clementine Hozier.

Clementine was twenty-three, the daughter of Lady Blanche Hozier, and her father was ... well, either Henry Montague Hozier or Captain William 'Bay'

Middleton, or Lady Blanche's sister's husband, Algernon Freeman-Mitford, or someone else entirely ... for Lady Blanche was known for having taken and discarded several lovers.

A graduate of the Sorbonne, Clementine was herself much pursued as a debutante, and was twice engaged to Sir Sidney Peel, engagements she broke off.

By a mere quirk of superstitious etiquette, then, Churchill was given the chance to make an impression on the woman who would help him wrestle not just with his own doubts but the doubts of others; who would believe in him but also rebuke him for bad behaviour; who would remain fiercely loyal to him and be regarded as a formidable force in his life; who, though not a politician, possessed skills and charm to rival those of the finest members of the House of Commons; and who would nurse him through the infamous 'black dog' of depression while suffering from her own demons. But, above all, she would always put his interests – and thus the interests of her country – before her own.

Winston and Clementine were a devoted couple. He affectionately nicknamed her 'Kat'; she called him 'Pug' or 'Pig'. Frequent periods apart meant they corresponded a great deal throughout their lives, often signing their letters with little drawings of their respective animals. For Clementine, marriage required more than the usual adjustments; she had become the wife of an MP, and one very much in the public eye. Within a few months of the wedding she was pregnant with their first child. Her parents' various infidelities had led to their separation when she was just six years old, so she was determined to create a stable home environment for her own family, including Winston himself.

Clementine gave birth to a girl, whom they named Diana, on 11 July 1909. However strong her desire for an idyllic domestic life, she found childbirth and motherhood traumatic. Winston, anxious about his wife's condition, supported her need for a break just a few weeks after Diana's birth, and Clemmie retreated to the countryside to stay with her sister, leaving the newborn baby at home with a wet-nurse. Recuperating alone eased her anxieties, and soon she felt confident enough to be reunited with her baby before eventually returning to London.

She found her husband deeply distracted, for almost as soon as Winston had secured the role of President of the Board of Trade, he lost the by-election for Manchester North West, suffering a humiliating defeat by the Conservatives. He was down but not out, and his relentless determination saw him immediately jump on a train to Scotland and stand for election in Dundee just over two weeks later – and win while he was at it. Relieved to have secured what most considered a very safe seat, he could now focus on implementing his radical plans for social reform, and successfully pushed for the principle of a minimum wage for the low-paid and the right of workers to a break for meals and refreshment. Initiatives to create unemployment insurance and labour exchanges soon followed. Churchill's political reputation had never been healthier, and neither had his relationships with fellow party members.

The Liberal Party only narrowly won the 1910 General Election. As predicted, Churchill was comfortably re-elected in his Dundee constituency, and was then offered the prestigious post of Home Secretary, but when the House of Lords (packed with Conservative peers) blocked the passage of the Liberals' Budget (packed with social reforms, many championed by Winston), Britain's new king, George V, stepped in and granted the Prime Minister, Herbert Asquith, permission to dissolve the Government and call the second General Election of 1910. Asquith hoped that the popularity of his party's proposed reforms would win it a larger majority in the House and enable it to pass the Parliament Act, which would thenceforth limit the power of the Lords. This was good news for the Liberals but terrible timing for Churchill, who was embroiled in the first of several major career crises from which he would not emerge unscathed.

Thousands of coal miners from the small village of Tonypandy, deep in the Welsh valleys, had gone on strike over working conditions. The situation had deteriorated rapidly and riots had broken out. The press denounced the Home Secretary for not sending in the military as soon as they were requested, and the Labour Party leapt on stories of police brutality, saying Churchill's response had been too heavy-handed. The story would remain an albatross around his neck for the rest of the twentieth century.

Things were no better for Winston back in London. In January 1911 a robbery-gone-wrong had resulted in the fatal shooting of three policemen by a gang of Russian criminals, who were now holed up in London's East End, firing indiscriminately from the windows of the house they had barricaded themselves into on Sidney Street.

The Scots Guards were drafted in to aid the police effort, and a telegram was sent to the Home Secretary. As soon as he was informed of the situation he rushed to join the fun. Pushing his way through the crowds of East End residents, Churchill, dressed in his top hat and fur-trimmed overcoat, made for a striking and conspicuous sight. When some of the first news footage ever recorded of the Metropolitan Police was screened in cinemas around the country to 'jeers' and 'boos'. It showed the brave force hard at work during the 'Siege of Sidney Street', while a bewildered-looking Home Secretary, looking more than a little incongruous, peeked around the corner of a building.

The news reporters mocked his action at Sidney Street, and the cartoonists of Fleet Street, aware that he would be a mainstay of their profession, refined their lampoons: Winston as Punch, Winston as Buffoon, Winston as Napoleon, Winston as Vagrant. His once good name was increasingly associated with missteps and blunders and miscalculations. Despite this, through some inbuilt over-confidence, he remained unfailingly certain of his own abilities.

Churchill, promoted to the role of First Lord of the Admiralty for his commendable response to a crisis in Morocco in mid-1911, was the man Asquith wanted to shake up the Navy. It was no mean task, and the new First Lord understood this more than most: 'I thought of the peril of Britain, peace-loving, unthinking, little prepared, of her power and virtue, and of her mission of good sense and fairplay. I thought of mighty Germany, towering up in the splendour of her Imperial State and delving down in her profound, cold, patient, ruthless calculations.' The Navy had to be strengthened in preparation for the now credible threat of 'attack by Germany as if it might come next day'.

This new post came with lavish perks like the Admiralty yacht, *Enchantress*, and grand accommodation at Admiralty House on The Mall, especially useful space when, on 28 May 1911, after another difficult and exhausting pregnancy for Clementine, the Churchills welcomed a son to continue the family name. They called him Randolph.

Beginning by creating a War Staff akin to the Army's War Office, Churchill sought advice from past First Lords, admirals and other senior naval personnel regarding the best possible practices and where people thought the weaknesses lay. He brought through a change in fuel from coal to oil to increase the speed of Britain's battleships. In total, he increased naval expenditure from £39m to over £50m, his main intention being to show 'the Germans that, whatever they built, Britain would build more'. Europe was now in the grip of a very public arms race that would see military spending increase by 50 per cent in the years preceding the First World War.

Churchill's Cabinet colleagues were aware of the rapid expansion of the German armed forces, but ministers were instead more focused on the easy ride they believed he was receiving from his old friend Lloyd George, now Chancellor of the Exchequer. According to Roy Jenkins,

Winston's 'foremost enemy' was none other than the Attorney-General, Sir John Simon, who immediately began suggesting to Asquith that the loss of Churchill, though regrettable, would not split the party, and, what's more, might even strengthen it by reassuring its anti-war and budget-minded factions.

Winston also met resistance from the public, and while he gave speeches hammering home the dangers posed by German naval expansion, the threat still seemed far off. As Michael Shelden writes in *Young Titan*: 'For many in Britain, the idea of these two highly civilised nations staging a naval Armageddon, with one group of dreadnoughts blasting away at the other, was almost unthinkable.' As confidence in the First Lord began to dwindle, the Liberals slowly started to retreat to their traditional anti-war stance. Even Lloyd George was now talking of Germany as a peace-loving nation. Winston found himself a lone sabre-rattler on the beach as the tide washed up a sudden sea of pacifists. But his resolve was unshaken, and when that fateful shot was fired in Sarajevo on 28 June 1914, he was listening, and he was ready.

'The lamps are going out all over Europe, and we shall not see them lit again in our lifetime.' These words were spoken by the British Foreign Secretary, Sir Edward Grey, the evening before Britain declared war on Germany on 4 August 1914.

The Navy suffered huge casualties in those first war months, with more than 5,500 lives lost. Churchill's handling of the initial stages was criticized heavily in both the press and the House of Commons. As during the Siege of Sidney Street, Britons were left confused by Winston's decision, at the Cabinet's request, to personally travel to the besieged port of Antwerp in Belgium with some fanciful belief he could rescue the city. After just over a day in the field, he telegrammed Asquith suggesting that he resign as First Lord 'and undertake command of relieving and defensive forces assigned to Antwerp'. Perhaps it was his experience of cavalry charges with the Army or the excitement he'd felt dodging bullets as a front-line journalist. Whatever the cause, Winston seemed incapable of not meddling in areas outside his remit. His offer of commanding the troops in Belgium was declined by the Prime Minister, who ordered him to return to England at once. Winston, believing that he was the only person capable of holding the fort, stayed for a further three days, avoiding all thought of abandoning his position as head of the Admiralty. He eventually arrived back in England on 7 October, just in time to have witnessed the fall of Antwerp, but missing the birth of his daughter Sarah, who had arrived the same morning.

The newspapers reported on his arrogant mission but still he remained unfailingly confident of his own abilities. What was to follow next is so infamous in British military history that all you need say is the name: Gallipoli.

The Ottoman Empire's 1914 anti-Russian alliance with Germany had thrust their territories into the forefront of the war as key battlegrounds. The proposed plan, seen by Churchill as a better alternative to chewing barbed wire in

Flanders, was for Britain to carry out a joint operation between the Army and Navy to force a passage through the Dardanelles strait, landing troops on the Gallipoli peninsula before mooring a fleet of ships in the landlocked Sea of Marmara, on the shores of Constantinople (today's Istanbul). Such actions, it was hoped, would induce the Turkish Government to withdraw from the war and make a peace deal, thereby opening up British access to its ally Russia via the Black Sea.

Churchill not only pushed the campaign hard among the Cabinet War Council, but also pressured the military leaders who were given the task of executing a plan they thought shaky at best. With the benefit of hindsight, it is clear that planning, or the lack thereof, was a major factor in the catastrophic outcome of the Dardanelles campaign. Instead of one cohesive, well-executed plan, there were three separate plans being pursued at the same time. Churchill favoured the 'ships alone' option; his second-in-command at the Admiralty, First Sea Lord Admiral Fisher, preferred a joint operation between the Army and Navy; third, the Secretary of State for War, Lord Kitchener, was pursuing an 'evolving army-based plan'. Matters were made worse by what Jenkins describes as the 'seething cauldron' of tension that had developed between the three men.

Used to getting his own way, Churchill was rewarded on 28 January 1915 when the War Council authorized his proposed naval attack. After several failed attempts to force through the minefield-littered Strait ended with the loss of three Allied battleships, it was decided that troops should be deployed and attempt to take the Gallipoli peninsula. Had sufficient plans for ground troops support been put in place when the naval operations failed, there would not have been such abject confusion over whether the Army or the Navy was running the operations when they landed on 25 April. Perhaps even more importantly, had the Allies been more organized from the outset, Ottoman and German forces would not have been given more than a month to prepare their defences for imminent invasion.

From the day troops landed on the Gallipoli peninsula, the conflict would take more than eight bloody months to come to an end, and result in nearly 400,000 casualties: 73,000 British and Irish, 36,000 Australian and New Zealand, 27,000 French, 4,800 Indian and 251,000 Ottoman. The Allies had not been prepared for the strength of resistance put up by the Turkish Army, and by January 1916 it was decided their only option was to evacuate.

Churchill's fate, rather than being tied to the end of the campaign, was decided long before, when the resignation of Sir John Fisher, the First Sea Lord, on 15 May 1915 prompted cries from colleagues who already blamed him for the fiasco for Winston's removal as First Lord of the Admiralty. In the light of so much criticism, the Prime Minister, Asquith, proposed a wartime Coalition Government with the Conservative Party, whose one condition was the removal of Churchill. Winston was dumped, demoted to the lowly position of Chancellor of the Duchy of Lancaster.

The failings of Gallipoli are impossible to lay solely upon him, but the widespread view – moored deeply in the collective need to find a scapegoat, and not dispelled by one public enquiry which found to the contrary – was that his stubborn overruling of his advisers, his bullying of Admirals, and failure to take basic safeguards were largely responsible. In his defence he was not, after all, Prime Minister, and he had put all his decisions in front of the War Cabinet, but he had pushed through his plans in spite of the objections of Kitchener and his own Admiralty colleagues. His own response was not one of contrition but of outrage: he told a friend, 'I am finished! . . . Finished in respect of all I care for – the waging of war, the defeat of the Germans.'

A diminished and humbled Churchill moved out of Admiralty House, and Clemmie and Winston found themselves cast adrift from the society they had enjoyed so much for five years. Clementine later told Churchill's biographer Martin Gilbert that this was one of the most painful moments of her husband's life, and she 'thought he would die of grief'. Furious at her husband's dismissal, she wrote to Asquith: 'If you throw Winston overboard you will be committing an act of weakness and your Coalition Government will not be as formidable a War machine as the present Government.' The Prime Minister was unmoved, and when a new War Cabinet was announced and Winston was not among its members, Churchill made the decision to resign from Government altogether and rejoin the army on the Western Front.

Initially, Churchill returned to his old brigade, the Queen's Own Hussars, but on arrival in France he was collected by a car and taken straight to General Head-quarters in Saint-Omer. Over a champagne dinner, he was offered a cushy role of Aide-de-Camp to the Commander-in-Chief, Sir John French, or an active commission at the Front. It is perhaps unsurprising that he chose front-line action, but the decision reflected more than his long-held sense of adventure. It gave him a chance to distinguish himself fighting for a cause in which he truly believed, and to rinse the blood of Gallipoli from his hands.

After only two weeks in France, Churchill requested that General French promote him to lead a brigade. With so little experience in such a role, and on the advice of the Prime Minister, who feared a backlash, French vetoed the idea and Winston was urged to take the lead of a smaller battalion instead, and so was given the rank of Lieutenant-Colonel in charge of Ninth Division, 6th Royal Scots Fusiliers. At the end of January 1917 his battalion travelled to the front in Belgium, and Churchill spent three and a half months in the trenches. This was not part of any major offensive, but there was no respite, for 'the German shell-fire was continuous, and machine-gun and rifle fire a constant hazard'.

Back home Clementine continued campaigning for her husband's political reputation, but with the Asquith Government in turmoil and Churchill's failed Gallipoli campaign being debated in the Commons, she feared it might be a while before hostility had subsided. Despite her own worries about his safety, she advised her husband not to rush his return, writing, 'To be great one's actions must be able to be understood by simple people. Your motive for going to the Front was easy to understand – Your motive for coming back requires explanation.' But after a disastrously received speech to the House of Commons during a week's leave in March 1917 left him in a worse position than before, Churchill ignored the advice of his wife and returned to London on 7 May to attempt to repair his tattered reputation.

It would take Churchill almost three years and a series of posts before he finally returned to a senior Cabinet position. In that time, the Armistice was signed between the Allies and Germany, and four days later, on 15 November 1918, Clementine gave birth to their fourth child, a girl named Marigold.

The recently re-elected Prime Minister, David Lloyd George, placed great faith in his old friend when he appointed him Secretary of State for War in January 1919. Almost at once he began campaigning behind the scenes for Allied troops still based in Russia to provide support for the White Army in the Russian Civil War. Churchill saw Bolshevism as one of the great threats to British democracy, and, as Jenkins explains, once again made plain his 'belief that will and optimism were more important than an adequacy of resources for the task envisaged'. His plan for an offensive in northern Russia to seize the trans-Siberian railway ended in withdrawal and total defeat, and solidified the now common view that he was a rash military adventurer not to be trusted.

Even Lloyd George lost faith in his War Secretary and moved him to Secretary of State for the Colonies in 1921.

This was still a senior Cabinet post, and at least it afforded Winston the opportunity to travel with Clementine to attend the Middle East Conference in Cairo that spring. It was a glamorous colonial affair, and while out there the pair made the acquaintance of none other than Colonel T. E. Lawrence ('Lawrence of Arabia') and the explorer Gertrude Bell. When Clementine returned to London in April, however, it was to the tragic news that her brother, Bill Hozier, a charming but well-known gambler, had shot and killed himself in a Paris hotel room. Clemmie and Winston had both been close to him, and the news hit the couple hard. Then, a few months later, Winston's mother died. After two such heavy losses, with their house already deep in mourning, Clementine received a telephone call: their youngest child, Marigold, was gravely ill with septicaemia.

The couple rushed to be with her, and kept a vigil throughout the night. On the evening of 22 August, Marigold regained consciousness for long enough to ask her mother to sing her 'Bubbles', her favourite song. Clemmie grasped every ounce of courage she had and began, 'I'm forever blowing bubbles . . . ' until Marigold put her hand on her mother's arm and said, 'Not tonight . . . finish it tomorrow.' She died the next morning, with her parents at her side. Winston later told his daughter Mary that 'Clementine in her agony gave a succession of wild shrieks, like an animal in mortal pain.'

It was a pain that would never leave them but was rarely spoken of. In true stiff-upper-lip fashion, Mary Soames describes how her mother 'did not indulge in her grief, rather, she battened it down, and got on with life'. She and Winston were advised to take a holiday and so travelled to France in January 1922, where Clementine discovered she was pregnant again. A little over a year after the death of Marigold, the Churchills welcomed Mary, their fifth and final child, just in time to visit the other new addition to their family: a country house thirty-five miles south of London called Chartwell, in Kent.

The house, which would become Churchill's most iconic address – after 10 Downing Street, perhaps – was somewhat rundown and would need a small fortune spent on it. Clementine loathed it, but she did her best to warm to it, knowing it fulfilled Winston's desire for a permanent country retreat of their own.

A safe haven couldn't have come at a better time for Churchill, for Lloyd George's coalition had reached breaking point and in October 1922 the Prime Minister was forced to resign. A general election was called, but Churchill was struck down with appendicitis and was too unwell to campaign for his Dundee constituency seat. The result was a disaster: 'His "life seat" of 1908 had crumbled in his hands.'

The couple decided to take an extended six-month holiday to the French Riviera so Winston could recuperate. He had taken up painting when he was removed from the Admiralty in 1915; now, his new-found unemployment gave him ample time to reconnect with his old hobby. The Churchills returned home in the summer of 1923 to supervise the final renovations at Chartwell. Clementine still had strong reservations about the finances, but the countryside was a place of solace for Winston. He could write and paint, and enjoyed helping with the renovations.

Winston being Winston meant he couldn't stay out of politics for long. In the run-up to the election campaign of 1924 he failed to secure a Liberal seat, and made an unsuccessful attempt to run as an independent. He believed that the Liberals and Conservatives should be working together, not opposing one another, and in April of that year was surprised to hear there was talk among Conservatives of bringing him into the party with an unopposed seat in Epping, London. After a minor hesitation, Churchill agreed to cross the floor once more. A Conservative he would remain for the rest of his life.

His campaign was run on a strongly anti-Soviet agenda, and he was highly critical of the Labour Party's desire for an Anglo-Soviet treaty. His stance struck a chord with voters and he won with a large majority. The new Prime Minister, Stanley Baldwin, rewarded him by making him Chancellor of the Exchequer. Upon accepting the role, he reportedly said to Baldwin, 'This fulfils my ambition. I still have my father's robe as Chancellor. I shall be proud to serve you in this splendid Office.' And splendid it was, coming with the welcome perk of accommodation at No. 11 Downing Street, a house that Clementine and the children adored, and would live in for four and a half years.

Churchill's ever-abundant confidence was unaffected by his time out of office and his various *faux pas*, but his period at the Treasury was marred by several controversies.

The first was a fiscal policy that would bring Britain's economy into recession and lead to strikes across the country. The idea of returning to the Gold Standard (Britain had abandoned it in 1914 to stop the rapid fall in value of the pound) had been circulating before the Baldwin administration took office, and Churchill initially had strong reservations. He undertook a thorough investigation and sought the advice of colleagues and academics. Among them was a bright young Cambridge economist named John Maynard Keynes, who produced a pamphlet entitled *The Economic Consequences of Mr. Churchill*, in which he argued that it would be disastrous for economic growth and employment if Britain were to return to this pre-war monetary system. Unfortunately, strong swathes of support from the Conservative Party and parliamentary committees won out, and with his family watching him from the Gallery of the House of Commons, Churchill restored the Gold Standard in his April 1925 Budget.

It is widely agreed that this was the most deeply misguided policy of Baldwin's Government, and Churchill's name was on the Bill. Keynes's predictions proved correct – the pound became too strong for exporting to take place – and the impact on Britain's industries, in particular coal, was catastrophic. At the height of the subsequent 1926 General Strike – Britain's only national strike – 1.75 million people withdrew their labour. Winston's response, to send in the army, was tempered by Baldwin's insistence that the soldiers be unarmed. As barbed wire was rolled out in Hyde Park, the white-collar class went to work, restoring some services: gentlemen with Eton ties acted as porters in Waterloo Station, drove railway engines and buses, delivered newspapers. Churchill himself went down to the docks in an attempt to quell the rioting. With fear growing of an outbreak of widespread violence the unions backed down and the strike was defeated in just ten days, but accusations of heavy-handedness were levelled at Churchill's door.

The General Strike lingered long in the memories of the nation, and with unemployment still high the Conservatives lost their majority at the 1929 General Election. Stanley Baldwin resigned, while Churchill retained his seat in Epping, but over the next two years he became estranged from his party through diverging opinions on core issues.

Winston retreated to Chartwell and resumed writing and painting. Without his Cabinet salary, and after suffering huge financial losses in the Wall Street Crash of 1929, the Churchills found themselves once more in the wilderness and – thanks to Winston's egregious overspending on cigars and champagne – tight for cash. It was an isolation that would last for ten years.

With his political status heavily pruned, there were subjects he felt he knew far too much about to deny the public his opinion of them, and in 1931 that subject was Indian Home Rule; but here again he was to find himself on the wrong side of history and of his own party by opposing India's request for Dominion status, similar to that of Canada, Australia and New Zealand. Churchill feared that as soon as any kind of Dominion status was granted, it would be the end of the British Empire in India – the new Indian Government would seek to remove Britain and Britons from the country as soon as possible.

On the opposing side of the argument was the Viceroy of India, Lord Irwin, better known to us as Viscount Edward Halifax. Despite Halifax's connections to the King and the upper echelons of the British aristocracy, his thoughts on this subject were surprisingly progressive. He was coming to the end of his tenure as Viceroy and truly believed that, following years of violence and civil disobedience, granting Dominion status was the way to work towards a peaceful settlement. Baldwin supported the Viceroy's proposal, and announced to the House that his party would consider it their 'one duty' should they return to power in the future. Having once been among the more liberal-minded of the Conservatives, Churchill felt compelled to resign from the Shadow Cabinet. As Roy Jenkins notes, 'The Indian issue remained at the centre of Churchill's politics, draining his energies, leading him further into a miasma of impotent isolation, for at least another three years.'

Back in the wilderness, Churchill focused on his writing and made tours of the United States, giving speeches and broadcasts. He was still a frequent speaker in the House of Commons on issues like finance and international security, but his views on India had made him seem out of touch. Many saw the end of the First World War as the end of the Empire anyway, but Churchill, as a child of the Victorian and Edwardian eras, retained an unbreakable allegiance to a global British presence.

*

Churchill's belief that Germany, under Hitler's fast-rising National Socialist Party, posed the greatest threat to Britain *did* come from a full understanding of the facts. Whereas he had not witnessed the present state of Indian society, he had travelled extensively through Germany, where he had seen '[a]ll these bands of sturdy Teutonic youths, marching through the streets and roads of Germany, with the light of desire in their eyes to suffer for the Fatherland'. It was clear to him: from their national desire to reclaim lost self-esteem would come the call for weapons; from this would come the call for the return of lost territories.

As early as April 1933 Churchill made a long and impressive speech to the Commons regarding the nature of the threat. He said he believed that 'Germany got off lightly after the Great War' and the Allies had been promised 'that she [Germany] would be a democracy with Parliamentary institutions', but:

all that has been swept away. You have a dictatorship – most grim dictatorship. You have militarism and appeals to every form of fighting spirit, from the reintroduction of duelling in the colleges to the Minister of Education advising the plentiful use of the cane in elementary schools. You have these martial or pugnacious manifestations, and also this persecution of the Jews, of which so many hon. Members have spoken and which appeals to everyone who feels that men and women have a right to live in the world where they are born, and have a right to pursue a livelihood which has hitherto been guaranteed them under public laws of the land of their birth . . .

Churchill continued to issue warnings such as this in Parliament, in newspaper articles, in the numerous letters to colleagues, but only once on BBC radio, where its founder, John Reith, saw Churchill as an extremist. Reith effectively banned Winston from speaking publicly on the matter. By 1935, however, the British Government had conceded that Germany had the right to begin rearmament and rebuild its Navy to a maximum of 35 per cent of Britain's under the Anglo-German Naval Treaty.

When the Conservative Ramsay MacDonald stepped down as Prime Minister in June 1935 due to ill-health, Churchill's old friend Stanley Baldwin succeeded him, but he too was a strong supporter of appeasement and the policies of his predecessor. The press were now reporting on the atrocities being carried out under the new Nazi regime, casting confusion into the minds of many in Britain who felt Germany had paid dearly for its loss of the First World War. However, fears of a Soviet threat still ran high, and as Martin Gilbert writes in *The Roots of Appeasement*, 'Hitler himself claimed to be acting as the principal guardian of Europe against the spread of communism', so the English upper classes in particular were loath to condemn him as dangerous.

Hitler's military ambitions continued, and in March 1936 German troops marched into the demilitarized zone of the Rhineland in defiance of the post-war treaties of Versailles and Locarno. The British were largely distracted by the crisis caused by the abdication of Edward VIII following his declared wish to marry the American divorcee Wallis Simpson – a matter that had once more placed Churchill – a supporter of the romantic union – on the opposite side to the Government. Aversion to the sheer idea of another war in any case meant the public found little issue with Germany taking back territories of German-speaking peoples.

Britain's Government had begun a process of rearmament in recent years, but the country was in no position to consider any kind of military sanctions in response to Hitler's latest move. Churchill warned that if Germany remained unchallenged it was only a matter of time before she would turn her gaze towards Austria, Poland, Czechoslovakia and Romania, and advised that Britain should rapidly increase its rearmament. Public support for him was beginning to grow, but he was still largely discredited and labelled a warmonger by the Baldwin Government. When Neville Chamberlain replaced Baldwin as Prime Minister in May 1937, Churchill remained outside the Cabinet largely because the pair had clashed constantly over the course of their political careers, most recently over relations with Germany and the Abdication crisis.

Though Chamberlain began taking an active interest in foreign policy, his policies towards Germany were no different from Baldwin's. The Foreign Secretary, Anthony Eden, however, shared Winston's view. Eden was already wary of Germany, and believed that both Chamberlain's policies towards Germany and his being soft on the Italian dictator, Benito Mussolini (following the Italian fascist's invasion of Abyssinia), were big mistakes. This distanced Eden from the new administration and that distance was only furthered when the Lord President of the Council, Lord Halifax, was encouraged by Chamberlain to have a stronger involvement in foreign affairs. In October 1937, the Prime Minister persuaded Halifax to accept an invitation to meet Hitler while he was visiting Germany for a hunting expedition.

Eden had been strongly against the proposed meeting and felt undermined by the new PM. He issued strict instructions to Halifax that he should take a hard line on the issue of Hitler's intentions towards Austria, Czechoslovakia and Poland. But since coming to power, Hitler had shown an exceptional ability to seduce British politicians – and Halifax was no different. He returned from his meeting in Germany singing the praises of the Führer and, contrary to Eden's advice, informed the Cabinet that he had taken the chance to confirm to Hitler that Britain would be very amenable to discussions regarding German accession of territories in Central Europe and the restoration of the former colonies that had been stripped from Germany by the post-war peace treaties. Halifax's assurances that he truly believed Hitler had no intention of starting a war held no weight with Eden, and marked the beginning of the end of Eden's position as Foreign Secretary.

Eden tendered his resignation on 20 February 1938, and Neville Chamberlain appointed Lord Halifax as his successor. Churchill was devastated and later recalled in his memoirs:

My heart sank, and for a while the dark waters of despair overwhelmed me . . . I have never had any trouble in sleeping . . . but now on this night of February 20, 1938, and on this occasion only, sleep deserted me. From midnight till dawn I lay in my bed consumed by emotions of sorrow and fear. There seemed one strong young figure standing up against long, dismal, drawing tides of drift and surrender, of wrong measurements and feeble impulses. My conduct of affairs would have been different from his [Eden] in various ways but he seemed to me at this moment to embody the life-hope of the British nation, the grand old British race that had done so much for men, and had yet some more to give. Now he was gone. I watched the daylight slowly creep in through the windows, and saw before me in mental gaze the vision of Death.

Two days later, with the German annexation of Austria underway and the possible loss of Czechoslovakia on the horizon, Churchill issued to the House a stark warning about the cost of appeasement: 'I predict that the day will come when at some point or another on some issue or other you will have to make a stand, and I pray God that when that day comes we may not find that through an unwise policy we are left to make that stand alone.'

There could be no uncertainty about Hitler's intentions now, and Churchill's fears were confirmed when, in September 1938, Neville Chamberlain travelled to Germany to present an Anglo-French proposal on the issue of the Sudetenland that both the Czech and Sudeten leaders had approved in principle. The plan backfired and, as Gilbert writes, 'Hitler, angry that the Sudetens were willing to accept autonomy inside Czechoslovakia, incited them to demand more. When they proved reluctant . . . Hitler publicly and violently denounced the proposal.'

With Churchill's predictions coming true, the Government finally welcomed him back into the fold – in a manner of speaking. Although not a member of the Cabinet, during the weeks that followed Chamberlain's unsuccessful meeting with Hitler, Churchill attended many meetings with the Prime Minister and the Foreign Secretary, but his parliamentary colleagues were still reluctant to accept his advice and concede that appeasement had failed.

Chamberlain pressed for further negotiations with Hitler, and travelled to Munich to attempt to settle the issues. Churchill pleaded with Chamberlain to 'tell Germany that if she set foot in Czechoslovakia we should at once be at war with her'. His pleas fell on deaf ears. When, on 30 September, Chamberlain returned after little more than a day of negotiations, a crowd of supporters was waiting at the airfield. He descended the steps of the plane, waving the signed piece of paper known as the Munich Agreement, and jubilantly announced to the waiting press that the agreement was 'symbolic of the desire of our two people never to go to war again'. Many felt that he had in fact acquiesced to all of Hitler's demands, and when the House of Commons met to debate the issue over four days, Churchill waited for the moment of greatest impact – at 5.10 p.m. on the third day of the proceedings – to deliver a crushing forty-five-minute speech on events five days earlier:

I will . . . begin by saying the most unpopular and most unwelcome thing. I will begin by saying what everybody would like to ignore or forget but which must nevertheless be stated, namely, that we have sustained a total and unmitigated defeat . . . The utmost he [Chamberlain] has been able to gain for Czechoslovakia and in the matters which were in dispute has been that the German dictator, instead of snatching his victuals from the table, has been content to have them served to him course by course . . . All is over. Silent, mournful, abandoned, broken, Czechoslovakia recedes into the darkness . . . What I find unendurable is the sense of our country falling into the power, into the orbit and influence of Nazi Germany, and of our existence becoming dependent upon their good will or pleasure . . . We do not want to be led upon the high road to becoming a satellite of the German Nazi system of European domination. In a very few years, perhaps in a very few months, we shall be confronted with demands with which we shall no doubt be invited to comply. Those demands may affect the surrender of territory or the surrender of liberty . . . I do not grudge our loyal, brave people, who were ready to do their duty no matter what the cost . . . but they should know the truth. They should know that there has been gross neglect and deficiency in our defences; they should know that we have sustained a defeat without a war, the consequences of which will travel far with us along our road; they should know that we have passed an awful milestone in our history, when the whole equilibrium of Europe has been deranged, and that the terrible words have for the time being been pronounced against Western democracies: 'Thou art weighed in the balance and found wanting.' And do not suppose that this is the end. This is only the beginning of the reckoning. This is only the first sip, the first foretaste of a bitter cup which will be proffered to us year by year unless by a supreme recovery of moral health and martial vigour, we arise again and take our stand for freedom as in the olden time.

Less than a year later, after Germany had invaded Czechoslovakia and Poland, Britain declared war.

Churchill's chilling words cannot have failed to echo through the minds of the architects of appeasement as the events of May 1940 unfolded, but few could have known on that day in October 1938 that this one intransigent man would be the saving of Britain.

FRIDAY, 10 MAY 1940

GERMANY INITIATES OPERATION 'FALL GELB'

—————

MOVES 4 MILLION TROOPS INTO POSITIONS ON BORDERS WITH HOLLAND, BELGIUM AND FRANCE

—————

SCRAMBLES ITS ONE-MILLION-STRONG AIR FORCE TO ENACT BLITZKRIEG

—————

CHAMBERLAIN GOVERNMENT FALLS

—————

3. A Leader Falls

As the evening of 9 May 1940 drew to a close, Churchill was readying himself for the colossal task of leading the nation, confiding to his son Randolph, who had telephoned the Admiralty, 'I think I shall be Prime Minister tomorrow.' At sunrise the next day, all thoughts of a smooth transition to leadership disappeared when – exactly one month after the embarrassment of Churchill's 'ramshackle' Norway campaign – Hitler once again launched a devastating attack in Europe.

A little after half-past five, it was not the arrival of his usual breakfast tray – with its glass of scotch and soda between the rack of toast and plate of eggs – that woke Churchill but the shattering news that Germany had invaded Holland. 'Boxes with telegrams poured in from the Admiralty, the War Office and the Foreign Office,' he recalled, and at 6 a.m. he telephoned the French Ambassador to discuss deploying troops into neighbouring Belgium. It swiftly became clear that Belgium, too, had been invaded, though both countries had declared neutrality when the war broke out. Churchill finished his call with the French and took a meeting with the Secretaries of State for Air and War, Sir Samuel Hoare and Oliver Stanley, to discuss Britain's possible response. Hoare recalled that Churchill's 'spirit, so far from being shaken by failure or disaster, gathered strength in a crisis, [and he] was ready as always with his confident advice'. He added, 'It was six o'clock in the morning, after a fierce House of Commons debate and a late sitting. Yet there he was, smoking his large cigar and eating fried eggs and bacon, as if he had just returned from an early morning ride.'

The three men then moved to the Upper War Room at the Admiralty where a Military Coordination Committee meeting was about to begin at seven o'clock. Situation updates were delivered in rapid succession, revealing the terrifying speed, scale and success of the German advance, which had begun at 3 a.m. GMT. The Luftwaffe was raining down bombs and parachuting in thousands of German soldiers across key targets in Holland, Belgium and now also Luxembourg. An order had been given by the Military Coordination Committee which saw the French and British Armies begin their march into Belgium. In the chaos of the moment, the Chief of the Imperial General Staff, Sir Edmund Ironside, recalled that when he entered another room he 'could not get out again. All the night watchmen were away and the day's men not there. Doors double and treble locked. [He] walked up to one of the windows and opened it and climbed out. So much for security.'

As Ironside was climbing through a window, the British people were making what they could of the 7 a.m. bulletin from the BBC Home Service. It had got wind of the invasion and announced: 'It is reported, but not yet *officially* confirmed, that the Germans have invaded Holland.'

Randolph Churchill, who was serving with his father's old regiment, the 4th Queen's Own Hussars, was at his barracks in Hull and telephoned his father at 7.30 a.m. to try to find out what was happening. Winston informed him that 'the German hordes are pouring into the Low Countries but the British and French armies are advancing to meet them and in a day or two there will be a head-on collision'. Randolph replied, 'What about what you told me last night about you becoming Prime Minister today?' His father was unequivocal: 'Oh I don't know about that. Nothing matters now except beating the enemy.'

But what indeed was going to happen regarding the question that had been burning for the past three days? Who would be Prime Minister? Chamberlain had said he would wait for Labour's decision before committing himself to resigning. If Labour would serve in a government led by him, then he would happily stay. As if unaware of the *Blitzkrieg* sweeping across Western Europe, Clement Attlee and Arthur Greenwood made the 11.34 a.m. train from Waterloo to Bournemouth and then went to the Labour conference. Chamberlain, it seemed, would get his answer that day, but not just yet.

Meantime, shortly before 8 a.m. Churchill walked his familiar route from the Admiralty across Horse Guards Parade, his jaunty pace matched by Stanley and Hoare as they made for No. 10 Downing Street, where the War Cabinet was convening the first of many meetings that day. Taking their seats around the mahogany table, the twenty ministers, military leaders and Cabinet secretaries reviewed the current situation. In the absence of official confirmation that he would become top dog, Winston decided simply to act like one. Neville Chamberlain was seated 'in the chair', but it was Churchill who commanded the room, confirming that 'the whole plan for the advance of the Allied forces into the Low Countries had been set in motion. The troops were not at the highest state of readiness, but would certainly be on the move quickly.'

In less than three hours Winston was running the war. You would think that Chamberlain, having witnessed such an assertive performance, would now accept the previous day's conclusion that Churchill should replace him as PM. You'd be wrong. Samuel Hoare and Churchill both noted that, after this meeting, Chamberlain confided to Sir Samuel Hoare that he believed he should 'withhold his resignation until the French battle was finished'. It was a staggering assertion, given that he uttered nothing worth minuting in the 8 a.m. War Cabinet meeting. Moreover, the British public had awoken to see the previous day's events splashed across the front pages:

CHAMBERLAIN TO RESIGN: CHURCHILL EXPECTED
TO BE NEW PREMIER

P.M.'S LAST BID FAILS: LABOUR 'NO'

PREMIER: LAST EFFORT. RESIGNATION
TO-DAY IF MOVE FOR ALL-PARTY GOVERNMENT
FAILS

SOCIALISTS AT NO. 10 LAST NIGHT

How could Chamberlain renege on everything he had agreed to? But then again, how could he let go? If Churchill succeeded him now, it would overturn everything he'd worked for, not just during the last three years as Prime Minister but throughout his dogged campaign of appeasement. It would prove him wrong. Wrong about everything. Wrong to ignore Churchill's *six years* of warnings. 'Peace in our time' – the four words Chamberlain spoke as he stepped off the plane from Munich on 30 September 1938 – now seemed so ridiculous. The flimsy piece of paper he clutched in his hand: ridiculous. It all looked ridiculous.

All except for one thing: Churchill. He alone had understood the threat; unlike members of the Royal Family and various aristocrats and gentry of England, he had not been seduced by Nazi charms; and he had refused to be silenced despite the slurs thrown at him. His reward? He was cast out from the political society he had helped shape and was labelled a warmonger. Yet he had stuck steadfastly to his principles: that one cannot negotiate with dictators.

One can only imagine what Chamberlain must have thought when he first heard the news that German tanks were sweeping across Western Europe – what it meant. What he now had to face. His last-ditch attempts to cling to power were the actions of a man humiliated. Chamberlain's actions and legacy have in recent years been viewed with less opprobrium than in the decades immediately after the war, but the next few months of his life must have been the hardest to take. After the first War Cabinet concluded, he approached the Chancellor of the Exchequer, Sir Kingsley Wood, with the idea of remaining in power.

It would be wrong to say that stubborn or naked ambition drove Chamberlain's attempts to stay on as leader. He had real reservations about Churchill. Like many of his colleagues and almost all of those who remained open to the idea of peace talks with Hitler – and these made for a powerful cabal which included Halifax – the very idea of Winston in charge was chilling. Winston *as supreme leader*? Winston *Churchill* in charge of everything? The 65-year-old word-spinner with a drinking problem and a decades-long history of misjudgement leading *the country*? Forget the country, you could forgive yourself for having reservations about lending such a man *bicycle*.

Chamberlain, in his last acts of resistance, was not thinking just of himself. He represented many powerful voices who felt that Britain needed, perhaps more than ever before, stable, sober, rational, calm, unexcitable leadership. Whatever you thought of Winston, you could not describe him thus. Churchill, willing in his bombast to commit legions of flesh-and-blood armies against terrible odds as though they were his own childhood lead soldiers, and with quatrains of heroic poetry ringing in his head, was surely capable of inflicting speedy ruin upon the entire nation.

In May 1940 the mere notion of Churchill as leader had many among even his most ardent fans quaking with apprehension. So when Chamberlain spoke with Kingsley Wood following the War Cabinet meeting, he had reason to hope for a last-minute show of support from friends who, if they would not acknowledge his strengths, must at least concede the weaknesses of his rival.

Highly unlikely. It was all too late. Britain needed a National Government, and the price of one, exacted by Labour, was nothing less than Chamberlain's head.

Kingsley Wood, cast as the messenger in this drama, thought it kinder to be cruel and delivered the blunt news that, 'on the contrary, the new crisis made it all the more necessary to have a National Government, which alone could confront it'. Hearing this from a man whom most viewed as his protégé, Chamberlain finally acquiesced.

The German Panzer divisions were making swift progress across the lowlands of Belgium, Luxembourg and Holland, with France in their sights, when the War Cabinet met for a second time at 11.30 a.m. and learned of the first casualties of German bombing at Nancy in France. But the information to hand was meagre and uncertain. Ironside informed the Cabinet that it was suspected the Germans planned to cross through Luxembourg and the Ardennes forest to the Belgian defensive line at the River Meuse, while also pushing an advance through Belgium towards Allied forces along the Albert Canal. In fact the Germans had already advanced much further than the Allies suspected, but, as Philip Warner explains in his book *The Battle of France*, Belgium's neutral status meant its troops had been unprepared and untrained for invasion 'along the Meuse [and] were so surprised by the arrival of the German gliders that at first they thought they were aircraft in difficulties; their first reaction was to help what they imagined were airmen in trouble'.

A second Defence Committee meeting was held back at the Admiralty at 1 p.m. to discuss the bombing strategy of targeting 'open towns in Belgium', with Churchill 'in the chair' once more. In response to the Belgian appeal for help from the Allies, General Sir Hastings Ismay, a staunch ally of Churchill, recalled how when the Supreme War Council had met in November 1939, it had decided that 'in the event of a German violation of Belgian territory, the plan known as Plan D would automatically be put into operation. This meant that without any further instructions the British Expeditionary Force [over 394,000 British Army men who had been deployed to France since the outbreak of war in September 1939] would very soon be on the move at top speed into Belgium.' Now such an hour was upon them, and the minutes of the meeting recorded 'that if the accumulated evidence went to show that the Germans had "taken off the gloves", the British Government were inclined to commence [bombing] attacks tonight, on oil refineries and marshalling yards in Germany'.

Churchill's marathon day continued, and after a brief lunch with his trusted friend Lord Beaverbrook he was back at No. 10 for a third War Cabinet meeting at 4.30 p.m. There a report by the Joint Intelligence Sub-Committee was presented detailing the latest German bombing targets in Holland, Belgium, France and Switzerland, as well as five locations in Kent (the first German bombs on England had been dropped in October 1939 on the East Coast). The previous meeting's discussion of retaliation attacks on German targets continued. It is here that we see how Winston paid attention to the most microscopic of details, as well as to the opinions of those trusted and experienced men sitting around the Cabinet table. Air Chief Marshal Sir Cyril Newall was in favour of immediate retaliation because the 'psychological effect of an immediate blow at the enemy's most vulnerable spot would be very great throughout the world'; he was supported by the Secretary of State for Air, Sir Samuel Hoare, who stated: 'If we did not strike Germany hard and immediately, world opinion would be very critical of us. There were a great number of instances in history of the postponement of a decision leading to its never being taken.' Despite the strong case put forward by the Air Force, Ironside was against, citing the view of Lord Gort, Commander-in-Chief of the BEF, that such an attack 'would have no effect on the land battle'. Hoare's comment about 'instances in history' must have rung in Churchill's ears like the bells of Big Ben, for he more than anyone understood what calamity could result from impetuous military actions, and so sided with a twenty-four-hour delay. The minutes then state that Chamberlain, 'after hearing the arguments . . . was in favour of postponing an attack . . . at any rate for 24 hours'.

As the meeting drew to a close, the Prime Minister announced that he had now received an answer from the Labour Party on the issue of a National Government. Its statement read: 'The Labour Party are prepared to take their share of responsibility as a full partner in a new

Government, under a new Prime Minister, which would command the confidence of the nation.' Chamberlain confirmed that 'in the light of this answer, he had reached the conclusion that the right course was that he should at once tender his resignation to The King. He proposed to do so that evening.' But despite everything that had transpired that day, he still could not bring himself to admit to the nineteen men around the table that the person he did not want to take power would now be taking the reins.

With the meeting adjourned, members of the War Cabinet returned to their respective offices as word of Labour's decision spread throughout the Conservative Party. One last desperate attempt to persuade Halifax to reconsider was made by a Tory Whip, but when he arrived at the Foreign Office he discovered that Halifax had gone to the dentist. Andrew Roberts notes in his biography of Halifax: 'Although [he] did have to see the dentist twice in two months in late 1939, he would hardly have left the Foreign Office if he had been at all amenable to these last-minute approaches.'

Chamberlain left for Buckingham Palace shortly after the War Cabinet meeting concluded. He met with King George VI to officially resign his seal of office and advise him who to send for to take his place. It was not the name His Majesty had hoped to hear. The King recalled in his diary:

How grossly unfairly I thought he had been treated, & that I was terribly sorry that all this controversy had happened. We then had an informal talk over his successor.

I, of course, suggested Halifax, but he told me that H was not enthusiastic, as being in the Lords he could only act as a shadow or a ghost in the Commons, where all the real work took place. I was disappointed over his statement, as I thought H was the obvious man, & that his peerage could be placed in abeyance for the time being. Then I knew that there was only one person whom I could send for to form a Government who had the confidence of the country, & that was Winston. I asked Chamberlain his advice, & he told me Winston was the man to send for.

The King offering temporarily to suspend a peerage so that Halifax could become Prime Minister? Constitutionally, this was an extraordinary means of getting the man he wanted. Chamberlain's staff at No. 10, whom Churchill would soon inherit, were as dismayed as His Majesty about the implications of events unfolding at the Palace. Jock Colville, Chamberlain's PPS, wrote in his diary:

It is a terrible risk, it involves the danger of rash and spectacular exploits, and I cannot help fearing that this country may be manoeuvred into the most dangerous position it has ever been ... Nothing can stop him [Churchill] having his way – because of his powers of blackmail – unless the King makes full use of his prerogative and sends for another man; unfortunately there is only one other, the unpersuadable Halifax.

Everybody here is in despair at the prospect.

The weight of these opinions must have been agony for Churchill. No amount of self-confidence could prevent him from feeling deeply the doubts of others. Could he ever escape his past failures, the lost lives people blamed him for, and achieve the glory that had eluded him? Strip away all of his bravado and we are left with an ageing man with an already full career behind him, now presented with a last opportunity to succeed where previously he had failed.

It was in this moment, walking back to Admiralty House from Downing Street, that Churchill's need for Clemmie's support and comfort was overwhelming. His daughter Mary recalls: 'During these tense and anxious days Clementine was away from London [at a funeral]. It was anguishing for her not to be with Winston during these days; and he, sensing that events were moving towards a climax, telephoned, asking her to return as soon as possible.' She arrived just before he left the Admiralty for the Palace, bolstering his belief that he was the only man who could become Prime Minister.

Shortly before 6 p.m. on 10 May 1940, as Winston was driven along the Mall, he reflected on how 'the public had not had time to take in what was happening either abroad or at home, and there was no crowd about the Palace gates'. But his growing excitement at assuming the office he had so long dreamed of put him in a somewhat cheeky mood when he met the King. He recalled:

His majesty received me most graciously and bade me sit down. He looked at me searchingly and quizzically for some moments, and then said, 'I suppose you don't know why I have sent for you?' Adopting his mood, I replied, 'Sir, I simply couldn't imagine why.' He laughed and said, 'I want to ask you to form a Government.' I said I would certainly do so.

This was a surprisingly good start, considering the views expressed at the King's earlier meeting with Chamberlain. Churchill, the King noted in his diary, was 'full of fire & determination to carry out the duties of Prime Minister'. It was fire he needed most, given the magnitude of the task ahead of him – and one he knew he must not fail.

When Churchill stepped out of his car for the first time as the Prime Minister of Great Britain, he turned to his police bodyguard, Detective Inspector W. H. Thompson, and said, 'God alone knows how great it is. All I hope is that it is not too late. I am very much afraid it is. We can only do our best.' Tears came into his eyes. As he turned away, he muttered something to himself. Then he set his jaw, and with a look of determination, mastering all emotion, he began to climb the stairs and begin planning his War Cabinet.

Politics really were in Winston's blood. Even after everything that had happened during the last three days, he knew that without the support of the Conservative Party his time as PM would be very short indeed. His grip on power was fragile. The atmosphere of the House had seen many a Tory get to his feet and scream for Chamberlain's removal, but that did not mean they were happy with the alternative. The Under-Secretary of State for Foreign Affairs, R. A. ('Rab') Butler, was said to have remarked, '[T]his sudden coup of Winston and his rabble was a serious disaster and an unnecessary one. They [senior Conservatives] had weakly surrendered to a half-breed American.'

It was perhaps with this in mind that Winston sat down at his desk at Admiralty House and wrote to Chamberlain.

My dear Neville,

My first act on coming back from the Palace is to write and tell you how grateful I am to you for promising to stand by me and to aid the country at this extremely grievous and formidable moment. I am under no illusions about what lies ahead, and of the long dangerous defile through which we must march for many months. With your help and counsel and with the support of the great party of which you are Leader, I trust I shall succeed. The example which you have set of self-forgetting dignity and public spirit will govern the action of many and be an inspiration to all.

In these eight months we have worked together I am proud to have won your friendship and your confidence in an increasing measure. To a very large extent I am in your hands – and I feel no fear of that. For the rest I have faith in our cause which I feel sure will not be suffered to fail among men.

I will write to you again tonight after I have seen the Labour Leaders. I am so glad you will broadcast to our anxious people.

Believe me,
Yours ever,
Winston S. Churchill

What a letter to write to the man who had gone out of his way to prevent him from becoming Prime Minister. It could be interpreted in so many ways: genuine, strategic, obsequious, pragmatic, forgiving, and so on. But whatever Winston's intentions, it was above all the smartest thing to do at that moment. Even if Chamberlain found it maddening, he could hardly criticize such an overture. Lord Halifax too received a letter along similar lines. However, his chimes harder because of Churchill's fateful comment: 'It gives me so much pleasure to feel that we shall be fighting this business through together to the end. I feel sure your conduct of Foreign Affairs is an essential element in our war strength. I am so grateful to you for being willing to continue your work in this great office of which you are at once the slave and the master . . . ' In the space of a few weeks, these words would come back to haunt Churchill as the two men clashed irreconcilably over the most important issue of their lives: peace with Hitler.

In the meantime, Churchill knew that he needed both these men inside his War Cabinet, keeping his friends close and enemies closer. Should even one of them resign, he was in no doubt that it would trigger a general mutiny that would end his premiership when it had barely begun. Chamberlain was to lead the House of Commons as Lord President of the Council, and Lord Halifax was to remain as Foreign Secretary. To complete the line-up, he invited the Labour Party's Clement Attlee to be Lord Privy Seal and Arthur Greenwood to be Minister Without Portfolio. In doing so, he hoped he could balance out the expected opposition from Chamberlain and Halifax. In *The Gathering Storm*, Churchill writes how he 'had known both Attlee and Greenwood for a long time in the House of Commons. During the eleven years before the outbreak of war, I had in my more or less independent position come far more often into collision with the Conservative and National Governments than with the Labour and Liberal Oppositions.'

His thoughts at this juncture seem to have been heavily focused around opposition and from what direction it would come. As we know from his time as First Lord of the Admiralty, Churchill was never able to do just the job he had been given, much to the ire of those around him. Now he decided to solve the problem of wading uninvited into other people's purviews from the start, and created the position of, and appointed himself, 'Minister of Defence, without however attempting to define its scope and powers'. This effectively gave him free rein to run the war, as well as the country. With this in mind he made three further key appointments that night: his close ally, Anthony Eden, was to be made Secretary of State for War; the Labour MP A. V. Alexander was made First Lord of the Admiralty; and the Leader of the Liberal Party, Sir Archibald Sinclair, became Secretary of State for Air.

With his War Cabinet complete, Churchill could pause for a moment to read the piles of letters and telegrams that had flooded in, congratulating him on his appointment. At 9 p.m. he turned his attention to the wireless, where Neville Chamberlain began to speak to the nation for the last time:

> Early this morning without warning or excuse, Hitler added another to the horrible crimes which already disgrace his name by a sudden attack on Holland, Belgium and Luxembourg. In all history, no other man has been responsible for such a hideous total of human suffering and misery as he. He has chosen a moment when perhaps it seemed to him that this country was entangled in the throes of a political crisis and when he might find it divided against itself. If he has counted on our internal divisions to help him he has miscalculated the mind of this people . . .
>
> Now as this is my last message to you from No. 10 Downing Street, there are one or two things that I should like to say to you. During the period, it's almost exactly three years, that I have been Prime Minister, I have borne a heavy load of anxiety and responsibility. As long as I believed there was any chance of preserving peace honourably, I strove to take it. When the last hope vanished and war could no longer be avoided, I strove equally hard to wage it with all my might. Perhaps you remember that in my broadcast of September 3, last year, I told you that we should be fighting against evil things. My words have proved to be insufficient to describe the vileness of those who have now staked everything on the great battle just beginning. Perhaps it may at least be some relief to know that this battle, though it may last

for days or even weeks, has ended the period of waiting and uncertainty. For the hour has come when we are to be put to the test, as the innocent people of Holland and Belgium and France are being tested already. And you and I must rally behind our new leader, and with our united strength and with unshakable courage, fight and work until this wild beast that has sprung out of his lair upon us, be finally disarmed and overthrown.

It was a dignified and rousing speech, and it garnered praise even from his critics. The broadcast was a little over five minutes in length, after which Winston returned to work for another six hours. He later wrote about this monumental day in *The Gathering Storm*:

During these last crowded days of the political crisis my pulse had not quickened at any moment. I took it all as it came. But I cannot conceal from the reader of this truthful account that as I went to bed at about 3 a.m. I was conscious of a profound sense of relief. At last I had the authority to give directions over the whole scene. I felt as if I were walking with destiny, and that all my past life had been but a preparation for this hour and for this trial. Ten years in the political wilderness had freed me from ordinary party antagonisms. My warnings over the last six years had been so numerous, so detailed, and were now so terribly vindicated, that no one could gainsay me. I could not be reproached either for making the war or with want of preparation for it. I thought I knew a good deal about it all, and I was sure I should not fail.

Therefore, although impatient for the morning, I slept soundly and had no need for cheering dreams. Facts are better than dreams.

Across town, in his plush suite at the Dorchester hotel, Edward Wood, aka Lord Halifax, was considering his own future. In recent days he had passed up having immense power – his ambitions to be Prime Minister would have to wait – but he had not given up on the principle that had defined his life: that every problem had a rational solution, and that the last thing that should ever be spent is blood. How worried he must have been to think that the man he had allowed to come to power in his place represented, in almost every way, the antithesis of his idea of leadership.

4. The Holy Fox

When Halifax turned down the premiership on 10 May 1940, Sir Henry ('Chips') Channon, a sharp-eyed American friend who had nested among the English upper classes, noted in his diary, 'I don't understand why, since a more ambitious man never lived, nor one with, in a way, a higher sense of duty and "noblesse oblige".'

So who was this man whom everybody wanted as leader but who, at the crucial moment, turned his back on such a great responsibility?

At six feet five inches tall, with pallid skin and deep-set eyes, Halifax cut an imposing, somewhat cadaverous figure. Added to this, a congenital defect left him with no left hand and a withered left arm, which he concealed with a prosthetic clenched fist clothed in a black leather glove. Despite his disability, Halifax was a renowned horseman and fanatical fox-hunter. In essence, he was a quintessential English aristocrat. Born Edward Frederick Lindley Wood on 16 April 1881, he was the fourth son of Charles Wood, 2nd Viscount Halifax. His childhood was spent in Yorkshire but was marred by the tragic early deaths of his three elder brothers before he was ten, leaving him the heir-apparent to the Halifax peerage.

The Woods were deeply pious High Anglicans. Halifax followed the traditional path of Eton College and Oxford University and, upon graduating, made the decision to go into politics in 1909. Having inherited several large London properties and two grand estates in Yorkshire, he was a natural fit for the Conservatives. That same year, he married Lady Dorothy Onslow, a woman described as 'a paragon amongst women' who was well known for her charm, friendliness, sympathy and kindness. The couple began their family, and in 1910 Halifax won the seat of Ripon in North Yorkshire.

When the First World War broke out, Halifax joined the Queen's Own Yorkshire Dragoons and took an active service commission in Flanders. The living hell of Flanders, the bloody loss of many friends, the pall of so much death, would haunt Halifax the whole of his life and inform his politics.

After the war ended he was one of 202 Conservative MPs who signed a telegram to the Prime Minister, David Lloyd George, who was attending the Paris Peace Conference, strongly urging him not to waver on the strict terms of reparation from Germany.

In April 1921 Halifax had his first political run-in with Winston Churchill, then the Secretary of State for the Colonies. At that time a member of the Liberal Party in the Government coalition, Churchill was unhappy about the suggestion of Halifax for Under-Secretary of State for the Colonies and so, for two weeks, resisted even meeting him. The usually tightly buttoned Halifax was furious with this treatment, and burst into Churchill's office to tell him, 'I have no desire to be your Under-Secretary, nor to have any other office. I am prepared to resign and leave this office tomorrow, but, so long as I remain here, I expect to be treated like a gentleman.' He was described by many as 'aloof, serious, devout, cunning— all of which coalesced in Churchill's characterization of him as the "Holy Fox"'. Despite this initial rocky start, the pair were able to settle their differences, for now, and Halifax assumed his first ministerial post, albeit a lowly one.

It was not until 1926 that he gained the first real post to garner him respect and status among his colleagues. He was appointed Viceroy of India, following in the footsteps of his grandfather, the 1st Viscount Halifax, who was Secretary of State for India from 1859 to 1866, and interestingly also in the footsteps of Lord Randolph Churchill, Winston Churchill's father. He assumed this office in 1926 and was created Baron Irwin at the same time. This new title elevated him to the House of Lords and he resigned his seat as an MP.

India defined Halifax. During his five years there he supported the idea of self-governance for the country, which was ruled entirely by Britain, advocating that it have full 'Dominion Status' as enjoyed by Australia and New Zealand. While making himself popular with the pacifist Indian leader Mahatma Gandhi, Halifax's view put him at sharp odds with almost all the big names in his party, among them Winston Churchill, to whom it became clear that Halifax was ready to put India before loyalty to the Conservative Party. But Halifax's plan, intended to further the Indian cause, backfired spectacularly when talks with leading Indian politicians over the proposals broke down and violent clashes erupted once more.

As civil disobedience raged on, Conservatives felt that Halifax's approach to India was far too weak, and the party leader, Stanley Baldwin, was warned by Churchill not to allow his friendship with Halifax 'to affect your judgement' on the situation. Undeterred, Halifax, in his last act as Viceroy, pushed through and signed the Gandhi–Irwin Pact on 31 March 1931. The pact brought an end to the period of civil unrest, allowed for the release of many imprisoned protestors and paved the way for the first Round Table Conference to consider Indian constitutional reform in London later that year, but it left him deeply unpopular with the imperialist factions in Britain, in particular with Churchill, who lambasted his colleague's 'catalogue of errors and disasters' as Viceroy of India. This difference of opinion caused an angry Churchill to break with the Conservative Party and begin his years in the political wilderness.

Upon returning to England in 1931, Halifax resumed his old life in the countryside. His interests centred mainly on fox-hunting, the church and politics. He made his maiden speech in the House of Lords in December that year. He was said to have 'carried himself as a senior member of the Government, even if strictly speaking he wasn't one'.

When his father died in January 1934, Lord Irwin became Viscount Halifax. This personal ascendancy was, a year later, followed by a professional one: he became Secretary of State for War under his old friend Stanley Baldwin, who had recently resumed his role of Prime Minister after Ramsay MacDonald resigned because of ill-health. After only five months, Halifax was promoted again, to Lord Privy Seal and Leader of the House of Lords following the Conservatives' November 1935 General Election win.

By now Herr Hitler had been Chancellor for two years. What of Halifax's attitude to the German leader?

Throughout this time Anthony Eden, the new British Foreign Secretary, had been warning of the potential implications of German rearmament. Halifax, who in 1918 had been supportive of harsh penalties on Germany, now – after India – expressed a certain sympathy for Germany over the penalties imposed by the Treaties of Versailles and Locarno. At the same time as Britain was gripped by the Abdication Crisis of 1936, in which King Edward VIII renounced his place on the throne, Hitler's tanks rolled into the demilitarized zone of the Rhineland in flagrant violation of the treaties of Locarno and Versailles.

Despite Eden's early fears regarding Hitler, he initially shared Halifax's opinion that the Rhineland occupation could be resolved through talks and negotiation, but when the pair attended a meeting with other Locarno Treaty governments in Paris on 10 March 1936, they were surprised, in Eden's words, to find 'that our policy of condemning the German action and then developing a constructive policy to re-establish the European settlement had no chance of acceptance'. It is here that we see Halifax first begin to cement in his mind the doctrine of a 'European Settlement': an idea that would stay with him through all the failures of appeasement and beyond the outbreak of war, and would erupt again in spectacular fashion in the War Cabinet meetings of May 1940.

The British Government ignored the warning signs of German rearmament and continued with its policy of negotiations, accepting the occupation of the Rhineland as a *fait accompli* that was not worth going to war over. When Hitler understood that he was not about to meet with resistance for violating Locarno sanctions, his plans for retaking former German territories lost after the First World War began to progress in earnest.

In Britain, the Soviet Union was seen as the greater threat by far. More importantly, a strong pro-German sentiment ran through large swathes of the English aristocracy, including the recently abdicated and newly created Duke of Windsor, who would meet Hitler less than a year after his abdication. Concern about Germany taking back territories populated by German-speaking peoples was not high on the British agenda, and many believed Hitler's intentions were honourable when he offered a non-aggression pact to France in an attempt to soothe that country's fears. At a Cabinet meeting in January 1937, Halifax is quoted as saying he would like to 'improve our contacts with Germany' and that 'he thought the Germans had some justification for their resentment against the sympathy expressed for France in this country and the criticism of Germany'.

When Stanley Baldwin retired in May 1937, his successor, Neville Chamberlain, who had been waiting in the wings for a long time, began actively to pursue an open policy of appeasement in an attempt to avoid a second world war. Halifax, in particular, had developed a good relationship with Chamberlain, so was quickly promoted to Lord President of the Council, and soon emerged as a favourite.

When the sensational invitation for Halifax to attend a fox-hunting expedition in Germany in November 1937, run by the founder of the Gestapo, Hermann Göring, was expanded to include a meeting with Hitler, it placed him in a difficult position, betwixt the opposing policies of the Prime Minister and the Foreign Secretary. Chamberlain's belief that the meeting was just an informal courtesy to be tagged on to the end of Halifax's trip set the suspicions of the Foreign Office racing over fears that someone from the pro-appeasement camp was being surreptitiously authorized by the Prime Minister to conduct a meeting in which myriad foreign policies could be discussed. Despite the objections raised by Eden, Halifax was permitted to attend but was warned to 'confine himself to warning comments on Austria and Czechoslovakia', the next two countries upon which Hitler clearly had designs. However, in a memo Halifax sent to the Foreign Secretary upon his return, Eden was horrified to read that he *had* discussed 'possible alterations to the European order which might be destined to come about with the passage of time. Amongst these questions were Danzig, Austria and Czechoslovakia.'

The meeting with Hitler had started with farce. After initially mistaking the Führer for a footman and nearly handing him his jacket, Halifax was quickly won over, 'both personally and politically'. Writing to his mentor, Stanley Baldwin, after returning to England, Halifax stated that 'Nationalism and Racialism is a powerful force but I can't feel that it's either unnatural or immoral! . . . I cannot myself doubt that these fellows are genuine haters of Communism, etc.! And I daresay that if we were in their position we might feel the same!'

Staggering words about the man who, when elected in 1933, rushed to implement national boycotts of Jewish businesses, removed citizenship from naturalized German Jews and outlawed interracial marriages. But the letter to Baldwin was tame compared to the sycophantic personal performance Halifax put on for Hitler. One line of vague disapproval was uttered when he said 'there was much in the Nazi system that offended British opinion (treatment of the Church; to perhaps a lesser extent, the treatment of the Jews; treatment of Trade Unions)', but the rest of the three-hour meeting was filled with nothing but compliments to Hitler for, in Halifax's own words, 'performing great services in Germany' and explaining that 'if the public opinion in England took up an attitude of criticism . . . it might no doubt be in part because the people of England were not fully informed' of the wonderful changes he had made.

While it was clearly Halifax's intention to avoid all subjects which might lead to conflict, his instigation of conversations regarding diplomacy that his Foreign Secretary had told him strictly not to go near, plus his effusive compliments to Hitler himself, show a man not just desperately out of his depth politically but worryingly detached from the reality of the situation. He wrote in his diary that Hitler 'struck me as very sincere, and as believing everything he said'. Even more charming to Halifax was Göring: 'His personality, with that reserve, was frankly attractive, like a great schoolboy ... a composite personality – film star, great landowner interested in estate, Prime Minister, party manager, head gamekeeper at Chatsworth.' Göring's status as a 'great landowner' played right into Halifax's pastoral heart, completely clouding any judgement that might have been trying to wrestle free from all the Teutonic honey that had been poured in his ears that day.

When he returned to London, it was too late. He had been successfully fooled by an artfully crafted German PR stunt. He reported to the Cabinet that war was 'inconceivable' and that 'The Germans had no policy of immediate adventure. They were too busy building up their country.' In the final part of his report, Halifax turned to the concept that would resurface in the most combative War Cabinet meetings between 25 and 28 May 1940: trades of colonial lands as part of a General European Settlement. But long before those meetings, it was an idea that formed the foundation for the policy of appeasement that Halifax and Chamberlain would now actively pursue.

In January 1938, Chamberlain officially announced his policy of colonial appeasement, and the Government began assessing what territories Europe could cobble together and give to Germany. The policy was openly derided by politicians and newspapers alike, and this public criticism even elicited complaints directly from Hitler himself. Staggeringly, Halifax stepped in to soothe Hitler and prevented the broadcast of several BBC radio programmes featuring leading anti-appeasers discussing their opposition to the colonial issue.

When Eden resigned in February 1938, over appeasement policies that favoured Hitler's designs in Austria and Mussolini's in the Mediterranean, Chamberlain offered the job to Halifax.

Just over two weeks later, on 11 March 1938, Hitler annexed Austria with the rapid operation he called *Anschluss*. Having known that this was coming, Halifax did very little to intervene until it was too late and the troops had marched into Vienna. The German Ambassador to Britain, Joachim von Ribbentrop, later went so far as to blame Halifax entirely for the *Anschluss*. In the memoirs he wrote from his cell while on trial at Nuremberg after the war, he referred to a comment made by Halifax in 1937 that he said effectively gave Hitler the green light to invade: 'the British people would never consent to go to war because two German countries wanted to merge'.

Following the *Anschluss*, all attention turned to the German-speaking Sudetenland in Czechoslovakia. How would Halifax respond to Hitler's intentions there?

Halifax at this time was described as being 'a man of uncertain judgement and vacillating opinions', who, along with Chamberlain and a cabal of titled appeasers – Sir John Simon, Sir Samuel Hoare, Sir Kingsley Wood, Sir

Thomas Inskip, Sir Reginald Dorman-Smith, Earl Stanhope – was described in Martin Gilbert's book *The Roots of Appeasement* as believing 'in the possibility of saving Anglo-German relations from the storm caused by rearmament, *Anschluss*, and anti-Semitism, into which international relations had been swept'. They concluded that it was impossible to guarantee any kind of British military response should Germany use force to annex a territory populated by a majority of ethnic Germans.

The summer of 1938 saw rumours swirling of German troops massing on the Czech border. When Hitler dismissed British and French proposals for a solution, a conference was called in Munich in September. By then Halifax – though not having lost faith in Hitler's potential rationality – wanted to hedge his bets and moved firmly behind a policy of rapid rearmament in Britain. But it was all too little too late.

In his biography *The Holy Fox*, Andrew Roberts writes:

[Halifax] made the disastrous error of trying to translate his Indian experiences of dealing with [the Indian] Congress into policy for dealing with the problems of Europe. He failed to appreciate the fact that Hitler believed in neither negotiation nor non-violence. Every single view [he] held in India . . . that ninety per cent of the problem was psychological . . . that face-to-face negotiations worked; that short-term humiliations were to be endured in the expectation of a general settlement; and that historical inevitability was ranged against him – worked well in the context of India. When Halifax went on to apply precisely these same criteria to his dealings with Nazi Germany, every one of these assumptions was to prove catastrophic.

When Chamberlain returned from Munich on 30 September, waving his little white piece of paper and declaring, 'Peace for our time!', Halifax joined the many in celebrating this seeming victory, but these celebrations failed to acknowledge that Hitler would be gifted if not Czechoslovakia (not just yet), then the Sudetenland as part of the deal.

So it turned out to be. Germany walked into the Sudetenland on 1 October 1938, without firing a shot.

Halifax's continual flip-flopping over what stance he should take in respect of Hitler showed a man still out of his depth with foreign policy. On 12 October 1938, less than two weeks after he had celebrated the success of Munich, he contradicted his own policies in a meeting with the American Ambassador, Joseph Kennedy, who reported back to Washington:

I spent an hour and a half with Halifax this afternoon drinking tea in front of his fireplace while he outlined to me what I think may be the future policy of His Majesty's Government. First of all, Halifax does not believe that Hitler wants to have a war with Great Britain and he does not think there is any sense in Great Britain having a war with Hitler unless there is direct interference with England's Dominions. The future of England, as he sees it, is to strengthen herself in the air, and 'by the way France should do the same,' so that nobody can get fresh with them from the air. Then after that to let Hitler go ahead and do what he likes in Central Europe . . . [while] fostering Dominion connections, and staying very friendly with the United States, and then, as far as everything else is concerned, Hitler can do the best he can for himself.

The events of *Kristallnacht* – when throughout Germany waves of anti-Jewish pogroms were carried out on 9 and 10 November – prompted Halifax immediately to think again. He convened an emergency meeting of the Foreign Policy Committee and announced that 'The happenings in Germany over the last few days following on from the sequence of events since Munich had made the position very difficult.' As he had informed Joseph Kennedy he would do, he instigated an immediate increase in aircraft production, and suggested – but was overruled by Chamberlain and the Chancellor of the Exchequer, Sir John Simon – a compulsory National Service Register.

At the Cabinet meeting of 15 December 1938, Halifax voiced his open opposition to Germany and stated that the 'ultimate end which he wished to see accomplished [was], namely, the destruction of Nazi-ism. So long as Nazi-ism lasted, peace would be uncertain.'

As the New Year, 1939, dawned, support for a Halifax premiership gathered momentum. Chamberlain was old and tired, and he was continuing to make one embarrassing mistake after another. Halifax was horrified when, without speaking to his Foreign Secretary first, the PM gave a briefing to the press in which he announced that the situation with Germany was better than it had been 'for some time', and that the two nations were discussing disarmament. Chamberlain again looked ridiculous when less than a week later German troops rolled into Prague, and Halifax pressed for Britain to guarantee Poland's safety should Hitler attempt to invade. This was something of a risky move, but it made the Foreign Secretary look even stronger as a potential future Prime Minister. Germany's invasion of Poland on 1 September 1939 placed Halifax in a much more culpable position when blame was distributed for Britain's being taken into war, but he believed that his constant efforts for peace over the previous years vindicated his decisions.

Throughout their careers leading up to the Cabinet crisis of May 1940, Halifax and Churchill had been like oil and water politically and personally. Long-held convictions, ideologies and morals died hard in these two most inflexible of men. Neither forgave the other for opposing opinions over Indian self-governance and appeasement. Yet they shared a superiority of belief that theirs was the right course for Britain, that no one could be more patriotic than they were, and that history had bidden them – virtually by Holy Writ – to protect their nation at its gravest hour.

Halifax later wrote of England in the Second World War:

> On our way home [we] sat in the sun for half an hour at a
> point looking across the plain of York. All the landscape
> of the nearer foreground was familiar – its sights, its

sounds, its smells; hardly a field that did not call up some half-forgotten bit of association; the red-roofed village and nearby hamlets, gathered as it were for company round the old greystone church, where men and women like ourselves, now long dead and gone, had once knelt in worship and prayer. Here in Yorkshire was a true fragment of the undying England, like the White Cliffs of Dover, or any other part of our land that Englishmen have loved. Then the question came, is it possible that the Prussian jackboot will force its way into this countryside to tread and trample over it at will? The very thought seemed an insult and an outrage; much as if anyone were to be condemned to watch his mother, wife or daughter being raped.

Such powerful, visceral words from a man so often cold and unemotional could have been written by Churchill. Both men loved Britain with a deep and abiding fervour, yet their differences remained: Winston believing in confronting conflicts head on with a display of strength; Halifax believing that if they left others – India, Germany, Italy – alone, their ambitions need not disturb Britain or the cause of civility. What Roberts terms Halifax's 'Whiggish' outlook meant that he believed 'that there was a rational solution to all problems and all that was needed was to find a *modus vivendi* comfortable to all parties ... A necessary precondition to that view of the world were [sic] national parties who sincerely wanted to reach solutions.'

Halifax's unshakeable faith in the essential rationality of people would, in the coming days, define his actions, his hopes and ultimately his legacy.

SATURDAY, 11 MAY 1940

CHURCHILL APPOINTS HIS WAR CABINET

GERMAN BLITZKRIEG HAMMERS HOLLAND AND BELGIUM

GERMAN TROOPS LOOM ON FRENCH BORDER

5. The Great 'Dictator'

Given the previous day's excitements, the new Prime Minister of Great Britain didn't get to bed until 3 a.m. Nor did he reward himself with a bit of time off before diving into his new role. First thing after he awoke that Saturday, he wrote again to Neville Chamberlain, requesting that 'you and Edward [Lord Halifax] would come to the Admiralty War Room at 12:30 p.m., so that we could look at the maps and talk things over'. Chamberlain agreed that they would, adding, 'Until you get your places filled we three will have to take the responsibility of directing the war.'

The day now presented something of a quandary for Churchill. He had just been handed power but was faced with the delicate balancing act of keeping both sides of this new National Government happy. On the one side were the effective kingmakers, Clement Attlee and Arthur Greenwood, who had not only refused to serve in a government under Neville Chamberlain, but also spelled it out to Winston that no reward be given to him for what they saw as his countless failings by including him in the War Cabinet or giving him a senior ministerial position. Having written his letters to Chamberlain and Halifax requesting their presence at 12.30 p.m., Winston then met with Attlee and Greenwood for a 'long interview' in an attempt to reconcile the decisions he now needed to make: namely, whether to include Chamberlain and Halifax in the War Cabinet and high office. When the meeting concluded, the pair believed that they had 'shaken Winston considerably', so that he agreed that he himself would become Leader of the House of Commons, and Chamberlain would serve under him as deputy and Lord President of the Council.

With this first compromise achieved, Churchill proceeded to his 'Meeting of Ministers' with Chamberlain and Halifax at the Admiralty. Also in attendance were Major-General Hastings ('Pug') Ismay, Churchill's close adviser, and a conduit between the PM and the armed forces, and the Cabinet Secretary, Sir Edward Bridges, along with the chiefs of staff: Chief to the Air Staff, Air Chief Marshal Sir Cyril Newall; First Sea Lord and Chief of Naval Staff, Admiral of the Fleet Sir Dudley Pound; Chief of the Imperial General Staff, General Sir Edmund Ironside; and Vice-Chief of the Imperial General Staff, General Sir John Dill.

The nine men proceeded to discuss such matters as the removal of British gold from Amsterdam; ongoing mine-laying operations in Mannheim; asking the King if he wished to offer the ex-Kaiser refuge from his current position in the Netherlands; despatching further armed divisions to France; attempting to persuade Sweden to enter the war on the side of the Allies; potentially arming the police in anticipation of an invasion of Britain; and interning 4,000–5,000 enemy aliens in camps in the southeast and east. With the general business of the war concluded, they agreed to meet again at ten o'clock that night.

It is interesting to note that Lord Halifax's diary account of the meeting states that Winston informed the ministers that 'the Labour People were trying to be difficult about Neville leading the House of Commons'. The Conservative MP and prolific diarist of the day Sir Henry ('Chips') Channon also wrote that:

> About one o'clock I heard that a terrific battle had been waging at the Admiralty, where Winston had summoned Neville and Halifax; for it seems that the Labour leaders ... announced that not only would they not serve under Chamberlain, but not with him either. Winston was in a dilemma as he had offered a post to Neville last night which he practically accepted, and announced as much in his speech. Now Winston may be forced to choose between Labour and Neville, and may thus be unable to form a Government at all. However after struggling all day, he was able to effect a last-moment compromise, and the Cabinet changes were announced.

Why wasn't this 'terrific battle' documented in the minutes? Enter the Cabinet Secretary, Sir Edward Bridges. He was chiefly responsible for the detailed minuting of all pertinent information discussed in the War Cabinet meetings during the Second World War. As the most senior civil servant in Britain, he was highly discreet, and noted by one of Churchill's telephonists, Ruth Ive, for 'always [being] particularly concerned with security leaks and indiscretions'. Unfortunately, his stringent approach to what might be considered sensitive comments often makes for a dry account of what were certainly ferocious debates, and here the personal diaries of the key players often provide a better and more visceral sense of the actual language deployed.

To make a true re-creation of these meetings and of the testy exchanges even harder, when the war ended Bridges burned all of his notes that didn't make it into the minutes. Given the heated discussions to come, the papers must have been highly flammable indeed.

As the afternoon of Saturday, 11 May, progressed, it began to dawn on the Conservative Party exactly what a Churchill premiership would mean, and speculation over who would serve in the new National Government intensified. Not only did the party have a leader that few wanted or trusted, but the necessary inclusion of Attlee and Greenwood in the War Cabinet was polarizing the ministerial offices lining the street of Whitehall. General Ironside believed that '[w]e want all the strength of the Labour benches to pull us through', but Halifax was of quite the opposite opinion, writing in his diary that 'Attlee and Greenwood take the place of Simon, Sam Hoare and Kingsley Wood. Certainly we shall not have gained on intellect.' Chamberlain even went so far as to write to Churchill, explaining that '[i]t is the personalities that matter, and although Greenwood would be amiable and agreeable enough I do not think he could contribute much else.' He had barely taken office, and already Churchill was facing opposition and interference from his own party.

As the barrage balloons were once again raised into the blue May skies above London – an ominous signal of the danger the capital faced – Lord Halifax, who had been given a key by the King himself, walked with his wife through the gardens of Buckingham Palace to the Foreign Office. As recorded in his diary, they 'ran into the King and Queen' en route.

> The Queen spoke very strongly about the House of Commons behaviour. The King told me that he had hoped if Neville C. went he would have had to deal with me, to which I replied with suitable expressions of gratitude, but also of hope that he had thought my reasons for judging differently are sound. On the whole he did not contest this, though he was clearly apprehensive of Winston's administrative methods.

Apprehension of Winston's methods was an understatement, and as news started to reach ministers about who he was to appoint, a collective groan could be heard all over Whitehall. The BBC made the announcement at 9 p.m., after which the Minister of Information, Sir John Reith, wrote in his diary: 'War Cabinet announced tonight, Churchill being defence minister as well as PM. Heaven help us. The three Service departments are Sinclair, Eden and Alexander. This is obviously so that Churchill can ignore them more or less and deal direct with the chiefs of staff. Awful.' It is perhaps not surprising that, the following morning, Sir John Reith received a letter from Churchill apologizing for sacking him . . . and for not giving him advanced warning for doing so.

> By the time you receive this letter, you will have been informed of the change which is taking place in this office . . . I am sure you will forgive me for not giving you previous intimation of the change I have thought it necessary to make. It is a matter of extreme national importance that the new Administration should be installed with the least possible delay.

The second 'Meeting of Ministers' on 11 May had been pushed back at the last minute to 10.30 p.m. and did not conclude until after midnight – something which irritated Halifax immensely. He noted in his diary that 'this night-life is no good to me'. Little did he and other ministers know that this was Churchill's method of working and the way he would run the war for the foreseeable future. The meetings held on Sunday, 12 May, were equally vexing. Halifax wrote:

> The meeting Winston had called for 6.30 [p.m.] was put off till 10.30 [p.m.]; quite intolerable . . . I shall tell him that if he wants midnight meetings he can have them without me. A long and rather discursive discussion, which left me uneasy as to Winston's methods. Got to bed at 1. These hours are bad enough for anybody, worst of all the Chiefs of Staff. I am seeking to organise a rebellion with Neville on the subject.

It was only Day Two, and Halifax was already planning rebellion with Chamberlain against Churchill.

Perhaps there is something in the water served to prime ministers? Margaret Thatcher famously claimed she slept for only four hours a night. Churchill at least had the excuse that Britain was at war and this was a time of national crisis. He recognized that he did not have time to stroll through the gardens of Buckingham Palace, taking in the unseasonably warm May weather, when the threat of invasion was being discussed in every meeting. However, instead of winning praise for his exemplary work ethic, the new Prime Minister seems to have been met with nothing but a series of complaints. As the staff of the Prime Minister's office officially transferred over to Churchill, his Principal Private Secretary, John 'Jock' Colville, who would later become one of his most trusted employees, noted a 'certain air of "malaise" about No. 10, which is largely due to the contrast between the fixity of the late P.M.'s habits and the inconsequential nature of Winston's. I suppose we shall get used to it; but the prospect of constant late nights – 2.00 a.m. or later – is depressing.'

In spite of the late nights, Churchill was also a relatively early riser, though he would often conduct business from his bed. Never one to stand on ceremony, he would remain there smoking cigars, which the War Office operations officer, Sir John Sinclair, recalled as making his 'stomach queasy at that time in the morning [7 a.m.]. I laid the map on his tummy, when it stopped wobbling, and told him how the British were disposed on the line of the Dyle.' Behaviour such as this was nothing new for Winston, as the staff at Chartwell knew all too well.

To ensure that he could function late into the night, Churchill religiously took a two-hour afternoon nap, which would then be followed by a hot bath (the second of the day) at 7 p.m. This had to be, as Clementine's biographer Sonia Purnell describes, 'two-thirds full and heated to precisely 98 F, rising to 104 F once he had plunged in . . . he did not like to lose water, but was fond of somersaulting in the tub – an alarming manoeuvre that caused gallons of displaced water to seep down onto the coats of visitors in the cloakroom below'. He would vigorously scrub himself with a brush and dictate speeches and memoranda to whichever awkwardly placed secretary was waiting outside the door. A former secretary, Chips Gemmell, recalled how she would be summoned to the bathroom door, where she would discreetly identify herself by a cough. Churchill would shout, 'Don't come in!' – so she would dutifully 'stand outside and you'd hear these wonderful bathroom noises, and you'd envisage the sponge being squeezed over the head and the sounds of water trickling down into nether regions. And occasionally he'd call out "Don't go away!" and you'd say, "no, no I'm still here" and the sounds of bathing would go on and sometimes . . . one really wasn't needed, he'd forgotten what he'd wanted to say.' Churchill's biographer Roy Jenkins noted an almost 'porpoise-like quality about him, which meant that one of his keenest physical pleasures, second only to alcohol, was submerging himself in either hot bathwater or lukewarm seawater'.

When he emerged from his beloved constitutional, he had no qualms about walking the connecting corridors of Admiralty House and No. 10 Downing Street, as his daughter Mary Soames recounted, 'robed like a Roman emperor in his bath towel, proceeding dripping from his bathroom across the main highway to his bedroom'. Staff should have counted themselves lucky that he chose to use a towel. When relaxed in the sanctum that was Chartwell, nudity was a frequent occurrence. As Purnell describes, '[f]ollowing his ablutions, Winston's valet would towel him dry, after which he refused to put on a dressing gown; if he wished to go to another room he would do so undressed. New members of staff would be shocked to see a very pink, sixteen-stone naked man with stooping shoulders scurrying towards them exclaiming "Coming through, don't look!"' The alternative announcement Elizabeth Gilliatt, another former secretary, recalled – 'I am coming out in a state of nature, you'd better watch it!' – would see secretaries fleeing down the corridors as fast as their heels would carry them.

When eventually he did decide to get dressed, exorbitant bills were run up at Army & Navy stores thanks to Winston's insistence that only the finest pale-pink silk underclothes would do, on account of his delicate skin. Jock Colville, one of Winston's private secretaries, remembers they made him look 'just like a rather nice pig'. Silk vests were paired with gloriously ostentatious silk dressing gowns embroidered with dragons or flowers. The legend of his lavish tastes and eccentric habits even spread to Berlin, where Joseph Goebbels noted in his diary: 'A book on Churchill reports that he drinks too much and wears silk underwear. He dictates messages in the bath or in his underpants, a startling image which the Fuehrer finds hugely amusing.'

It can't have hurt Churchill to have the Nazis consider him a joke – for it is no bad thing to be underestimated by one's enemy. But those who knew him maintain that he was not a drunk. He had been drinking alcohol for so long that his tolerance was remarkable – with just an occasional slip. When asked once how he managed to drink during the day his reply was simply 'Practice.'

So what was his actual drinking regime?

He would have his first, albeit very weak, whisky and soda around an hour after finishing his morning tray of bacon and eggs. During the war, his hatred of condensed milk was so strong that he stopped drinking tea as a traditional accompaniment to breakfast and replaced it with a glass of sweet German white wine: not, then, the usual breakfast tray. A bottle of Pol Roger champagne would be consumed at lunch, and another bottle at dinner, chased by a fine port or brandy digestif into the wee hours. He would maintain this regime every day throughout his long life, with few exceptions. How could such a man guide the country through its most perilous hours in this state, you might well join the Nazis in asking?

This iconic image of a cigar-chomping poet with a glass of scotch always in one hand – one Winston himself did much to promote – may seem amusing now, but on Sunday, 12 May 1940, his spotted reputation was no laughing matter. To his Conservative colleagues he was a different kind of joke – one whose last military campaign had ended with disaster in the Dardanelles, and one who surrounded himself with courtier friends from 'raffish worlds'. With this in mind, Lord Hankey, Minister Without Portfolio, wrote to fellow appeaser Sir Samuel Hoare to tell him how upon visiting the Admiralty:

> I found complete chaos this morning. No one was gripping the war in its crisis. The Dictator [Churchill], instead of dictating, was engaged in a sordid wrangle with the politicians of the left about the secondary offices. NC [Chamberlain] was in a state of despair about it all. The only hope lies in the solid core of Churchill, Chamberlain and Halifax, but whether the wise old elephants [Chamberlain and Halifax] will ever be able to hold the Rogue Elephant [Churchill], I doubt.

Churchill was conscious of how dangerous these opinions could be. His every move was being scrutinized, and if he was to remain as Prime Minister he would have to find a way of winning over the dissenters.

Public support for him was extremely strong. It was almost a year since the newspapers had begun calling for his inclusion in the Government and posters appeared around London stating: 'What price Churchill?' But he needed more than the support of the nation to succeed. Charm offensives had been launched the previous day with his gracious letters to Chamberlain and Halifax upon succeeding to the premiership. After all, Chamberlain was still leader of the Conservative Party and so, in spite of Labour opposition, Lord President of the Council.

Another kindness to Neville was the Churchills' decision not to move immediately into No. 10 Downing Street. Instead, Winston would stay at the Admiralty for another month to enable Mr and Mrs Chamberlain to move themselves out gradually. Churchill did everything he could think of to smooth over fractious party relationships, especially as he was scheduled to speak to the House of Commons for the first time as Prime Minister the following day, 13 May.

General Ismay recalled how:

> two or three days after he became Prime Minister, I walked with him from Downing Street to the Admiralty. A number of people waiting outside the private entrance greeted him with cries of 'Good luck, Winnie. God bless you.' He was visibly moved, and as soon as we were inside the building, he dissolved into tears. 'Poor people,' he said, 'poor people. They trust me, and I can give them nothing but disaster for quite a long time.'

With the task of forming a Government out of the way, Winston's thoughts now turned to what he could offer not just his fellow politicians, but also the nation in its darkest hour.

MONDAY, 13 MAY 1940

GERMAN TROOPS
INVADE FRANCE THROUGH
THE ARDENNES FOREST

———

DUTCH QUEEN WILHELMINA
FLEES TO ENGLAND

6. Blood, Toil, Tears and Sweat

It had been just over two days since Winston Churchill had 'kissed the King's hand' and assumed his role as Prime Minister. Despite having a war to run and a Government to assemble, there was another pivotal task looming: his maiden speech to the House of Commons as the new PM.

Despite the triumph of taking office, Winston had found himself on shaky ground during the preceding days. The speech needed to silence the critics in Whitehall and generate some desperately needed support. It had, in short, to be a beauty.

And he knew it.

The House had not sat since the drama of the Norway debate on 9 May and the following day's invasion of the Low Countries, and a large number of Conservative MPs were feeling deeply remorseful about their actions. Many who had voted against the Government did so out of frustration and to vent their anger, not quite realizing that it would lead to the fall of Neville Chamberlain. It was this same group of penitent and distrustful individuals who now, experiencing a version of 'buyers' remorse', looked down upon their new Prime Minister as he entered the Chamber. His reception was muted, with some thin cheers from the Labour and Liberal benches but little applause and even stony silence from the Conservatives.

The House of Commons had been in a state of chaos for days. Chips Channon described the atmosphere in his diary:

Absurdly dramatic and very Winstonian: first of all we were summoned by a telegram signed by the Speaker, and asked not to mention the meeting. But as both Houses were summoned, over 1300 telegrams must have been sent, and must have been seen by literally thousands of people.

I arrived at 2.15 and found an atmosphere of confusion and embarrassment. No-one knew who had been re-appointed, dropped or changed. It was 'Crazy Week'; I joined a group of bewildered Ministers . . . They chattered, amused, apprehensive, uninformed.

Neville entered with his usual shy retiring little manner, MPs lost their heads; they shouted; they cheered; they waved their Order Papers, and his reception was a regular ovation.

Just as there had been upheaval at home, reports on the war front the past weekend had revealed a progressively worsening situation across Holland, Belgium and France. The tension in the House was palpable. It was now up to Winston to attempt to allay this 'confusion and embarrassment', and disarm members' fears with words, words alone.

Churchill couldn't have designed the moment better himself, and to some extent, of course, he had.

At 2.54 p.m. he rose to his feet, stood in front of the despatch box and began to speak:

I beg to move,

That this House welcomes the formation of a Government representing the united and inflexible resolve of the nation to prosecute the war with Germany to a victorious conclusion.

So far so good – a little wordy, but unquestionably stately. His serve had landed in and the rally had begun . . .

On Friday evening last I received His Majesty's commission to form a new Administration. It is the evident wish and will of Parliament and the nation that this should be conceived on the broadest possible basis and that it should include all parties, both those who supported the late Government and also the parties of the Opposition. I have completed the most important part of this task. A War Cabinet has been formed of five Members, representing, with the Opposition Liberals, the unity of the nation. The three party Leaders have agreed to serve, either in the War Cabinet or in high executive office. The three Fighting Services have been filled. It was necessary that this should be done in one single day, on account of the extreme urgency and rigour of events. A number of other positions, key positions, were filled yesterday, and I am submitting a further list to His Majesty tonight. I hope to complete the appointment of the principal Ministers during tomorrow. The appointment of the other Ministers usually takes a little longer, but I trust that, when Parliament meets again, this part of my task will be completed, and that the administration will be complete in all respects.

I considered it in the public interest to suggest that the House should be summoned to meet today. Mr. Speaker agreed, and took the necessary steps, in accordance with the powers conferred upon him by the Resolution of the House. At the end of the proceedings today, the Adjournment of the House will be proposed until Tuesday, 21st May, with, of course, provision for earlier meeting, if need be. The business to be considered during that week will be notified to Members at the earliest opportunity. I now invite the House, by the Motion which stands in my name, to record its approval of the steps taken and to declare its confidence in the new Government.

To form an Administration of this scale and complexity is a serious undertaking in itself, but it must be remembered that we are in the preliminary stage of one of the greatest battles in history, that we are in action at many other points in Norway and in Holland, that we have to be prepared in the Mediterranean, that the air battle is continuous and that many preparations, such as have been indicated by my hon. Friend below the Gangway, have to be made here at home. In this crisis I hope I may be pardoned if I do not address the House at any length today. I hope that any of my friends and colleagues, or former colleagues, who are affected by the political reconstruction, will make allowance, all allowance, for any lack of ceremony with which it has been necessary to act. I would say to the House, as I said to those who have joined this Government: 'I have nothing to offer but blood, toil, tears and sweat.'

We have before us an ordeal of the most grievous kind. We have before us many, many long months of struggle and of suffering. You ask, what is our policy? I can say: It is to wage war, by sea, land and air, with all our might and with all the strength that God can give us; to wage war against a monstrous tyranny, never surpassed in the dark, lamentable catalogue of human crime. That is our policy. You ask, what is our aim? I can answer in one word: It is victory, victory at all costs, victory in spite of all terror, victory, however long and hard the road may be; for without victory, there is no survival. Let that be realised; no survival for the British Empire, no survival for all that the British Empire has stood for, no survival for the urge and impulse of the ages, that mankind will move forward towards its goal. But I take up my task with buoyancy and hope. I feel sure that our cause will not be suffered to fail among men. At this time I feel entitled to claim the aid of all, and I say, 'Come then, let us go forward together with our united strength.'

After speaking for just seven minutes, Churchill resumed his seat.

His closing appeal for unity and strength had not been powerful enough for his opponents to rush to support him, and Channon noted in his diary that the speech – widely regarded now as one of the greatest ever given by a politician – 'was not well received'. While the House was not assuaged, Lloyd George wished to pay his respects to the new PM:

> I congratulate the country upon his elevation to the Premiership at this very, very critical and terrible moment. If I may venture to say so, I think the Sovereign exercised a wise choice. We know the right hon. Gentleman's glittering intellectual gifts, his dauntless courage, his profound study of war, and his experience in its operation and direction – perhaps the reverse ... He is exercising his supreme responsibility at a graver moment and in times of greater jeopardy than have ever confronted a British Minister for all time.

This high praise from a former wartime Prime Minister caused Churchill to weep, and according to Harold Nicolson MP he 'mop[ped] his eyes', but in this speech, and in the ones that followed, Channon noted that 'only references to Neville raised enthusiasm'.

Diary entries from the day are more generous. Nicolson described Churchill's speech as '[v]ery short . . . but to the point'; Jock Colville called it a 'brilliant little speech'; and Channon noted, 'The new PM spoke well, even dramatically . . . ' But none were confident enough to acknowledge the real power of what is now considered as masterful a display of political rhetoric as the Gettysburg Address.

Churchill's disappointment is understandable. He had worked hard on the speech, knowing that history was listening. He had refined the text again and again, weighing, with a poet's sensitivity, phrase and metre and word. He even slipped the key phrase – the one by which the speech is now known – into earlier conversations during preceding days to test its impact. Malcolm MacDonald, one of the ministers whom Winston had appointed earlier that day, recalled how:

> I entered the presence. The great man was striding up and down the Chamber with his head thrust forward in deep thought on his massive shoulders and his hands gripping the lapels of his jacket, as if he were making a speech in the House of Commons.
>
> He looked round, caught sight of me, and said rather oratorically without halting his pacings, 'My dear Malcolm, I'm glad to see you. I've nothing to offer you except . . .' For a moment he hesitated deliberately in his utterance. I felt disappointed, thinking he could have no more senior office to give me than that of Postmaster General or some similar minor job. Then he continued, ' . . . blood and toil, tears and sweat.'
>
> I was taken aback, wondering whether he had created a new war-time Ministry, and was asking me to become Secretary of State for Blood, Toil, Tears and Sweat.
>
> He glanced at me to observe my reaction, stood still, and then in a voice suddenly changed to friendly informality remarked, 'I want you to be Minister of Health in my government.'
>
> [Leo] Amery awaited me in the private secretary's office . . . and then asked, 'Did he also offer you blood and sweat and toil and tears?'

I answered 'Yes'; and Amery remarked that he had received the same proposition. 'He must be rehearsing his speech for Parliament this afternoon.'

It is in this account that we get a glimpse of the process and methods used by Churchill the orator – pacing around the room gripping his lapels, dummy-running his speech over and over again. Jock Colville remembered that 'the composition of a speech was not a task Churchill was prepared either to skimp or to hurry'. Indeed, it was said that one hour's work went into every minute of speech delivered. In this case, though the circumstances of the past four days had interfered with Churchill's preparations significantly, they had not done so irreparably, for he had been preparing for this speech in actual fact his entire life.

During his period of self-education in India in 1896, Churchill had studied myriad great thinkers and historians, but it was in the works of Socrates, Plato and Aristotle that one subject in particular caught his eye: the art of rhetoric. In an unpublished essay written a year later entitled 'The Scaffolding of Rhetoric', the 23-year-old Churchill wrote: 'Rhetorical power is neither wholly bestowed nor wholly acquired, but cultivated. The peculiar temperament and talents of the orator must be his by nature. Their development is encouraged by practice.' More than forty years of practice, in fact.

We can trace the origins of 'blood, toil, tears and sweat' back to Cicero's *De Divinatione II* (44 BC) and Livy's *History of Rome* (c.29 BC), when 'sudor et sanguis' (sweat and blood) were first and frequently coupled together.

Centuries later John Donne wrote in his 1611 poem 'An Anatomy of the World': 'That 'tis in vain to dew, or mollify it with thy tears, or sweat, or blood'. In 1823 Lord Byron wrote: 'Year after year they voted cent per cent, Blood, sweat, and tear-wrung millions – why? for rent!'; and in Robert Browning's poem 'Ixion' of 1883 are the words: 'Tears, sweat, blood – each spasm, ghastly once, glorified now.'

Speeches by politicians and military leaders influenced Churchill too. In 1849 the Italian revolutionary and patriot Giuseppe Garibaldi gave a rousing speech to his besieged soldiers in St Peter's Square, Rome; one sentence of it translates as: 'I offer neither pay, nor quarters, nor provisions; I offer hunger, thirst, forced marches, battles and death.' Nearly fifty years later, Theodore Roosevelt's speech to a naval war college in 1897 described how 'Because of the blood and sweat and tears, the labor and the anguish, through which, in the days that have gone, our forefathers moved on to triumph.'

'Amateurs borrow, professionals steal' – as either Picasso or T. S. Eliot famously said, depending on who stole the line from whom.

In 1900 Churchill began to ruminate on his own version when writing of his time spent in a Boer prisoner of war camp. In *London to Ladysmith via Pretoria* he confidently predicted British victory in the South African war as being 'only a question of time and money expressed in terms of blood and tears'. Clearly pleased with the phrase, he used it again in a newspaper article for the *Saturday Evening Post* the same year: 'It will all seem very sad and brutal in times of peace, but there will be less blood and tears when the next war comes.'

That 'next war' turned out to be the First World War, about which Churchill wrote his five-volume history entitled *The World Crisis*. In the final volume, published in 1931, he described the devastation suffered on the Eastern Front and how the pages of his book will '[r]ecord the toils, periods, sufferings and passions of millions of men. Their sweat, their tears, their blood bedewed the endless plain.' Two years later 'follies in blood and toil' appeared in his biography of the Duke of Marlborough; and in a 1939 article about General Franco's war in Spain, he wrote of the 'new structures of national life erected upon blood, sweat and tears, which are not dissimilar and therefore capable of being united'.

The visceral impact of these four words on Churchill over the course of forty years is undeniable. In his prescient essay of 1897, the young Winston described how 'the orator is the embodiment of the passions of the multitude. Before he can inspire them with any emotion he must be swayed by it himself. When he would rouse their indignation his heart is filled with anger. Before he can move their tears his own must flow. To convince them he must himself believe.' So it would seem Churchill was prepared for the stony reception he received in the House of Commons on 13 May – was perhaps even expecting it, because he was not just speaking to fellow politicians. He was speaking to the nation, the world, and indeed to history.

Churchill needed to convey both the gravity of the situation the nation now faced and also to ask the people to trust him to lead them safely through to the bitter end. After the official preamble, the core of his speech follows an undulating climactic pattern of rhetoric: he begins by making it clear how dangerous the peril is, but then presents himself as the hope that will work tirelessly and fearlessly for them. He repeats this with two more stark assessments of danger but ends on a high note of courage and optimism. Classic stuff. Winston wanted his listeners to feel their new reality keenly but not to be afraid. He showed himself as a defiant leader, humbling himself to his people.

Churchill skilfully employs two key rhetorical devices here, both drawn from antiquity. One is anacoenosis, a figure of speech in which an appeal is made to one's listeners or opponents for their opinion or judgement as to the subject under discussion. He uses this in 'You ask, what is our policy?' and 'You ask, what is our aim?', bringing his listeners into the drama with him. The other device is anaphora, repetition of a word or words at the beginning of two or more successive verses, clauses or sentences. He repeats, 'To wage war, by sea, land and air . . . to wage war against a monstrous tyranny' and, 'It is victory, victory at all costs, victory in spite of all terror, victory, however long and hard the road may be, for without victory there is no survival.'

In *The Roar of the Lion*, the historian Richard Toye describes how 'the repetition of that single word "victory" five times within one sentence created an impressive sense of Churchill's single-mindedness and determination; he did not promise victory, but he did promise to not stop short of it, and this meant that his warnings of blood and terror were accompanied with a sense of optimism'.

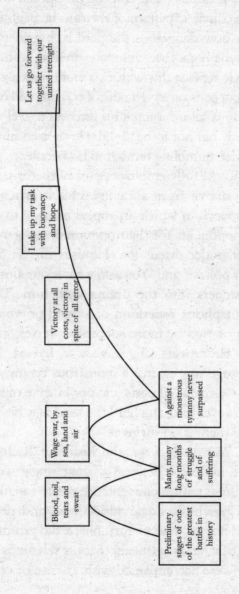

The Triple Jump of Rhetoric

Let us go forward together with our united strength

I take up my task with buoyancy and hope

Victory at all costs, victory in spite of all terror

Against a monstrous tyranny never surpassed

Many, many long months of struggle and of suffering

Wage war, by sea, land and air

Blood, toil, tears and sweat

Preliminary stages of one of the greatest battles in history

In this way, Churchill appealed to the long-held tradition of British stoicism. Drawing on thoughts from his 'Scaffolding of Rhetoric' again, he knew that great oratory is a kind of clever trick, fooling the audience with 'a series of vivid impressions which are replaced before they can be too closely examined and vanish before they can be assailed'.

We are left with an emotion, then, but may not be quite sure how we came by it, and may not be inclined to understand why. How easily, down through the ages, have citizens been so beguiled.

Structurally, we can see how these rhetorical techniques have been passed down from within the House of Commons too. In his book *The History of the English-Speaking Peoples,* Churchill referenced a speech given in 1800 by William Pitt when debating the British conflict with Napoleon during the French Revolution:

> [Mr. Fox] defies me to state, in one sentence, what is the object of the war. I know not whether I can do it in one sentence; but in one word I can tell him that it is 'security': security against a danger, the greatest that has ever threatened the world. It is security against a danger which never existed in any past period of society. It is security against a danger which in degree and extent was never equalled; against a danger which threatened all the nations of the earth; against a danger which has been resisted by all the nations of Europe, and resisted by none with so much success as by this nation, because by none has it been resisted so uniformly and with so much energy.

In stark contrast to Hitler's egomaniacal speeches – which emphasized the word 'I' – Churchill, whose years of study had honed his keen understanding of the nation he was now leading, knew the power of 'We' when exhorting the British public to take up such a fearful struggle. If the trial was to be presented in this speech as a clear battle between two empires – one democratic and good, the other totalitarian and utterly evil – then he knew that '*We shall*' would far better serve than '*Ich werde*'. The short, simple Anglo-Saxon phrases came in cannonades of plural pronouns: '*we* have before *us*', 'with all *our* might', 'come then, let *us* go forward *together* with *our* united strength'. His business was to flatter a frightened people by casting them in lead roles in the great world drama; and, as we know, flattery will get you everywhere.

In 'The Scaffolding of Rhetoric' he wrote about how 'the unreflecting often imagine that the effects of oratory are produced by the use of long words. The error of this idea will appear from what has been written. The shorter words of a language are usually the more ancient. Their meaning is more ingrained in the national character and they appeal with greater force to simple understandings . . . ' The words in his speech followed such a method exactly: 'battle'; 'blood, toil, tears and sweat'; 'war'; 'victory'; 'terror'; 'survival', 'urge'; 'hope'; and 'united strength'.

It was Plutarch, citing Plato, who wrote that rhetoric is 'the art of working upon the souls of men by means of words, and that its chief business is the knowledge of men's characters and passions which are, so to speak, the strings and stops of the soul and require a most skilful and delicate touch'. With this speech, Churchill succeeded in his objective of winning over his key audience – the public – and was rewarded with a rapturous response the following day. Contrary to the first-hand accounts from within the Chamber, both the *Daily Telegraph* and the *Evening Standard* reported that Churchill's statement was 'loudly cheered'. The *Standard*'s publication of an iconic cartoon by David Low would set the tone for the nation's confidence in its new Prime Minister.

As the newspapers went to print, the War Cabinet convened at No. 10 Downing Street to discuss the latest updates from the continent. Churchill informed the meeting that 'he felt an air attack on their country was inevitable. Whatever course the war in France took', it was now time for him to make a personal approach detailing the 'seriousness of the situation' to a man he hoped had been listening to his defiant speech: President Franklin D. Roosevelt.

ALL BEHIND YOU, WINSTON

HOLLAND IS OVERWHELMED AND IS PREDICTED TO BE IN GERMAN HANDS WITHIN DAYS

AFTER A FIERCE TWO-DAY BATTLE, GERMAN PANZERS CROSS THE RIVER MEUSE INTO FRANCE

CONFUSION PERSISTS OVER GERMAN STRATEGIC INTENTIONS

THE SUPREME COMMANDER OF THE FRENCH ARMY, GENERAL MAURICE GAMELIN, IGNORES WARNINGS THAT GERMANY IS SETTING A TRAP, AND CONTINUES THE ADVANCE OF SOLDIERS INTO THE LOW COUNTRIES, LEAVING THE MAGINOT LINE POORLY DEFENDED

———

7. The Worsening Situation

The British people awoke on 14 May to newspapers heralding Churchill's masterful performance in the Commons, echoing that cartoon message: 'All behind you, Winston.'

But the situation of the war was darkening fast. The largest invasion the world had ever seen – 3 million German troops in rapid advance (with another 2 million at home in uniform at the ready) – was happening so quickly that the Allies, with their primitive field telephones and telegrams and mud-caked motorbike despatch riders, struggled to grasp the sheer scale of the terror, or how best to counter so many threats.

The daily routine of smoke-filled War Cabinet, Defence Committee and Chiefs of Staff Committee meetings continued unabated as fragments of the full picture emerged. In the War Rooms, the cramped underground bunker beneath Whitehall that served as the operational planning centre for Britain throughout the war, Churchill, in the Map Room, watched as coloured pins (green for Germany) were pressed into the large wall maps of Western Europe, only to be pulled out and advanced westward as each new telephoned report came in. Churchill described these first days as 'peculiar' on account of how 'one lived with the battle, upon which all thoughts were centred, and about which nothing could be done'.

The War Cabinet assembled at No. 10 Downing Street at 11.30 a.m. to hear the latest updates. By now the Western Front was taking the brunt of the German assault, with the French Army withdrawing to Antwerp and trying to hold the line with the Belgians against German armoured and motorized divisions. The most serious thrust of attack was farther south on the Namur–Sedan (Belgian–French) front, where German soldiers had crossed the river Meuse into France. News such as this shook the War Cabinet to its core, for the Meuse since Roman times has served as a barrier, protecting the plains of France, Belgium and Holland from the ancient threat of invasion from the east.

Holland could not resist for long. Lord Halifax informed the War Cabinet that earlier that morning he had been approached by the French Ambassador, who expressed serious concerns regarding a message received from Queen Wilhelmina of Holland, now installed in Buckingham Palace by King George VI. The French had interpreted her words as an indication that the Dutch were considering peace negotiations with Germany. In an attempt to allay French fears, Halifax had said that his interpretation of the message was quite the opposite and that the attitude of the Dutch Government was unyielding: they showed no appetite for peace talks.

As for Italy's threat to enter the war at Germany's side, Halifax alerted the War Cabinet to a telegram he had received from the British Ambassador in Rome, advising that 'we should not regard any verbal provocation from Italy as so intolerable as to drive us into a declaration of war [with Italy] ... Unless Signor Mussolini has already decided to take the plunge, there are three or four weeks left for him to make up his mind on military performance whether to come in or not.' The intentions of Mussolini would prove critical far sooner than three or four weeks, and would cause an irreparable schism between the War Cabinet's two leading figures, Halifax and Churchill. In the meantime, there were more urgent matters at hand.

Churchill attended the Chiefs of Staff Committee at 6 p.m. and the War Cabinet at 7 p.m., informing each of them of a telephone message from the French Prime Minister, Paul Reynaud:

Germany intends to deliver a mortal blow towards Paris. The German Army has broken through our fortified line south of Sedan. The reason is we cannot resist the combined attacks of heavy tanks and bomber squadrons. To stop the German drive whilst there is still time and to allow our counter-attack to succeed, it is necessary to cut off the German tanks and bombers supporting them. It can only be done by an enormous force of fighters. You were kind enough to send 4 squadrons which is more than you promised, but if we are to win this battle, which might be decisive for the whole war, it is necessary to send at once, if possible to-day, 10 more squadrons. Without such support, we cannot be sure of stopping the German advance between Sedan and Paris. Between Sedan and Paris there are no fortifications left to be compared with the line to be re-established at almost any cost.

I am confident that in this crisis the English help will not fail us.

The ease with which the Germans crossed the river Meuse had come as a shock to the French. To cross so quickly General Ironside believed they must have had 'amphibious tanks protected by armour impervious to the fire of the French tanks'. Again, the 'situation was too obscure' to enable the War Cabinet to commit to sending further troops to France. Instead they deemed it 'essential that information should be obtained at the earliest possible moment, not only about what had happened but also regarding the future intentions of the French' and whether or not they were even capable of mounting a sufficient counter-attack.

Since the morning's War Cabinet, Lord Halifax had received confirmation from a British naval attaché in Rome that 'merchant vessels were being assembled and armed at various ports . . . and that mines and net defences were being laid'. But a contradictory report had also come from the British Ambassador in Rome that a reliable source with the 'highest Fascist standing had quoted Signor Mussolini as having categorically declared that Italy would *not* go to war'. Discussions ensued over whether it was better to do nothing or to explore protective measures such as closing the Suez Canal to prevent the passage of Italian supplies. Churchill concluded that 'the most prudent course would be to wait and see what action the Italians took and to take our decision in that light'. The meeting then adjourned until the following day, and Winston returned to the Admiralty to continue working.

A makeshift personal 'war room' had been set up for Churchill in the drawing room at Admiralty House. Jock Colville recalled that amid the 'curious ugly dolphin furniture' which prompted Churchill to call the place the 'fish room', space was made for a private secretary and one of Winston's specially trained 'night-women-typists'. 'At the side of his desk stands a table laden with bottles of whisky etc. On the desk itself are all manner of things: toothpicks, gold medals (which he uses as paperweights), special cuffs to save his coat sleeves from becoming dirty, and innumerable pills and powders.'

At around 10.30 p.m. a 'motley gathering appeared', comprised of General Ismay; Anthony Eden, Minister for War; Sir Arthur Sinclair, Minister for Air; David Margesson, the Tory Chief Whip, whom Churchill had decided to keep on; Lord Beaverbrook, recently appointed Minister of Aircraft Production; and Joseph Kennedy, the American Ambassador (and father of JFK). Colville called them 'strange bedfellows indeed!' and listened while they discussed the German advance – with noted 'alarmist and ... untrustworthy opinions of Mr. Kennedy'.

Churchill once more worked well past 1 a.m., but was up at 7 a.m. on 15 May to speak with the French Prime Minister. The news was terrible. Reynaud was described by Churchill as being in a 'very excited mood';

late the previous evening the French counter-attack south of the Sedan had failed, so 'the road to Paris was open and the battle was lost. He even talked of giving up.' The last thing Churchill needed was his country's strongest ally losing its head, surrendering the fight and leaving Britain alone against the brute force of the Nazis. Churchill set about talking Reynaud down off the ledge:

> He [Reynaud] must not be misled by panic-stricken messages [military despatches] of this kind; that only a small proportion of the French Army was yet engaged and that the Germans who had broken through would be in a vulnerable position. He also said several times that, whatever the French did, we would continue to fight to the last.
>
> M. Reynaud asked that we might send further troops to their assistance. The Prime Minister pointed out that, as he well knew, this was impossible. .
>
> The Prime Minister asked and obtained M. Reynaud's permission to speak direct to General Georges [France's Commander-in-Chief of the North East Front]. General Georges rang up later on, shortly after 9 a.m.

Fortunately, Churchill's conversation with the General proved infinitely more calm, and he subsequently informed the 10 a.m. Chiefs of Staff Committee meeting and the 11 a.m. War Cabinet that while 'the situation was undoubtedly serious ... the Germans had broken through on a fairly wide front, but this was now plugged'.

Plugged? The good news was pounced upon and passed on.

But the relief was short-lived. Lord Halifax had troubling news. Firstly, the Netherlands Minister in London had called him that morning to inform him that the Dutch would be 'announcing the surrender of Rotterdam and Utrecht in order to save further useless loss of life'. Alfred 'Duff' Cooper, Churchill's new Minister for Information, immediately sensed the possible PR disaster should the British people hear of the Dutch proclamation in the press and panic that the Netherlands was now out of the war. Churchill agreed that 'it should be made clear that the action announced . . . amounted to no more than a military capitation in a particular area'.

Halifax's second piece of bad news for the War Cabinet concerned a report from Joseph Kennedy, who had been informed by a colleague in Rome that:

> the situation had become so serious that . . . now he thought that the odds were 10 to 1 on her [Italy] going in with Germany . . . Signor Mussolini had already made up his mind. He was convinced that the information in regard to military operations which Herr Hitler had given to Signor Mussolini in the past had always been correct; and the information which Herr Hitler had sent that day showed a complete German victory in Belgium and the Netherlands.

A grave mood fell over the room. If Italy entered the war, then France, facing *two* enemies, would be even less likely to survive. In this context, Britain might soon be the only nation standing between Hitler and his total domination of Europe. General Ironside wrote in his diary:

> The war is coming nearer and nearer to us and it makes one think all the more. We are living in a new phase of history the course of which no man can foresee. Nobody believed we should be engaged in war, certainly not in a death struggle so soon. We made no preparations, even for war industry to be developed, and we cannot now catch up. It is too late. The year may see us beaten, but it cannot bring us to the defeat of Germany, unless it is by economic means.

Halifax, who increasingly looked to Italy for a ray of hope, suggested that it 'might be of some value if the Prime Minister . . . were to send a communication to Signor Mussolini'. Churchill readily agreed to do so, as well as outlining the 'particulars of the personal message which it had been agreed he should send to President Roosevelt informing him of the seriousness of the situation'.

How the sweat must have run down Chamberlain's forehead in the stuffy, smoky Cabinet Room at Downing Street. To the twenty-two other men seated around the table, and who were now witnessing Churchill desperately trying to pick up the pieces and save England from the same fate as Europe, his failures must have been palpable. When the long meeting was over, Chamberlain returned to Halifax's room to talk. In his diary, Halifax describes the ex-PM as being 'a good deal shaken by political events . . . He told me that he had always thought he could not face the job of being Prime Minister in war, but when it came he did; and yet now that the war was becoming intense he could not but feel relieved that the final responsibility was off him.'

With that vast responsibility now on his shoulders, Churchill sat down to write to President Roosevelt. Unlike Halifax, he regarded the United States as Britain's most immediate bulwark against the Nazis.

Churchill, during his time as First Lord of the Admiralty, had developed a strong rapport with Roosevelt, and so spoke frankly now:

Although I have changed my office, I am sure you would not wish me to discontinue our intimate, private correspondence. As you are no doubt aware, the scene has darkened swiftly. The enemy have a marked preponderance in the air, and their new technique is making a deep impression upon the French. I think myself the battle on land has only just begun, and I should like to see the masses engage. Up to the present, Hitler is working with specialised units in tanks and air. The small countries are simply smashed up, one by one, like matchwood. We must expect, though it is not yet certain, that Mussolini will hurry in to share the loot of civilisation. We expect to be attacked here ourselves, both from the air and by parachute and air-borne troops in the near future, and are getting ready for them. If necessary, we shall continue the war alone, and we are not afraid of that. But I trust you realise, Mr President, that the voice and force of the United States may count for nothing if they are withheld too long. You may have a completed subjugated Nazified Europe established with astonishing swiftness, and the weight may be more than we can bear. All I ask now is that you should proclaim non-belligerency, which would mean that you would help us with everything short of actually engaging armed forces . . .

He then outlined six immediate needs, ranging from a loan of forty or fifty old American destroyers, to several hundred of the 'latest types of aircraft' and anti-aircraft equipment, to the purchase of US steel and other raw materials. All of which, he explained, 'we shall go on paying dollars for as long as we can, but I should like to feel reasonably sure that when we can pay no more, you will give us the stuff all the same'.

Churchill also requested 'the visit of a United States Squadron to Irish ports' as a deterrent against a German invasion of Britain via Ireland; finally he requested that the President 'keep that Japanese dog quiet in the Pacific, using Singapore in any way convenient'. Signing the letter 'with all good wishes and respect', all he could do now was wait for the President's response.

Since the beginning of Hitler's aggressive rule in 1933, the United States had maintained a steadfastly neutral position, with Roosevelt openly declaring that his country would have no part in any future European conflict. Indeed, during the late 1930s, Congress passed several Neutrality Acts to ban trading or financial loans to belligerent countries. When war eventually did break out in 1939, these terms were revised and a 'cash-and-carry' basis of sale (excluding arms) was legalized, enabling the US to provide unofficial support to Great Britain and France, which were considered the only two countries able to pay in 'cash' and 'carry' the items home themselves.

Two weeks before Churchill took up his pen to write to Roosevelt, Britain had secured a purchase of 324 Curtis P-40 fighter planes for the Army and eighty-one Grumman fighter planes for the Navy. The official line was that the planes were currently 'being built in and for the United States'. Britain requested permission for one of its aircraft carriers to collect the aircraft from a US port, but this was denied by Roosevelt because of the Neutrality Act conditions; he did, however, suggest that 'we [America] could arrange to have the aircraft flown to the Canadian border, pushed across that border and flown on to Botwood [Newfoundland]'. Push them across the border? Yes. The rules prohibited any mechanical assistance. But such an almost comical offer, in its makeshift complexity, was also an extraordinary display of determination to get around his own Neutrality Act. Roosevelt's landslide election victory in 1936 had been won on the basis of a strong anti-war stance, and Churchill knew that despite strong public support in America for the Allied cause, that country's overt involvement in war at this juncture would be difficult.

Churchill, as he mentioned in his letter to the President, now expected that fascist Italy *would* come into the war alongside Hitler. The intimacy with which he'd written to Roosevelt was therefore not extended to Mussolini when, on the morning of 16 May, he sent a brief and somewhat theatrical letter to his soon-to-be enemy in Rome:

Now that I have taken up my office as Prime Minister and Minister of Defence I look back to our meetings in Rome and feel a desire to speak words of goodwill to you as chief of the Italian nation across what seems to be a swiftly-widening gulf. Is it too late to stop a river of blood from flowing between British and Italian peoples? We can no doubt inflict grievous injuries upon one another and maul each other cruelly, and darken the Mediterranean with our strife. If you so decree it must be so; but I declare that I have never been the enemy of Italian greatness, nor ever at heart the foe of the Italian law-giver. It is idle to predict the course of the great battles now raging in Europe, but I am sure that whatever may happen on the Continent, England will go on to the end, even quite alone, as we have done before, and I believe with some assurance that we shall be aided in increasing measure by the United States, and, indeed, by all the Americas.

I beg you to believe that it is in no spirit of weakness or of fear that I make this solemn appeal which will remain on record. Down the ages above all other calls comes the cry that the joint heirs of Latin and Christian civilisation must not be ranged against one another in mortal strife. Hearken to it I beseech you in all honour

and respect before the dread signal is given. It will never
be given by us.

It would seem that old grudges were dying hard not only
with Hitler but with Mussolini too, and when he replied,
two days later, Mussolini made his feelings clear:

> I reply to the message which you have sent me in order to
> tell you that you are certainly aware of grave reasons of a
> historical and contingent character which have ranged
> our two countries in opposite camps. Without going
> back very far in time I remind you of the initiative taken
> in 1935 by your Government to organise at Geneva sanc-
> tions against Italy engaged in securing for herself a small
> space in the African sun without causing the slightest
> injury to your interests and territories or those of others.
> I remind you also of the real and actual state of servitude
> in which Italy finds herself in her own sea. If it was to
> honour your signature that your Government declared
> war on Germany, you will understand that the same
> sense of honour and of respect for engagements assumed
> in the Italian–German treaty guides Italian policy today
> and tomorrow in the face of any event whatsoever.

Having just begged for help from America, and for
decency from Italy, Winston headed straight to the War
Cabinet meeting at 11.30 a.m. on 16 May. Once again the
news there was grim.

General Ironside informed the room that the Germans
had surprised the French by breaking through the Maginot

Line and 'there was no doubt that the situation was most critical . . . All now depended on whether the French would fight with vigour in the counter-attack which General Gamelin proposed to launch.' The French had drastically underestimated the capacity of the German tanks to cross the weakest point of the line, near the Ardennes forest, assuming the terrain would prove too difficult. Opinion had been that the line's 85-mile-long series of fortresses and strongpoints was near-impenetrable. The line had cost a staggering 7,000 million francs to build when it was completed in 1935 but left a vast 250-mile frontier of unprotected border between France and Belgium. The walls were well built, therefore, but the back door had been left open.

Knowing first hand the agitated state of the French PM, Paul Reynaud, Churchill agreed that four fighter squadrons should be despatched to France ahead of his own journey that afternoon to an emergency crisis meeting of the Supreme War Council at the Quai d'Orsay in Paris. He had decided that Britain's old friend needed to be roused to a heroic resistance.

Accompanied by General Ismay and the Vice-Chief of the Imperial General Staff, General Sir John Dill, Churchill flew across the Channel in his trusty Flamingo plane, accompanied by two Hurricane fighter jets. On route he polished his weapons of diplomacy and decided to add to France's misery by speaking French. (Just as Winston invented new words such as 'paintatious' to describe landscapes that begged to be painted, he often spoke 'franglais' intentionally, coining memorable phrases such as when, during a heated discussion with General Charles de Gaulle in Casablanca, in January 1943, he said, '*Si vous m'obstaclerez, je vous liquiderai!*' 'If you obstruct me, I will liquidate you.')

Ismay recalled the trip in his memoirs:

From the moment we set foot at Le Bourget airfield, there was an unmistakable atmosphere of depression . . . As we drove through the streets, the people seemed listless and resigned, and they gave no sign of the passionate defiance that had inspired the cry, '*Ils ne passeront pas*' ['They shall not pass'], in the previous struggle. They showed little interest in our heavily-escorted cavalcade, and there were no cheers for Churchill . . . The Quai D'Orsay . . . was even more depressing. M. Reynaud, M. Daladier [Minister of Defence and former Prime Minister] and General Gamelin were awaiting us in a very large room, looking out on to a garden which had appeared so lovely and well kept on my last visit, but which was now disfigured with clusters of bonfires. The French archives were already being consigned to the flames.

Churchill entered the room in a dominant mood. French morale was desperately low, and he needed to act quickly to prevent its complete capitulation. He telegraphed the War Cabinet to inform them of the panic in Paris and 'again emphasise the mortal gravity of the hour'. His suggestion was that 'we should send squadrons of fighters demanded (i.e. six more) tomorrow', and requested they meet at 11.00 p.m. that night to discuss the proposal in his absence, sending their reply by midnight. Such a strategy had until now been rejected because it would seriously weaken Britain's defences, but Paris had been left almost completely undefended and no other option remained. Thirty minutes later, the War Cabinet telephoned back their agreement. Ismay recalled:

> [Churchill was] delighted that the War Cabinet had endorsed his recommendation so promptly, and we thought that he would telephone the good news to M. Reynaud at once. But not at all. He was determined to tell it to him face to face. This was in character. We all know the delight that it gives some of our friends, especially our younger friends, to watch our expressions as we open their gift parcels. That was Mr. Churchill's motive at this moment. He was about to give Reynaud a pearl beyond price, and he wanted to watch his face when he received it.

Churchill and Ismay duly raced over in the middle of the night to give Reynaud the news before leaving for London at 7 a.m. on 17 May. But Reynaud was not at his office; nor was he at home with his wife. He was with his mistress, Mme la Contesse de Portes, in her modest apartment on the Place du Palais Bourbon, where they found him luxuriating in a bathrobe. Winston, apparently undaunted, wanted a bigger audience for his message and insisted that Daladier, the War Minister, be asked to join them. But Daladier was not at home with his wife either. It was Mme la Marquise de Crussol who would pass the phone to Daladier, her lover, and tell him that M. Churchill wished to speak with him on a matter of some urgency.

Relief, gratitude and fervent handshakes greeted Churchill's offer of more planes, but all three men doubted it would change very much. Winston's greatest fear in this hour was that France would soon opt for a peace deal with Hitler. Then the full weight of resistance would fall on Britain and its Empire alone.

Upon arrival back at Downing Street, the Prime Minister convened the War Cabinet at 10 a.m. to recount the visit to France. Churchill expressed his regret that they 'had been faced with the gravest decision that a British Cabinet had ever had to take', but the War Cabinet's reply 'had hardened [the French] to a very considerable degree'.

The meeting in Paris had not been easy. The British commitment to send six fighter squadrons was exceedingly generous considering they only had thirty-nine for the protection of England. Churchill had described the squadrons to the French as 'the life of the country' and explained how they needed to be conserved, the British having already lost thirty-six aircraft in defence of the Meuse. The French counter-argued that they 'had begun the battle with 650 Fighters, and they now had only 150 left', to which Churchill replied that 'we had bombarded all the places we had been asked to, and were anxious to attack only such vital objectives as would stop the enemy from attacking by day. It was not reasonable that the

British aircraft should be required to take on German armoured fighting vehicles. This should be done by ground action.' Churchill concluded his account of the Supreme War Council meeting, and then read aloud the reply he had just received from President Roosevelt.

Alas, it was not the life-saving communiqué he had wished for. Roosevelt explained that he was 'of course giving every possible consideration to the suggestions made in your message', but any efforts to aid the Allies would 'take time'.

But for Western Europe time had all but run out. The War Cabinet agreed that under the present circumstances a declaration of a state of 'supreme emergency' should be made to the British people. It could be put off no longer. Chamberlain 'invited the Prime Minister to broadcast a statement on the following day'.

On the morning of Sunday, 19 May, Clementine Churchill returned early from a church service at St Martin-in-the-Fields in central London, having walked out when the preacher delivered a pacifist sermon. Winston told her, 'You ought to have cried "Shame", desecrating the House of God with lies!' At a time like this, pacifism was exactly the opposite of what the nation needed to hear – and the opposite of what Churchill was preparing to say to them. Later that day, Colville noted that in his frustration and after 'a gruelling week, [Churchill] retired to Chartwell . . . for a few hours' sunshine and sought distraction by feeding his surviving black swan (the remainder had been eaten by foxes)'. However, he was almost immediately summoned back to Downing Street for a War Cabinet meeting at 4.30 p.m.

France had still not mounted any credible counter-attack, and with the German Army rapidly advancing to the coast, discussions began among the military about a possible withdrawal of the nearly 400,000-strong British Expeditionary Force (BEF) from near the Belgian border in Northern France to the port of Dunkirk. This suggestion provoked serious consternation among the Cabinet, and Winston believed that if the BEF were forced into such a position they 'would be closely invested in a bomb-trap, and its total loss would be only a matter of time . . . We must face the fact that the Belgian Army might be lost altogether, but we should do them no service by sacrificing our own Army.'

The War Cabinet concluded, and at 6 p.m. Churchill finally began to write his speech.

He sat, alone, in his office at the Admiralty, pen in hand, sheaves of blank stationery in front of him. Again he faced the challenge: what words, in what order? What notes to sound, what to avoid?

How his pen and imagination must have flown, for only three hours later he sat down in front of the BBC microphone, his heavily marked-up pages before him, to attempt once more to galvanize the support of a jittery nation.

One aspect of the speech rehearsal that the public never saw veers into farce. As biographer William Manchester tells it: 'After forty years in the House of Commons, Churchill instinctively swung his head from left to right [as he spoke]. That would not do on the BBC, so Tyrone Guthrie of the Old Vic [theatre, London] stood behind him and held [Winston's] ears firmly as he spoke at a desk in a small room . . . '

Held his ears? Preserve this image in mind, then, as we see the BBC wall clock strike 9.00 p.m., and hear Churchill, under a green light, begin to speak into the microphone:

I speak to you for the first time as Prime Minister in a solemn hour for the life of our country, of our empire, of our allies, and, above all, of the cause of Freedom. A tremendous battle is raging in France and Flanders. The Germans, by a remarkable combination of air bombing and heavily armoured tanks, have broken through the French defences north of the Maginot Line, and strong columns of their armoured vehicles are ravaging the open country, which for the first day or two was without defenders. They have penetrated deeply and spread alarm and confusion in their track. Behind them there are now appearing infantry in lorries, and behind them, again, the large masses are moving forward. The re-groupment of the French armies to make head against, and also to strike at, this intruding wedge has been proceeding for several days, largely assisted by the magnificent efforts of the Royal Air Force.

We must not allow ourselves to be intimidated by the presence of these armoured vehicles in unexpected places behind our lines. If they are behind our Front, the French are also at many points fighting actively behind

theirs. Both sides are therefore in an extremely dangerous position. And if the French Army, and our own
Army, are well handled, as I believe they will be; if the
French retain that genius for recovery and counter-attack
for which they have so long been famous; and if the British Army shows the dogged endurance and solid fighting
power of which there have been so many examples in the
past – then a sudden transformation of the scene might
spring into being.

It would be foolish, however, to disguise the gravity of
the hour. It would be still more foolish to lose heart and
courage or to suppose that well-trained, well-equipped
armies numbering three or four millions of men can be
overcome in the space of a few weeks, or even months,
by a scoop, or raid of mechanized vehicles, however formidable. We may look with confidence to the stabilization
of the Front in France, and to the general engagement of
the masses, which will enable the qualities of the French
and British soldiers to be matched squarely against those
of their adversaries. For myself, I have invincible confidence in the French Army and its leaders. Only a very
small part of that splendid Army has yet been heavily
engaged; and only a very small part of France has yet
been invaded. There is a good evidence to show that
practically the whole of the specialized and mechanized
forces of the enemy have been already thrown into the
battle; and we know that very heavy losses have been
inflicted upon them. No officer or man, no brigade or
division, which grapples at close quarters with the
enemy, wherever encountered, can fail to make a worthy

contribution to the general result. The Armies must cast away the idea of resisting behind concrete lines or natural obstacles, and must realize that mastery can only be regained by furious and unrelenting assault. And this spirit must not only animate the High Command, but must inspire every fighting man.

In the air – often at serious odds, often at odds hitherto thought overwhelming – we have been clawing down three or four to one of our enemies; and the relative balance of the British and German Air Forces is now considerably more favourable to us than at the beginning of the battle. In cutting down the German bombers, we are fighting our own battle as well as that of France. My confidence in our ability to fight it out to the finish with the German Air Force has been strengthened by the fierce encounters which have taken place and are taking place. At the same time, our heavy bombers are striking nightly at the tap-root of German mechanized power, and have already inflicted serious damage upon the oil refineries on which the Nazi effort to dominate the world directly depends.

We must expect that as soon as stability is reached on the Western Front, the bulk of that hideous apparatus of aggression which gashed Holland into ruin and slavery in a few days will be turned upon us. I am sure I speak for all when I say we are ready to face it; to endure it; and to retaliate against it – to any extent that the unwritten laws of war permit. There will be many men and many women in the Island who when the ordeal comes upon them, as come it will, will feel comfort, and even a pride, that they are sharing the perils of our lads at the Front – soldiers, sailors and airmen, God bless them – and are drawing away from them a part at least of the onslaught they have to bear. Is not this the appointed time for all to make the utmost exertions in their power? If the battle is to be won, we must provide our men with ever-increasing quantities of the weapons and ammunition they need. We must have, and have quickly, more aeroplanes, more tanks, more shells, more guns. There is imperious need for these vital munitions. They increase our strength against the powerfully armed enemy. They replace the wastage of the obstinate struggle; and the knowledge that wastage will speedily be replaced enables us to draw more readily upon our reserves and throw them in now that everything counts so much.

Our task is not only to win the battle – but to win the war. After this battle in France abates its force, there will come the battle for our Island – for all that Britain is, and all that Britain means. That will be the struggle. In that supreme emergency we shall not hesitate to take every step, even the most drastic, to call forth from our people the last ounce and the last inch of effort of which they are capable. The interests of property, the hours of labour, are nothing compared with the struggle for life and honour, for right and freedom, to which we have vowed ourselves.

I have received from the Chiefs of the French Republic, and in particular from its indomitable Prime Minister, M. Reynaud, the most sacred pledges that whatever happens they will fight to the end, be it bitter or be it glorious. Nay, if we fight to the end, it can only be glorious.

Having received His Majesty's commission, I have formed an Administration of men and women of every Party and of almost every point of view. We have differed and quarrelled in the past; but now one bond unites us all – to wage war until victory is won, and never to surrender ourselves to servitude and shame, whatever the cost and the agony may be. This is one of the most awe-striking periods in the long history of France and Britain. It is also beyond doubt the most sublime. Side by side, unaided except by their kith and kin in the great Dominions and by the wide empires which rest beneath their shield – side by side, the British and French peoples have advanced to rescue not only Europe but mankind from the foulest and most soul-destroying tyranny which has ever darkened and stained the pages of history. Behind them – behind us – behind the Armies and Fleets of Britain and France – gather a group of shattered States and bludgeoned races: the Czechs, the Poles, the Norwegians, the Danes, the Dutch, the Belgians – upon all of whom the long night of barbarism will descend, unbroken even by a star of hope, unless we conquer, as conquer we must; as conquer we shall.

Today is Trinity Sunday. Centuries ago words were written to be a call and a spur to the faithful servants of Truth and Justice: 'Arm yourselves, and be ye men of valour, and be in readiness for the conflict; for it is better for us to perish in battle than to look upon the outrage of our nation and our altar. As the Will of God is in Heaven, even so let it be.'

As he had done six days earlier, Churchill proved himself a master of rhetoric, capable of rousing people to his cause at the most crucial of moments.

The response from fellow politicians this time was overwhelmingly positive. Anthony Eden wrote to him that evening to tell him, 'You have never done anything as good or as great. Thank you, & thank God for you.' As Captain Claude Berkley, a member of the War Cabinet Secretariat, noted in his diary, 'The PM gave a magnificent broadcast address last night, which has at last put the true position before the people. He is being "sublime" at every stage and after narrowly averting a serious collapse in Paris four days ago has been galvanising everybody here.' The former Prime Minister, Stanley Baldwin, wrote to Churchill to say, 'I listened to your well known voice last night and I should have liked to have shaken your hand for a brief moment and to tell you that from the bottom of my heart I wish you all that is good – health and strength of mind and body – for the intolerable burden that now lies on you.'

Churchill would need these words of support more than he knew, for the first German tanks had reached the French coast at Abbeville and their crews were looking across the Channel, just fifty miles to England.

**THE COLLAPSE OF THE ENTIRE FRENCH
NINTH ARMY HAS CRUSHED ALL HOPE OF
A COUNTER-ATTACK**

———

**THE BRITISH EXPEDITIONARY FORCE HAVE NO
CHOICE BUT TO ATTEMPT A FIGHTING RETREAT TO
THE COASTAL PORTS . . . ESPECIALLY DUNKIRK**

———

**CHURCHILL HAS THE IDEA TO ORDER THE
ADMIRALTY TO PREPARE A LARGE FLEET OF
CIVILIAN VESSELS TO SAIL TO FRENCH PORTS IN
CASE OF AN EVACUATION**

8. Fear, Doubts and Pressures from Within

What had been unthinkable when the Germans invaded the Low Countries ten days before – the fall of France – was now becoming a reality, and Churchill's frustration with the distinct lack of solid intelligence was beginning to show. General Ismay recalled:

> It is always difficult to get accurate information about a fast-moving battle, and for those who have to wait far from the scene, there is nothing for it but to exercise patience, and to remember that the commander in the field is preoccupied with the conduct of the engagement, and often has neither the time nor the knowledge to report details of its progress. This truism was never fully accepted by my impetuous chief; nor did he always make sufficient allowance for the fact that, in the fog of war, the commander himself does not know from hour to hour what is happening at every point on an enormous front.

Churchill despatched General Ironside to France, hoping that he, as the Chief of Imperial General Staff, might shed some light on the precise situation faced by the French, Belgian and British armies. Meanwhile, the War Cabinet met at 11.30 a.m. on 20 May to discuss once more the options for military support of Britain's Allies.

Sensing that a Nazi invasion of Britain might well be imminent, Churchill agreed with the War Cabinet that Britain had 'already reached the absolute limit of the air assistance that we can afford to France, if we are to have any chance of protecting the United Kingdom, the Fleet, our sea-borne trade, our aircraft industry, and all the vital centres throughout the country on which we must depend for our ability to continue the war.' This was of course a reasonable conclusion, but it also presented the very real prospect that, without further support over the next few days, the French Army 'may give up the struggle'.

French surrender might be staved off if the United States would agree to supply the planes the British had requested. Churchill had the previous evening sent 'a telegram for those bloody Yankees', and was waiting for the President's reply, but time for an eleventh-hour rescue was running out and the Prime Minister abandoned his usual 'soothing words', and advised Roosevelt:

In no conceivable circumstances will we consent to surrender. If members of the present Administration were finished and others came in to parley amid the ruins, you must not be blind to the fact that the sole remaining bargaining counter with Germany would be the Fleet, and, if this country was left by the United States to its fate, no one would have the right to blame those responsible if they made the best terms they could for the surviving inhabitant. Excuse me, Mr. President, putting this nightmare bluntly. Evidently I could not answer for my successors, who in utter despair and helplessness might well have to accommodate themselves to the German will.

General Ironside returned from France on the morning of 21 May, having narrowly escaped with his life when a German bomb had hit his hotel in Calais, and came straight to the 11.30 a.m. War Cabinet to update his colleagues. There was only bad news to report. He had found the French High Command 'in a state of indecision', struggling to make sense of events due to poor communications. Ironside wrote in his diary that he 'lost his temper and shook Billotte [French Commander in Chief of the armies in the north] by the button of his tunic. This man is completely beaten.'

He reported that the roads were heavily congested with 'hundreds of thousands of refugees from Belgium and the northern French towns', who greatly slowed the movement of Allied troops. The German thrust to the coastal town of Boulogne now meant that the British and Belgian forces positioned in the north of France had been all but completely cut off from the French Army and the bases holding all of their supplies. Without either the means or leadership, any possibility of reconnecting the fighting Allied forces looked less likely by the minute.

The whole situation was chaos.

Churchill decided there was nothing for it but to return to Paris early the next morning, 22 May, to meet with Weygand and Reynaud, and to attempt to shake them into some form of order. He was deeply infuriated by the lack of information. 'In all the history of war, I have never seen such mismanagement,' he told Jock Colville, who noted in his diary that he had 'not seen Winston so depressed', and to make matters worse, as he was retiring to bed at 1.30 a.m. that night, Churchill was informed that General Billotte had been involved in a high-speed car accident, plunging the French Command into further disarray.

The British Expeditionary Force's position was now worse than it had ever been and the proposed withdrawal to the Channel ports would have to be attempted without the necessary supplies of munitions and food. If and when the force did eventually reach the coast, there remained the problem of how to evacuate 300,000 men and their considerable stock of armaments. The Luftwaffe controlled the skies, and a beach was no safe haven.

When Churchill arrived in Paris on 22 May, he was relieved to find a new lease of energy from the new French Supreme Commander, General Weygand, seventy-three years old, who 'in spite of his physical exertions and a night of travel . . . was brisk, buoyant, and incisive. He made an excellent impression upon all', and proceeded to unfold 'his plan of war'.

Britain had already despatched the maximum active Army units to the continent, reserving only what was required for the defence of the nation. They had landed at Boulogne that day and were now taking measures to protect the French ports of Calais and Dunkirk to the north. Weygand assured Churchill during the meeting that 'there were at Calais three French infantry battalions and that the command at Dunkerque [sic] was in the hands of a particularly vigorous Admiral, who had sufficient forces at his disposal to protect the town', and having assessed the front in person, he [Weygand] concluded that 'there could be no question of asking the Anglo-Franco-Belgian forces in the North, consisting of over forty divisions, simply to retreat Southwards in an attempt to join up with the main French Army. Such a movement would be found to fail and the forces would be condemned to certain disaster.' Churchill agreed but explained to the French Prime Minister and General Weygand that he understood relations between General Billotte and Lord Gort to be 'not entirely satisfactory', so work needed to be done to restore these essential lines of communication between Allied forces to the north and south of the German advance.

After just over an hour, the Supreme War Council meeting concluded, as Ismay recalled, 'on a note of restrained optimism', and he departed with Churchill for London.

Ironside noted in his diary, with some surprise, that during the 7.30 p.m. War Cabinet meeting the Prime Minister was 'almost in buoyant spirits, having been impressed by Weygand'. Others in the room did not share his upbeat mood. It was already clear that the BEF had 'lost a chance of extricating itself and [was] very short of food and ammunition'. Moreover, General Ismay, who was in possession of battlefield intelligence, rather than French predictions, saw more closely the writing on the wall, and informed Jock Colville that he was 'really worried' and could foresee the moment when France might give up the struggle. Colville, borrowing some of Winston's optimism, thought Ismay was being 'unduly alarmist, because I cannot see the French shaming themselves quite to that extent'.

The War Cabinet were informed that the Supreme War Council in France had agreed on a joint offensive to begin the following day, 23 May, with British and French armies attacking to the south-west, and the French Army Group attacking northwards. But Ironside 'observed that, so far as was known, no preparations had been made for these attacks at noon that day'; he thought the attacks 'would take some time to mount'. Anthony Eden also expressed concern, having received a telephone call at five o'clock that afternoon relaying a message from Lord Gort that the French 'were not prepared to fight, nor did they show any sign of doing so'. In his diary Eden later noted that it 'seemed to me a deadly commentary on the increasing confusion which we had neither the authority nor the reserves to mend. The only hope was a joint offensive from the north and south, if there were the will and the means to mount it.'

But when the War Cabinet met again the following morning at 11.30, residual optimism quickly evaporated. A skeletal report had finally come in from the front. Churchill informed his colleagues that 'very much larger German forces had succeeded in getting through the gap than had at first been supposed'. General Ironside had been instructed to remain at the War Office rather than attend the meeting because the situation had 'become so critical'.

Again, a lack of information as well as the lack of a credible response by the French was destroying the Allied hope of survival. The Prime Minister explained that 'the whole success of the plan agreed with the French depended on the French forces taking the offensive. At present they showed no signs of doing so.'

Boulogne was now under heavy German bombardment and the enemy forces were perilously close to surrounding the town, cutting off the Allies completely. Calais was in no better shape and was described to the War Cabinet as a 'seething mass of French troops and refugees, all of whom seemed completely demoralised'. Supply ships had been sent to the Channel ports of Calais, Dunkirk and Boulogne, but the Luftwaffe was making it impossible to unload.

Neville Chamberlain had remained relatively quiet over the past few days' meetings but now, with many looking to him for a seasoned opinion, he voiced his concerns that Britain, rather than counter-attacking, would do better to execute a speedy retreat. Britain, he feared, would be left completely defenceless if it missed the opportunity to evacuate the BEF safely. Britain was, he said, 'in danger of falling between two stools and that neither the plan agreed with General Weygand would be effectively carried out, nor would we use our forces to the best advantage in retaining our hold on the Channel Ports'.

Lord Halifax, as ever falling in line with Chamberlain, further supported these concerns when he read out a telegram to the War Cabinet from the British Ambassador in Rome, outlining suspicions that 'Signor Mussolini was only awaiting the establishment of the Germans in the Channel Ports to declare war.' Halifax, it was becoming clear, saw Italy as having a key role in what happened next to Western Europe. Rather than view Italy as an enemy-in-waiting, he wished to exploit the small window of opportunity that existed before Mussolini entered the war and bend it to a different purpose: towards peace.

Churchill, in the meantime, needed officially to update the House of Commons. The severity of a defenceless British Army in full retreat, the collapse of France and a new enemy in Italy demanded it.

Speaking at 3 p.m., the Prime Minister informed his fellow MPs that Abbeville was now in enemy hands and Boulogne would soon follow. When asked by a fellow Conservative MP, Mr Gurney Braithwaite, if the Government 'renews and reiterates its predecessor that no peace will be concluded with the enemy except in agreement and co-operation with the Government of the French Republic', Churchill answered simply, 'Yes, Sir.'

On record, then, came the first suggestion of a peace deal with Nazi Germany. That it would be entertained only with France's participation does not detract from the magnitude of such a suggestion. Unlike his 13 May address, there was no talk of 'victory at all costs', no argument that survival was impossible without victory. If there was one word to sum up this exchange, it was not victory, but defeat.

Having been assured that Weygand's plan would be executed first thing that morning, Churchill was shocked to discover when he returned to Downing Street that 'the Germans were already in Boulogne, Gort's attack southwards to Arras had made no progress, the British Expeditionary Force had been forced through lack of supplies to go on half rations, and Weygand's northward offensive had not yet begun'.

Calls were made to Reynaud and eventually to Weygand himself at 6 p.m. He reassured the Prime Minister that his plan had begun and his forces had successfully recaptured three French towns. We now know that this information was false, but as Colville later wrote, 'there was no reason to doubt Weygand's report, and gloom gave way to elation'. As Churchill's biographer Martin Gilbert notes, '[T]he reason for Weygand's deception has been a matter of considerable concern to those who were involved in the crisis of May 23, or who witnessed it at the time. Colville, who was at Downing Street throughout that day . . . later reflected: "Weygand was determined, if the BEF could not go southward [to aid French forces], that *we* should go under if *they* did."'

The elation must have been short-lived. When Churchill sat down at the 7 p.m. War Cabinet, he admitted – after many moments of valuable indecision on his own part – that he had 'been giving further consideration' to the concerns raised by Neville Chamberlain at their last meeting. In a sign that this bulldog was capable of changing his mind, even as he wished to stamp his authority on a War Cabinet so full of doubters, he conceded that it was perhaps time for the 'BEF to fall back on the Channel Ports' and an evacuation should be attempted. The situation in Boulogne was now described as 'catastrophic', but 'General Weygand had demanded that the operation should continue'. General Ironside agreed that Lord Gort's attack southwards should carry on as requested by the French, for 'if the BEF were to retire on the Channel ports, it was unlikely that more than a small part of the force should be got away'. Churchill concluded that 'there was as yet little ground for confidence. He felt, however, that we had no choice in the matter but to do our best to conform to General Weygand's plan.'

The choices facing Winston and Britain were stark and binary: continue with a failing plan, or attempt a perilous evacuation that would save only a fraction of the British Expeditionary Force. In a black mood, the Prime Minister travelled to Buckingham Palace to inform the King of the situation.

In his diary, King George VI wrote:

The Prime Minister came at 10.30 p.m. He told me that if the French plan made out by Weygand did not come off, he would have to order the BEF back to England. This operation would mean the loss of all guns, tanks, ammunition, & all stores in France. The question was whether we could get the troops back from Calais and Dunkirk. The very thought of having to order this movement is appalling, as the loss of life will probably be immense.

Churchill would later quip, 'War is usually a catalogue of blunders and this one is proving no exception', but his mood did not allow for jest as he returned to the

Admiralty to be updated with yet more grim news of the chaotic Weygand plan. He sent quick messages to General Weygand and Paul Reynaud, warning them that Belgian headquarters had still 'received no directive' and Lord Gort had 'no (repeat no) ammunition for a serious attack'. Churchill made his irritation plain: 'We have not here even seen your own directive, and have no knowledge of the details of your northern operations. Will you kindly have this sent through French Mission at earliest?' He noted that 'time is vital as supplies are short'.

As the night wore on, 1,000 British soldiers were evacuated from Boulogne during a relentless German attack, but 200 were left behind.

Just over twenty miles up the coast, Brigadier Claude Nicholson and his garrison at Calais were facing constantly conflicting orders. What had become clear was that if Boulogne fell, the defence of Calais was essential to keep the Germans from reaching Dunkirk. The roads out of the town were now blocked and Calais was completely surrounded. As the soldiers looked east towards Dunkirk, bonfires had been lit by the German soldiers of 1 Panzer Division as a signal to the approaching Luftwaffe planes.

At the following day's War Cabinet meeting on 24 May, Lord Halifax began to make his presence felt, mapping out a route whereby diplomacy might at least keep Italy out of the fray.

Sensing an opportunity to subtly advance this aspect of his peace agenda – part one of his grand design to reach a general pan-European peace deal – he read a telegram from the British Ambassador in Paris, outlining a request from the French Government that:

> President Roosevelt should be asked to make another approach to Signor Mussolini . . . to ask what his reasons are for being on the brink of entering the war against the Allies. If Signor Mussolini recited his grievances, the United States Ambassador in Rome would then say that the President would be prepared to communicate the Italian claims to the Allied Governments or some other words which would at least have a delaying action.

Halifax's opinion was that not much would come of it, but that Britain should:

> reply that we fully endorse the suggestion of another approach by President Roosevelt . . . provided it was quite clear that President Roosevelt were acting on his own responsibility . . . The Allies were ready to consider reasonable Italian claims at the end of the war, and would welcome Italy at a Peace Conference on equal terms with the belligerents, and that the United States were willing to guarantee that the Allies should carry out these under-takings so long as Italy and the United States of America did not become engaged in the war on opposite sides.

So assuredly did Halifax present his argument that the War Cabinet, without debate, agreed 'that a reply should be made on these lines'.

Chalk one up for Halifax.

As the situation in France worsened, and the direct danger to Britain increased, the pressure on the Prime Minister began to take its toll physically. By noon, he had returned to his bed on the advice of his doctor. But he proved a poor patient. From his bed Churchill learned that an evacuation of Calais had been proposed by General Ismay. Brigadier Nicholson telegraphed at 2 a.m. to confirm this. Even though the proposal was cancelled three hours after it was sent, Churchill – still awake and blowing steam about the idea – wrote to Ismay to complain: 'The only effect of evacuating Calais would be to transfer the [enemy] forces now blocking it to Dunkirk. Calais must be held for many reasons, but specifically to hold the enemy on its front.'

Even though ill and abed, Churchill was sketching out in his head the first outlines of a desperate rescue plan – and having the garrison at Calais fight on to the death, inviting the enemy's wrath and drawing their attention away from Dunkirk, was becoming a critical part of it. The only question was: how much longer could Calais perform this function?

Later that day, when the Defence Committee met at 5 p.m., General Ironside informed the room that 'German tanks had penetrated past the forts on the west side of Calais and had got between the town and the sea'. Despite this news, the troops at Calais were to remain and fight off the approaching German advances, in order that they might buy the Allies in Dunkirk more time.

Nicholson was still hoping for an evacuation and, unaware of this decision, gallantly continued to attempt to defend the town, but his men were forced to retreat to the citadel located within the Old Town walls. He telegraphed a last-ditch message at 7.05 p.m.: 'Reinforcements urgent if whole garrison be not overwhelmed.' He received a reply at 11.23 p.m. telling him that no evacuation had yet been ordered. 'You must comply for the sake of Allied solidarity. Your role is therefore to hold on . . . No reinforcements . . . You will select best position and fight on.' General Ironside sent a separate message, telling Nicholson that the evacuation had been forbidden and that his were 'all regular troops, and I need not say more'.

All we know of Nicholson's reaction to this message is that he immediately told his staff to burn his remaining tanks.

When Churchill learned of these messages he was furious. To his mind, these were not words that would motivate someone to make the ultimate sacrifice. The following day he wrote to Anthony Eden and General Ironside: 'Pray find out . . . by whom was this very lukewarm telegram I saw this morning drafted, in which mention is made of "for the sake of Allied solidarity." This is not the way to encourage men to fight to the end.' Knowing he could withhold this decision no longer, Churchill drafted a response, which Eden sent just after 1.50 p.m. on 25 May:

To Brigadier Nicholson. Defence of Calais to the utmost is of the highest importance to our country as symbolising our continued cooperation with France. The eyes of the Empire are upon the defence of Calais, and H.M.

1. Churchill leaves a cabinet meeting with Anthony Eden (*right*) and Sir Kingsley Wood (*left*), May 1940. (© *H. F. Davis/Topical Press Agency/Getty Images*)

2. Viscount Halifax (*left*) at Hitler's house in the Bavarian Alps, The Berghof, 1937. (© *Ullstein Bild*)

3. Neville Chamberlain (*right*) returns 'victorious' from the Munich conference, 1938, greeted by Halifax. (© *Hulton Archive/ Getty Images*)

4. (*below*) Chamberlain and Halifax meet with the Italian dictator Mussolini, 1939. (© *Popperfoto/Getty Images*)

5. Churchill, the writer, in his study at Chartwell, Kent, England. (© *Kurt Hutton/ Picture Post/Getty Images*)

6. (*below*) Churchill, May 1940. (© *Fox Photos/Hulton Archive/Getty Images*)

7. Churchill speaks to the nation. (© *Keystone-France/Gamma-Keystone via Getty Images*)

8. The new Prime Minister with Clementine on their way to take up residence at 10 Downing Street, 25 May 1940. (© *H. F. Davis/Topical Press Agency/Getty Images*)

9. Supreme War Council Meeting in Paris, May 1940: Clement Attlee (*third from right*) and French Premier Paul Reynaud (*extreme right*). (*Alamy D995B5* © *World History Archive/Alamy Stock Photo*)

10. The War Cabinet Rooms, below Whitehall. (© *IWM*)

11. Churchill the warrior inspects a 'tommy gun'. (© *Capt. Horton/IWM via Getty Images*)

12. Londoners listen to Churchill. (© *Felix Man/Picture Post/Getty Images*)

13. (*left*) 'V for victory'.
(© *Popperfoto/Getty Images*)

14. (*below*) Churchill
at the Albert Hall.
(© *Universal History
Archive/UIG via
Getty Images*)

15. (*above*) Churchill the orator, full flow, addresses a Conservative Party meeting. (© *Keystone-France/ Gamma-Keystone via Getty Images*)

16. (*right*) Churchill and Clementine at Epsom horse races. (© *Central Press/ Hulton Archive/Getty Images*)

17. (*below*) Churchill's body language, accentuating the power of his words. (© *Fox Photos/Hulton Archive/ Getty Images*)

Government are confident you and your gallant regiments will perform an exploit worthy of the British name.

That was how you did it – no paltry talk of compliance, or of holding on. Rather, make these doomed men aware that this was their chance to go down in history, to – paraphrasing Shakespeare – make their names as familiar in the mouths of Britons as household words.

In London, Churchill had received a telegram from Paul Reynaud informing him that the British Army was no longer conforming to General Weygand's plan and had withdrawn towards the Channel ports. Without the British attacking southwards, the road to Dunkirk was now wide open. The prospect of a full retreat and evacuation now looked certain, so Lord Halifax – ready to intensify the pressure on Winston – returned to the French suggestion of a proposed approach to Mussolini.

For the pacifists in the Tory Party, and there were many – more each day, in fact, who were keen to preserve their ancestral country estates and British autonomy, even if the ultimate price was Central and Western Europe – the idea of an approach to Mussolini, asking him to name his terms to stay out of the war and also to broker future negotiations with Hitler, was a viable, welcome and entirely rational plan. It certainly made a lot more sense than fighting on, if this meant, as looked likely, the loss of almost all of Britain's professional army.

With this in mind, and confident of widespread support for his case, Halifax informed the War Cabinet on

25 May that a meeting had taken place at the Italian Embassy in London, where it was said that:

> [an] Italian diplomat, alleging that he was speaking without instructions, had said that there are still a great many influential people in Italy who desired to see a peaceful solution of the Mediterranean problem. If His Majesty's Government saw their way to make an approach to the Italian Government, with a view to exploring the possibilities of a friendly settlement, there need be no fear of their meeting with a rebuff.

Halifax again expressed his belief that 'very likely nothing might come of all this. Nevertheless, even if the result were merely to gain time, it would be valuable. The French would certainly be pleased with such a move on the part of His Majesty's Government, which was in line with their own policy.'

In his reply to Churchill one week earlier, Mussolini had entirely dismissed the prospect of peaceful negotiations with the Allies: 'If it was to honour your signature that your Government declared war on Germany, you will understand that the same sense of honour and of respect for engagements assumed in the Italian–German Treaty guides Italian policy today and tomorrow in the face of any event whatsoever.' But with France now teetering on the brink of collapse and the desperate rush to evacuate the BEF, Churchill agreed 'to an approach of the character suggested', but stressed that 'it must not, of course, be accompanied by any publicity, since that would amount to a confession of weakness'. He remained deeply suspicious of the Italian leader and suspected that 'it was very probable that at any moment Signor Mussolini might put very strong pressure on the French, with a view to obtaining concessions from them. The fact that the French were denuding their Italian frontier of troops put them in a very weak bargaining position.'

The British people would have been horrified to know that their leaders were exploring peace terms with a fascist dictator, but the fact was they were kept almost entirely in the dark about the terrible progress of the war. As Sir Alexander Cadogan, Halifax's right-hand man at the Foreign Office, noted in his diary: 'the public don't grasp the situation at all'. Newspapers from the time show something of the gulf between what was reported and the reality on the ground. On 25 May, for example, the *Manchester Guardian* published an advertisement for a weekend away in the French capital:

STAY IN PARIS: NEAR THE OPERA AND GRAND
BOULEVARD . . . SPECIAL RATES FOR MEMBERS
OF THE ALLIED FORCES

On 26 May, two days after Boulogne had fallen, in the *News of the World*:

ALLIES POUNDING GERMANS NEAR
CHANNEL COAST — FRENCH SAY, 'BOULOGNE
STILL IN OUR HANDS'; CALAIS BEING
STRONGLY DEFENDED

On the same day, in the *Sunday Express*:

FRANCE SACKS 15 GENERALS — COMMUNIQUE
DECLARES 'WE HAVE DOMINATED THE ENEMY'

And in the *People*:

NAZIS CLAIM ALLIED ARMIES ARE RINGED IN
FLANDERS, BUT PARIS REPORTS RECAPTURE OF
AMIENS, AND ENORMOUS ENEMY LOSSES

On 27 May, a day after Calais had fallen, in the *Daily Mail*:

NAVY GOES INTO ACTION SHELLING GERMAN
TROOPS ACROSS BOULOGNE — CITADEL HELD IN
STREET BATTLE — CALAIS AND DUNKIRK ARE
FIRMLY IN ALLIED HANDS

CALAIS IS HELD: NAVY SHELLS ENEMY

In the *Evening Standard*:

'ENORMOUS' GERMAN LOSSES IN VIOLENT
FIGHTING AT MENIN — CALAIS STILL
HELD TO-DAY

In the *Daily Express*:

FIGHTING IN THE STREETS OF CALAIS — NAVY
SHELLS SMASH GERMAN ARMOURED DIVISIONS

As dawn broke on 26 May, the news from France dominated Churchill's thoughts, and those of his advisers and staff. The road to Dunkirk lay open to both British and German troops. As Churchill himself described it, 'the march to the sea' had begun.

Paul Reynaud was on his way to London for crisis talks with Churchill, who informed the 9 a.m. meeting of the War Cabinet that they should:

> be prepared for M. Reynaud in his interview that day to say that the French could not carry on the fight. He would make every endeavour to induce M. Reynaud to carry on, and that he would point out that they were at least honour bound required to provide, as far as lay in their power, for the safe withdrawal of the British Expeditionary Force.

Lord Halifax could no longer stay silent. Ever more sure of his opinions, he told the Cabinet in no uncertain terms that 'we had to face the fact that it was not so much now a question of imposing a complete defeat upon Germany but of safeguarding the independence of our own Empire'. To continue with Churchill's crusade of 'victory at all costs' now seemed ludicrous. His message was blunt: We are losing the war, and if we have an opportunity to prevent losing more young lives, how can we not take it?

Driving home his advantage, he informed the Cabinet that he had met the Italian Ambassador, Signor Giuseppe Bastianini, the previous evening and had been informed that 'Mussolini's principal wish was to secure peace in Europe'. Halifax had replied that this was an objective Britain desired too, and 'we should naturally be prepared to consider any proposals which might lead to this, provided our liberty and independence were assured'. This representation of the British Government's stance in respect of Italy was far in advance even of Churchill's most forward position concerning a negotiated peace with Hitler. Now, clearly fused in Halifax's mind and in his language were both the smaller idea of keeping Italy out of the war and the bigger one of getting Hitler to lay down his guns. Henceforward, for Halifax, all approaches to Italy would be synonymous with the solution he called (to Bastianini) the 'general European settlement', wherein Italy would be offered *nothing* unless it was tied to this wider deal.

Churchill too now understood that his approval of any formal approach to Italy meant sending Britain down a slippery slope that would lead down, down, down towards peace talks with Berlin. He replied to Halifax, '[P]eace and security might be achieved under a German domination of Europe. That we could never accept. We must ensure our complete liberty and independence. [I am] opposed to any negotiations which might lead to a derogation of our rights and power.'

Halifax had repeatedly pointed out that there was no question of accepting such a derogation, and added now that if France and Britain presented a united front at such a negotiation, then this would be 'a powerful lever to obtain favourable terms which might be of great value to us . . . If the French intended to come to [peace] terms, they had a very strong card to play if they made it clear to Hitler that they were bound not to make a separate peace.'

Winston, who believed that separate deals were more likely to be offered, replied that 'the Germans would make the terms of any peace offer as attractive as possible to the French, and lay emphasis on the fact that their quarrel was not with France but with England'.

The Chiefs of Staff had prepared a paper outlining possible outcomes if France did surrender. It made for bleak reading. The paper, Halifax pointed out, said that 'our ability to carry on the war single-handed against Germany would depend in the main on our being able to establish and maintain air superiority over the Germans'. However, if the Germans now had control of the French Army, they would not need to plough all their resources into a European land battle and 'would be then free to switch the bulk of their effort to air production'. This was a terrifying thought, and a strong argument for suing for peace immediately. The Luftwaffe already had considerable air superiority. Should it get any stronger, the RAF would be powerless to oppose it. Peace talks or no, Halifax suggested that as a 'last resort we should ask the French to put their [aircraft] factories out of gear'.

The Cabinet concluded with no real resolution on the issue. The pressures on Churchill were mounting now that it was clear, even to him, the incorrigible optimist, that he was completely at the mercy of France. His options had all but gone.

*

When the War Cabinet met again at 2 p.m. on 26 May, talk shifted to the imminent prospect of the fall of Paris.

Churchill reported that Reynaud had told him that 'while he would obey orders and fight it out as long as he was told to do so, and would be prepared to go down fighting for the honour of the Flag, he did not think that France's resistance was likely to last very long against a determined German onslaught'. The French had fifty divisions against the Germans' 150, and 'it was clear that the war could not be won on land'. Reynaud had asked Churchill 'where then, could France look for salvation? Someone had suggested that a further approach should be made to Italy.' Reynaud speculated that Italy would extract, as the price for peace, 'the neutralisation of Gibraltar and the Suez Canal, the demilitarisation of Malta, and the limitation of naval forces in the Mediterranean' – which the French believed *should* be offered if it would keep Italy out of the war.

Churchill was desperate to raise Reynaud's spirits, for he needed the French to fight on if the BEF were to escape. He had told the Premier that 'we were not prepared to give in on any account. We would rather go down fighting than be enslaved to Germany. But in any case we were confident that we had a good chance of surviving the German onslaught. France, however, must stay in the war.'

Churchill now suggested that someone ought to leave the meeting and go to the Admiralty and meet with Reynaud himself. The man he chose to do this was Halifax, the peace-maker. Effectively, while talking tough himself with Reynaud, he despatched his most ardent pacifist to continue the vital conversation. Were there mixed messages here?

Talking to the War Cabinet, Winston was more realistic: he was still convinced that Britain had a slim chance of coming out of this in one piece, but only if France would 'stick things out for another three months . . . the position [then] would be entirely different'. Here was another admission of how bleak his assessment of Britain's chances of survival really was.

Halifax, slow to leave the meeting, and seizing upon this rare bout of realism in his leader, again urged that *an approach to Italy* – with all this signified – must now be made. He insisted that 'the last thing that Signor Mussolini wanted was to see Herr Hitler dominating Europe. He would be anxious, if he could, to persuade Herr Hitler to take a more reasonable attitude.' Finally, the Prime Minister – backed into a corner in the fencing duel that characterized his long argument with Halifax – said that he 'doubted whether anything would come of an approach to Italy', but conceded – in the first of what would become a stunning series of concessions that challenge our image of him – that 'the matter was one which the War Cabinet would have to consider'.

At last, one for Halifax. How very far Winston had come, in just a few days, from the man who would brook no thought, nor allow anyone else to think, of parley or surrender. But this was the cumulative effect of the avalanche of bad news and collegial pressure that had steadily collapsed all his early hopes.

Lord Halifax duly left to meet with Reynaud at the Admiralty, and the War Cabinet joined him there when the French Premier had left.

In a quirk of fate, the Cabinet Secretary, Bridges, was not present for the first fifteen minutes of this meeting, so there is no direct record of what was said during this time. But it is clear that the extreme tension was showing on Churchill, and there is a clue, hidden in the minutes of the following day's War Cabinet meeting and in Chamberlain's diary account of the day, that Winston may have made his most startling statement on the question of peace talks to date.

Sir Alexander Cadogan, who was there at 5 p.m., described Churchill as being 'too rambling and romantic and sentimental and temperamental'. Why, we might ask, was he this way?

Chamberlain's diary supports the notion that on this day, and most likely at this hour, Churchill reached a major turning point in his consideration of peace talks with Germany. The diary records him saying 'it was incredible that Hitler would consent to any terms that we could accept – though if we could get out of this jam, by giving up Malta & Gibraltar & some African colonies, he [Winston] would jump at it'.

A collaborating note in the War Cabinet minutes of the following day (27 May) shows Halifax recalling:

In the discussion the previous day [26 May] he [Halifax] had asked the Prime Minister, if he was satisfied that matters vital to the independence of this country were unaffected, he could be prepared to discuss terms. The Prime Minister said that he would be thankful to get out of our present difficulties on such terms, provided we retained the essentials and the elements of our vital strength, even at the cost of some cession of territory.

The reason for suspecting that Churchill said all this in the missing fifteen minutes before Bridges arrived to take up history's pen is because it seems unthinkable that such a significant yielding by Churchill would not merit a single mention in that day's War Cabinet minutes, even though two other sources verify it. Were it not for Halifax's officially documented reminder of Churchill's concession – but only during the 27 May meeting – it would have survived only in the unpublished pages of Chamberlain's diary, accessible to modern readers via the Birmingham University archives.

A conspiracy? Churchill's official biographer, Martin Gilbert, makes no mention at all of the paradigm-shifting notion of Winston saying he would be thankful for a reasonable peace offer from Hitler.

True to form, once Bridges had resumed his minutes, Winston waxed aggressive once more – perhaps out of his fear that his true thoughts might become public knowledge.

The first new matter on record, then, is Winston singing an old tune. Trusting that Hitler would offer any kind of respectable peace deal with Britain was absurd, he argued, adding that 'there was no limit to the terms which Germany would impose on us if she had her way'. He obviously hoped that France would hold out, but 'at the same time we must take care not to be forced into a weak position in which we went to Signor Mussolini and invited him to go to Herr Hitler and ask him to treat us nicely. We must not get entangled in a position of that kind before we had been involved in any serious fighting.'

Lord Halifax, perhaps exasperated by all this to-ing and fro-ing, rounded on Churchill and forcefully but calmly reiterated that he attached 'perhaps rather more importance than the Prime Minister to the desirability of allowing France to try out the possibilities of European equilibrium'. He added that he was 'not quite convinced that the Prime Minister's diagnosis was correct and that it was in Herr Hitler's interest to insist on outrageous terms'. As an Englishman, Halifax would of course not agree to 'any suggestion of terms which affected our independence', but if, as he suspected, 'Signor Mussolini was as alarmed as we felt that he must be in regard to Herr Hitler's power, and was prepared to look at matters from the point of view of the balance of power, then we might consider the Italian claims. At any rate, he could see no harm in trying.'

Such a fundamental disagreement between the two men in the moment when they should have been working together was dangerous. The others in the room added little to this fierce debate, in which the stakes were no less high than the future of Britain, Europe and the world.

In essence the two positions were this: Hitler in control of Western Europe but with Britain's autonomy secured by a peace deal was something that Halifax could live with, even now welcome. In this he represented, he felt, the will of a large part of his own party, the public, and – moreover – anyone with a sober grasp of the facts on the battlefield. Winston, for his part, was beginning to accept that a peace deal might be a way out – indeed, if the terms were favourable, he would be thankful to find such a way out. But the million-pound question remained. *When* might be the best time to strike for such a deal: now, or later?

A Labour Party minister, Arthur Greenwood, was not convinced that Mussolini could be of any help; he told the War Cabinet that he doubted it was in his power to 'take a line independent of Herr Hitler'. Chamberlain said he believed that Mussolini 'could only take an independent line if Herr Hitler was disposed to conform to the line which Mussolini indicated', and in an attempt to make peace within the room added that 'the problem was a very difficult one, and it was right to talk it out from every point of view'.

This speculation was getting them nowhere, and Churchill said he 'thought it was best to decide nothing until we saw how much of the Army we could re-embark from France. The operation might be a great failure. On the other hand, our troops might well fight magnificently, and we might save a considerable portion of the Force.'

The path of peace negotiations that Halifax was proposing with gusto – with parts of the map used as bargaining chips – could, in Churchill's opinion, only benefit Germany, which would gain colonial territories and be granted concessions in the Mediterranean, whereas 'no such option was open to us. For example, the terms offered [by Germany] would certainly prevent us from completing our re-armament.' Halifax tried to assure him that if this was in fact the case, then Britain would of course refuse the deal, but Churchill was adamant that 'Herr Hitler thought that he had the whip hand. The only thing to do was to show him that he could not conquer this country.' If what Churchill expected from Reynaud came true, and France could no longer continue the fight, then 'we must part company'.

Among those in the War Cabinet meeting room were several men who had for years labelled him a warmonger. To completely shut down the idea of exploring peace terms now would only cement that reputation and alienate him from men like Halifax and Chamberlain whose support he desperately needed. Weighing his slim options, he conceded: 'At the same time . . . [I do] not raise objection to some approach being made to Signor Mussolini.'

Gradually, then, Winston's language and heart were changing, moving from words like 'never' to words like 'consider', and agreeing to 'not raise objection' to the first step being taken in the peace process – a step whose key aim was to establish what price Italy would ask in order to mediate in peace talks between Germany and Britain, the expectation being that France was most likely out of the picture.

Greenwood and Chamberlain both believed that the Italian leader would grab this opportunity to make demands not just in Malta, Gibraltar and Suez, but also in Somaliland, Kenya and Uganda. They were very likely right. In his letter to Churchill on 18 May rejecting the Allied cause, Mussolini had, of course, used the example of Britain's harsh treatment of Italy in Africa. Greenwood also added that with France's situation worsening by the minute, and 'if Paris was likely to be taken within a short time, was there really any chance that negotiations would serve any purpose?' Halifax warned the Cabinet that if they 'found that we could obtain terms which did not postulate the destruction of our independence, we should be foolish if we did not accept them'. He could not have been clearer. For him, only a very 'foolish' person would not now entertain a deal with the Germans that allowed for an independent Britain.

Winston, offering no immediate counter-argument, no doubt tapped his ring finger busily against the varnished wooden arm of his chair. (After the war it was discovered that this agitated tapping had worn away many layers of lacquer during six years of excruciating deliberations.) What would he say now? What would he do?

The record tells us.

At the end of a meeting that had lasted over four hours, and during which the deepest aims and most strongly held principles of powerful men had been pitched against each other in well-reasoned battle, Winston called the meeting to a close with his agreement that Halifax could circulate a draft – a memorandum – outlining his suggested approach to Italy, for discussion the following day.

Halifax had been victorious.

And how relieved he must have felt. How much closer peace must have seemed to him, now that the clock of diplomacy had been set running at last. He escaped the Cabinet room and set to creating a draft memorandum that might just – just – restore a shattered Europe to a state of practical peace.

Churchill, however, had been forced by events and by political pressures to give up considerable ground. He had never been comfortable on the back foot! While Halifax was busy drafting his draft, Winston shifted his focus back onto his own alternative escape strategy.

In essence, it was this. Save the Army. Without it, Britain could not even insist on decent peace terms, let alone live to fight another day. The country would be in the same dire position that France was now in, with no choice but to accept whatever terms Germany felt disposed to offer. They key was to ensure that the evacuation of the BEF from Dunkirk was a success. But how?

Roosevelt once said of Churchill, 'He has a hundred ideas a day. Four are good, the other 96 downright dangerous.'

Six days earlier one of these four ideas had been – in the parlance of the day – a belter. And it bore all the hallmarks of a great Winston idea: surprising, grand, feasible if risky, potentially vastly costly to human life, and more than a little eccentric at first glance.

At the morning War Cabinet meeting of 20 May, the situation of the Army, en route to Dunkirk, had again been discussed. Three hundred thousand men were about to arrive at a harbour blocked by burning British ships. The British Navy could not get close enough to the shore to effect a rescue, not without coming under blistering air attack from the Luftwaffe. The best prediction offered by Ironside was that they'd be lucky to get 10 per cent of their men out alive.

The minutes of the meeting record the following response: 'The Prime Minister thought that as a precautionary measure the Admiralty should assemble a large number of small [civilian] vessels in readiness to proceed to ports and inlets on the French coast.'

Small vessels? Winston's brainwave – for which he has never, to my knowledge, been credited (amazingly not in any biography or news report) – was to ask members of the public, or at least those who could get their hands on a boat of useful size, to sail in a grand if ragtag civilian armada across the channel to save the stranded British Army.

It is seldom observed, by the public or even by historians, that the father of this colossally risky idea – what has become known as the 'Little Ships Rescue', was Churchill himself.

Within hours of Winston's brainwave, Vice-Admiral Bertram Ramsay, the Flag Officer in command of Dover and an old comrade who had come out of retirement at Churchill's request, was instructed to assemble a fleet of civilian ships that could sail to the Channel ports and evacuate the BEF to England.

So it was that six days later – as Halifax, with the bit between his peace-making teeth, drafted words of finessed supplication to an unhinged dictator – Winston made haste to the Admiralty. Desperate to find alternatives to the Halifax plan, he was described in those hours by Captain Claude Berkley, a member of the War Cabinet Secretariat, as 'hurling himself about, getting his staff into hopeless tangles by dashing across to Downing St without a word of warning, shouting that we would never give in'. By this time, Ramsay, from deep within the naval headquarters below Dover Castle, had managed to put out the public call for boats over the BBC and had so far gathered more than 800 so-called little ships to take part in one of the most daring efforts of the war.

Thus, at 6.57 p.m., on 26 May 1940, Churchill gave the order: 'Operation Dynamo is to commence.'

It was a huge gamble with civilian lives, but Winston felt – with justification – that if he had an army to either fight or bargain with, then Britain could yet be saved from the wreck.

At the same time as Dynamo was commencing, Churchill sent another telegram to Brigadier Nicholson's garrison at Calais, officially informing them that there would be no evacuation and they must 'fight it out until the bitter end'.

Nicholson and his garrison obeyed. They refused to surrender and continued their resistance until the very last as the swastika was raised above the bell-tower of the Hôtel de Ville. After they were eventually overwhelmed that same day, Nicholson's men were led out of the citadel in single file by the Germans with their hands raised above their heads, and into the courtyard. There they were lined up in front of machine-guns. Prisoners of war. The brave men of Calais were taken to camps in which the lucky ones would spend the duration of the war, and the unlucky would die. Brigadier Nicholson died three years later after falling from a window in a possible suicide at the prisoner-of-war camp in which he was interned.

In his memoirs, Anthony Eden described the decision not to evacuate the Calais garrison as 'one of the most painful of the war'. Churchill, more than most, felt this pain keenly, having given the order to sacrifice over 2,000 men in the hope of saving several hundred thousand. When he returned to Admiralty House with Eden, Ismay and Ironside, Ismay recalled how he was 'unusually silent during dinner that evening, and he ate and drank with evident distaste'.

What was on his mind? Calais, surely. Halifax, definitely. Hitler, always. Dynamo, with its little civilian navy just then chopping through the waves towards Dunkirk, assuredly. His own leadership abilities, possibly. Self-doubt, guilt, remorse, exhaustion must all have played their part.

As the men rose from the table, a deep sadness came across Churchill's face as he told them, 'I feel physically sick.' Sickness from the guilt of condemning brave men to a terrible fate, sickness from the worry of losing an entire army, sickness from the fear of there being no way out but through the strangling terms of enemies. It was his lowest ebb, but the following day would only present him with further pressures and an irreparable split within the War Cabinet.

MONDAY, 27 MAY 1940

**WORD REACHES CHURCHILL THAT
THE KING OF BELGIUM IS CONTEMPLATING
SURRENDERING TO GERMANY**

**LORD HALIFAX CONSIDERS PEACE DEAL
WITH GERMANY AND HAS COMPLETED
HIS MEMORANDUM ENTITLED 'SUGGESTED
APPROACH TO ITALY'**

**SS TROOPS CAPTURE AND MURDER
NINETY-SEVEN BRITISH SOLDIERS
NEAR LE PARADIS, FRANCE**

9. Cabinet Crisis and Leadership

Having issued the order for Operation Dynamo to begin the previous evening, the first message that reached Churchill at 7.15 a.m. on 27 May did not bode well. The naval garrison in Dover informed him that 'a bad situation is developing between Calais and Dunkirk. The enemy have mounted 40 guns as far as Gravelines [the small town between Calais and Dunkirk] and are shelling shipping approaching Dunkirk . . . ' If the ships could not even make it into the harbour to collect the soldiers, the British troops would soon be completely surrounded, with no means of escape.

The previous evening, Lord Halifax, now deep in his contemplation of peace deals, had been visited by the Counsellor of the Belgian Embassy in London to inform him that 'the King of the Belgians appeared to imply that he considered that the war was lost and was contemplating a separate peace with Germany'. King George VI's cousin, King Leopold III, had remained with his troops when his government had 'transferred themselves to foreign soil [France] to continue the struggle'. Halifax relayed this news to the 11.30 a.m. War Cabinet, who 'considered that the action of the King was tantamount to dividing the nation and delivering it into Herr Hitler's protection'. Churchill immediately telegraphed Admiral Sir Roger Keyes, liaison officer to King Leopold III, to request that he 'impress on him [Leopold] the disastrous consequences on the Allies and to Belgium of his present choice'. The Belgian Army was mostly concentrated in the north of France, fighting alongside the BEF, but it had not yet been informed of the decision to evacuate. Churchill understood the magnitude of what he was asking of the Belgians, but he also knew that their surrender at this moment would leave the Allied left flank completely exposed and endanger the British withdrawal to the coast. In a separate message to Lord Gort, the BEF's Commander-in-Chief, the Prime Minister, admitted, '[W]e are asking them to sacrifice themselves for us.'

With the prospect of further Allied surrenders, thoughts turned once more to the United States. The British Ambassador to Washington had telegrammed Halifax to suggest that 'we should cede some of our possessions in the New World to the United States in part payment of our war debt', because 'an offer of this kind made by us would make a deep impression in the United States and add to our security'. Halifax believed that this was another interesting alternative that should be explored, but Churchill was again opposed, remarking, 'The United States had given us practically no help in the war, and now that they saw how great was the danger, their attitude was that they wanted to keep everything which would help us for their own defence.' These continued suggestions of deals were wearing the Prime Minister down, and he concluded the War Cabinet meeting by saying he would 'issue a general injunction to Ministers to use confident language. He was convinced that the bulk of the people of the country would refuse to accept the possibility of defeat.' Churchill then asked Ismay to have the Chiefs of Staff once more examine 'what are the prospects of our continuing the war alone against Germany and probably Italy' in advance of their next meeting.

When members of the War Cabinet took their seats, it was not the usual twenty attendees discussing endless points of order. The 4.30 p.m. meeting on 27 May consisted of Churchill, Halifax, Chamberlain, Clement Attlee, Arthur Greenwood, Sir Alexander Cadogan, Sir Archibald Sinclair and Sir Edward Bridges. There was just one topic to discuss: the suggested approach to Mussolini.

Churchill's inclusion in the line-up of the Liberal Party leader, Sinclair – a long-time critic of appeasement and an old friend – was in defiance of protocol and clearly an attempt to strengthen a hand weakened by the facts on the battlefield.

The ensuing discussion would finally pitch Halifax and those who supported him – a large proportion of the ruling Conservative Party – full force against one of their own: Winston, whose stubborn will to fight on alone seemed, to Halifax, impervious to reason and hard evidence and against the country's best interests.

Following Paul Reynaud's suggestion the previous day that the governments of Britain and France should make a direct approach to Signor Mussolini and attempt to keep Italy out of the war, Lord Halifax had, prior to the meeting, circulated a memorandum discussing the possible options:

If Signor Mussolini will co-operate with us in securing a settlement . . . we will undertake at once to discuss, with the desire to find solutions, the matters in which Signor Mussolini is primarily interested. We understand that he desires the solution of certain Mediterranean questions: and if he will state in secrecy what these are, France and Great Britain will at once do their best to meet these wishes.

The War Cabinet was now informed by Halifax that 'President Roosevelt had made an approach on the lines set out in the Memorandum.' This was what the British had requested some time ago, believing it would have had a positive outcome then, but now, with the French on the brink of collapse, Chamberlain was convinced it was too late, and that Italy already had her eyes on the spoils of a German victory and was waiting for France to fall before jumping in with her greedy demands.

As for the French, who had requested permission under the Anglo-French pact to make their own approach to Italy, Churchill felt that 'nothing would come of the approach, but that it was worth doing [allowing them to make it] to sweeten [our] relations with a failing ally'.

The ministers then took it in turn to voice their opinions. Sir Archibald Sinclair – Winston's secret weapon at the table – now played his part, saying he felt strongly that any approach to Italy in which Britain was involved would show a weakness that 'would encourage the Germans and the Italians', but that Britain should do all it could to 'strengthen the hands of the French'. Both Labour ministers were strongly against sending the Italian letter, with

Clement Attlee stating that 'the suggested approach would be of no practical effect and would be very damaging to us. In effect, the approach suggested would inevitably lead to our asking Signor Mussolini to intercede [between Germany and Britain] to obtain peace-terms for us.'

Attlee saw correctly that the ultimate subject under discussion was whether Britain should enter into peace talks with Berlin.

Arthur Greenwood, seeing the same thing, took up the point: 'If it got out that we had sued for [peace] terms at the cost of ceding British territory, the consequences would be terrible ... The Prime Minister and M. Reynaud had already made approaches to Italy which had not been well received. It would be heading for disaster to go any further with those approaches.'

Sensing that the tide had been turned in his favour, Churchill responded strongly. It is clear from this that what had originally started as a request from Reynaud for Britain and France to make an approach to Italy to keep her from joining the war had very quickly evolved into a discussion about negotiated peace and about Halifax's 'European Settlement' with Hitler.

The secretary's précis records Churchill's response:

He was increasingly oppressed with the futility of the suggested approach to Signor Mussolini, which the latter would certainly regard with contempt. Such an approach would do M. Reynaud far less good than if he made a firm stand. Further, the approach would ruin the integrity of our fighting position in this country ... Personally he doubted whether France was so willing to give up the struggle as M. Reynaud had represented. Anyway, let us not be dragged down with France. If the French were not prepared to go on with the struggle, let them give up, though he doubted whether they would do so. If this country was beaten, France became a vassal State; but if we won, we might save them. The best help we could give to M. Reynaud was to let him feel that, whatever happened to France, we were going to fight it out to the end.

At the moment our prestige in Europe was very low. The only way we could get it back was by showing the world that Germany had not beaten us. If, after two or three months, we could show that we were still unbeaten, our prestige would return. Even if we were beaten, we should be no worse off than we should be if we were now to abandon the struggle. Let us therefore avoid being dragged down the slippery slope with France. The whole of this manoeuvre was intended to get us so deeply involved in negotiations that we should be unable to turn back. We had gone a long way already in our approach to Italy, but let us not allow M. Reynaud to get us involved in a confused situation. The approach proposed was not only futile, but involved us in a deadly danger . . . If the worst came to the worst, it would not be a bad thing for this country to go down fighting for other countries which had been overcome by the Nazi tyranny.

Such an emotional argument caused a sudden rift in the room. The old strategic and ideological battle lines that had separated Winston from the appeasers since the mid-1930s were once again starkly exposed.

Neville Chamberlain, rallying behind the suddenly isolated Halifax, rowed back on his original objections to the proposed approach and came to the Foreign Secretary's defence, suggesting that 'while he agreed that the proposed approach would not serve any useful purpose, he thought that we ought to go a little further with it, in order to keep the French in a good temper. He thought that our reply should not be a complete refusal.'

The Cabinet Secretary, Bridges, noted that a discussion then ensued. He did not document precisely what was said, only that 'it was generally agreed that a reasoned reply on these lines was the best course to take'.

Halifax, despite this interjection from Chamberlain, had reached the limit of his appetite for Churchillian rhetoric, and wrote in his diary of this meeting that 'it does drive one to despair when he [Churchill] works himself up into a passion of emotion when he ought to make his brain think and reason'.

Churchill's remark that it was better to 'go down fighting for other countries which had been overcome by the Nazi tyranny' was a step too far for Halifax, especially as he truly believed that a potential solution of peace existed and Britain could avoid sacrificing so many young lives. Besides, Churchill had just performed a massive about-face. Only the day before, he had calmly approved the drafting of this memorandum and said he would be 'thankful' if peace talks offered a way out of this crisis. Now he was describing the proposed letter, and Halifax's very position, and perhaps even Halifax himself, as a 'deadly danger'.

Halifax knew he was being hung out to dry for all in the room to see, and he didn't like it. It was this very inconsistency of mood and opinion that he and the other appeasers had feared when Churchill was given power. Now they were seeing it in action. Clearly angered that what he believed was his quite reasonable and patriotic proposal was being misrepresented as terrifying and unpatriotic, Halifax sought to make clear his 'profound differences of points of view', and to have them documented for all time. He would leave no one in any doubt that he was ready to fight for his ideas, for their good sense, and for their morality, saying that:

> He could not recognise any resemblance between the action which he proposed, and the suggestion that we were suing for terms and following a line that would lead us to disaster.

After then referencing the PM's comments of the previous day – in which Churchill had both said he'd be 'prepared' to discuss peace terms, and even be 'thankful' to find a peaceful way to settle things by territorial trades with Germany – Halifax went on:

> On the present occasion, however, the Prime Minister seemed to suggest that under no conditions would we contemplate any course except fighting to a finish. The issue was probably academic, since we were unlikely to

receive any offer which would not come up against the fundamental conditions which were essential to us. If, however, it was possible to obtain a settlement which did not impair those conditions, he, for his part, doubted if he would be able to accept the view now put forward by the Prime Minister. The Prime Minister had said that two or three months would show whether we were able to stand up against the air risk. This meant that the future of the country turned on whether the enemy's bombs happened to hit our aircraft factories. He was prepared to take that risk if our independence was at stake; but if it was not at stake he would think it right to accept an offer which would save the country from avoidable disaster.

The crucial conversations of the previous day, in which the Prime Minister had said 'he would be thankful to get out of our present difficulties', are not documented in any of the minutes, so it would seem that this is what was discussed in the fifteen minutes before Bridges arrived at the 'Informal Meeting of War Cabinet Ministers'.

Neville Chamberlain's diary also confirms that 'WC [Churchill] said we would try and find some formula on which Musso [Mussolini] would be approached but we must have time to think. With this R [Reynaud] had to be content . . .' In addition, he records Churchill's clear position on giving up Malta and Gibraltar and some African colonies.

Jump at a peace offer from Hitler?

It seems we can be confident that this had been

Churchill's mood and position the previous day. Certainly, this would explain Halifax's anger that Churchill's position, seemingly so open, so welcoming, so enthusiastic, had in one day closed shut.

What was Churchill playing at? Were his earlier remarks just an attempt to buy time, or had he been sincere about peace talks during these dark days?

Despite everything he had fought for since 1933, after all the speeches and all the rhetoric about victory, we see that at the 26 May meeting Winston too considered a deal with Hitler possible, even welcome. Just look at the pressures urging such a deal. Dynamo had begun, but the outlook was grim. The destruction of virtually the entire British Army looked likely. In that moment Winston had agreed it was worth exploring a possible negotiated settlement, provided Britain maintained her sovereignty. Now, Halifax's frustration that Winston was reneging on this less than twenty-four hours later is clear. As Halifax's biographer Andrew Roberts notes:

> Wars fought for ideas, in which nations exhausted themselves and risked their own extinction in pursuit of the enemy's annihilation, were completely alien to Halifax's nature. Hitler had clearly won the first round in what could be a decade-long struggle, and it seemed only common sense to Halifax to attempt to obtain at least a breathing-space along the lines of the Treaty of Amiens [which had suspended the Napoleonic Wars for fourteen months]. If this could save the British Expeditionary Force and much of France, so much the better.

It was Churchill's turn to reply.

Halifax's passion had clearly dented the PM's swagger, as had Chamberlain's loyal solidarity with Halifax. Perhaps Winston hesitated before speaking, aware that history's pen – currently in the fist of Bridges – would record his words, words that would represent another major shift in position, both from the view he had only just finished expressing and from our general understanding of him. He began:

> If Herr Hitler was prepared to make peace on the terms
> of the restoration of German colonies and the overlord-
> ship of Central Europe, that was one thing . . .

Let us press the pause button there for one second.

This was *some* admission. Winston, here, is willing to say, on record, that he can live not only with a situation that saw Britain in a peace arrangement with a continentally victorious Nazi Germany, but also one that would concede to Hitler *overlordship* of Central Europe. When one then injects his words from the previous day – along with 'thankful' and the either verbatim or paraphrased 'jump at it' – this more or less scuppers the long-held position of historians that Winston never wavered, never took seriously the notion of peace talks, and never took any real steps to advance them.

In typical Churchillian fashion, however, he followed this major concession to history and to Halifax with a caveat: that 'it was quite unlikely that he would make any such offer'. But Halifax was determined to stop Churchill right there, stop him again wriggling out of commitments he had made to peace the previous day, and to link for ever the Italian letter to an overall Europe-wide peace strategy. Cabinet minutes indicate that Halifax then stated for the record:

> The Foreign Secretary said he would like to put the following question. Suppose the French Army collapsed and Herr Hitler made an offer of peace terms. Suppose the French Government said 'We are unable to deal with an offer made to France alone and you must deal with the Allies together.' Suppose Herr Hitler, being anxious to end the war through knowledge of his own internal weaknesses, offered terms to France and England, would the Prime Minister be prepared to discuss them?

This is a strikingly confrontational challenge from Lord Halifax, especially given that his words have been filtered through the pen of Bridges. In fact, Halifax wrote in his diary: 'I thought Winston talked the most frightful rot, also Greenwood, and after bearing it for some time I said exactly what I thought of them, adding that if that was really their view, and if it came to the point, our ways would separate.'

Had Bridges been a more faithful servant of history, what dialogue might we now have been bequeathed?

In its absence, we can speculate on how the exchange might have run:

> WINSTON: Viscount Halifax, as I said yesterday, the approach you propose is not only futile, but involves us in a deadly danger.

HALIFAX: THE DEADLY DANGER HERE IS THIS ROMANTIC FANTASY OF FIGHTING TO THE END!!! What *is* 'the end' if not the destruction of all? There is nothing heroic in going down fighting if it can be avoided. Nothing even remotely patriotic in death or glory if the odds are on the former; nothing inglorious in trying to shorten a war that we are clearly losing.

WINSTON: Europe is still –

HALIFAX (*cutting him off*): EUROPE IS LOST! Lost. And before our forces are wiped out completely, this is the time to negotiate in order to obtain the best conditions possible. It would not be in Hitler's interests to insist on outrageous terms. He will know his own weaknesses. He will be reasonable.

WINSTON (*unable to bear this talk*): When will the lesson be learned? How many more dictators must be wooed, appeased – good God, given immense privileges – before we learn . . . that you can't reason with a tiger when your head is in its mouth!

HALIFAX: Prime Minister. I feel I must have it on record, that if all you can foresee is fighting to the end, and you would not even be prepared to discuss peace terms should Hitler offer them, then you should know that I feel we must part ways.

Part ways?

Churchill knew full well that Halifax's resignation at this time would be catastrophic. Deprived of Halifax's cooling counsel, the Prime Minister, still viewed by many as a loose cannon, would almost certainly face a vote of no confidence in the House, a vote he would in all likeli-hood lose. The entire Conservative Party would split along pro-peace and anti-peace lines. So he was, in the moment, facing not only a well-reasoned argument (a pat-riotic one just as potent as his own), but also a decision upon which his premiership teetered.

Halifax wrote in his diary that Churchill 'surprised and mellowed' when he said 'that he would not join France in asking for terms but if he were told what the terms offered were, he would be prepared to consider them'.

This would be the zenith of Halifax's power and influ-ence, for he had steered a reluctant leader from almost histrionic talk of victory at all costs to a serious embrace of the notion of peace talks, to a consideration of *when*, not *if*, such talks should take place.

With Winston's capitulation to Halifax, the War Cab-inet quickly agreed that a reply would be sent to the French consenting to an approach of some kind to keep them 'in good temper' and because 'we had heard that President Roosevelt had now made an approach on the lines indi-cated. It would only confuse the issue and might jeopardise our chances of getting a favourable reply from President Roosevelt if we were now to barge in on our own.'

As soon as the meeting was over, the victorious but still exasperated Lord Halifax requested a private meeting with Churchill in the gardens of No. 10. As he was walking out of the Cabinet Room, he confided to Cadogan, 'I can't work with Winston any longer.' To this Cadogan replied, 'Non-sense: his rodomontades probably bore you as much as they do me, but don't do anything silly under the stress of that.'

Roberts writes in *The Holy Fox*:

> the hyperbole which did so much to stiffen the public
> morale in 1940 struck Halifax as melodramatic and best
> reserved for public broadcasts. He had heard it all through-
> out his political life and it smacked to him of the histrionic
> and dangerous posturing which illustrated all the famous
> Churchillian lack of judgement ... Halifax was keenly
> aware that the imminent onslaught probably spelt the end
> of Britain's empire and way of life and he also – probably
> wrongly – thought it may have been avoidable.

When he retired to the garden with Churchill, he again
threatened his resignation but found Winston 'full of
apologies and affection'.

His threats had achieved their desired outcome, at least
for now, and Halifax returned to the Foreign Office. Over
tea, he recounted the meeting to Cadogan, who told him he
'hoped he really wouldn't give way to an annoyance to which
we were all subject and that, before he did anything, he would
consult Neville'. Halifax agreed that he would, reassuring
Cadogan that 'he wasn't one to take hasty decisions'.

Back at Downing Street, word of the heated meeting
spread quickly. Jock Colville wrote in his diary: 'The Cabinet are feverishly considering our ability to carry on the
war alone in such circumstances, and there are signs that
Halifax is being defeatist. He says that our aim can no
longer be to crush Germany but rather to preserve our
own integrity and independence.'

The Defence Committee met at 7 p.m. to discuss the latest news from France. Churchill described the situation now faced by the BEF as 'even more desperate, and their only choice would be to fight their way in retreat back to the coast, taking as heavy a toll of the enemy as they could on the way'. This present danger should, Churchill added, bring no reproach upon Britain, which had done everything possible in her power to support her Allies. He outlined in detail the failings of the French military leaders and the weaknesses of the Belgians, which the British 'were now paying the price for' and which had contributed 'to the disaster with which our Army was now faced'.

When the meeting concluded, Churchill received yet another difficult update. It was confirmed by Major-General Sir Edward Spears that the King of Belgium had 'telegraphed to his Chief of Staff to send a plenipotentiary to the Germans to ascertain under what conditions an armistice could be arranged, and had suggested "cease fire" at midnight tonight, the 27th–28th May'. The Defence Committee agreed that the British and French Governments would immediately dissociate themselves from the Belgian armistice, and the War Cabinet was summoned for 10 p.m. that evening.

Churchill informed the War Cabinet of this latest news and confirmed that British and French forces had been ordered to fight on. There was strong sympathy for Leopold III, despite his surrender, and the Prime Minister stressed the 'importance of ensuring the King's safety . . . Any grounds for recrimination lay rather in the Belgian action on the outbreak of war than in the more immediate past.' The Belgians' insistence on neutrality and their subsequent resistance in allowing the Allies to enter the country had wasted a vital opportunity to establish a strong presence on the country's western frontier at a time when 'the bulk of the German Army had been engaged in Poland'. This had left the BEF in 'the most serious peril', for 'Lord Gort had no troops with which to close the gap and prevent the Germans breaking through to Dunkirk'.

The Minister for Information, Duff Cooper, suggested that with this new development 'a statement should be issued referring to the gallant defence by the British troops . . . and the public should be given some indication of the serious position in which the B.E.F. had been placed'. He made particular reference to the 'cheerful tone' that still existed in the French communiqués reported in the British press, and that 'there was no doubt that the public were, at the moment, quite unprepared for the shock realisation of the true position'. Churchill agreed 'that the seriousness of the situation should be emphasised but he would depreciate any detailed statement or attempt to assess the results of the battle, until the situation had been further cleared up. The announcement of the Belgian Armistice would go a long way to prepare the public for bad news.' Cooper did not think this was strong enough, and argued that there was a real danger in suddenly making an announcement that so thoroughly contradicted what the public had been reading in the papers. He suggested that 'it would be as well to remind the public of the constant German efforts to drive a wedge between the two peoples. At the same time editors could be asked to tone down the French announcements.' Churchill concluded the meeting with the suggestion that 'it would be necessary for him to make a full statement in Parliament, although it might be another week before the situation had cleared sufficiently to allow him to do so'.

He returned to Admiralty House with Jock Colville and 'at midnight, after reading a few papers and after saying "Pour me out a whisky and soda, very weak, there's a good boy", he went up to bed'.

What price would we pay to know his thoughts, to know the depths of his fears and self-doubts as he lay on the single bed, willing sleep to carry him off. Was Halifax right? Was he himself wrong? Had he done the right thing or would he and the nation live to regret his decision to let his Foreign Secretary move forward with his plan for a negotiated peace?

Lord Halifax described Tuesday, 28 May, as 'a very black day'. Admiral Sir Roger Keyes had returned to London following the cease-fire of the Belgian Army at four o'clock that morning. Churchill invited him to brief the 11.30 a.m. War Cabinet.

There Keyes made it clear that he, too, believed that the 'Belgian Government were entirely responsible for the chaos caused . . . [and that] only the King's personality had held the Belgian Army together for the last four days. If the King had left when pressed to do so by His Majesty's Government three days ago, the morale of the Army would have cracked at once.' Churchill read out the terms of the German–Belgian armistice:

(1) All Belgian troops movements forbidden. Belgian troops must line up on the side of the road to await orders. They must make known their presence by means of white signs, flags, &c.
(2) Orders must be given forbidding destruction of war material and stores.
(3) German troops must be allowed to proceed to the coast.
(4) Free passage to Ostend is demanded and no destruction permitted.
(5) All Resistance will be overcome.

If Britain desired a foretaste of what the Germans might demand of it, here it was.

'Considerable numbers' of British troops had now begun to arrive at Dunkirk, and the First Sea Lord relayed a report from Vice-Admiral Ramsay at Dover that '11,400 men had arrived the previous night and 2,500 more were in passage across the Channel'. The first reports of the infamous lines of soldiers waiting for evacuation were confirmed, with '2,000 troops on the beaches and 7,000 among the sand dunes' of Dunkirk, which was now 'covered with a pall of smoke'. However, the Cabinet were informed that the Air Officer Commander-in-Chief, Sir Hugh Dowding, had sent a message to say he was 'deeply concerned' with the current aircraft losses incurred by the RAF protecting the BEF on the beaches of Dunkirk, and that 'our fighter defences were almost at cracking point'. He stressed that 'if this exceptional effort had to be repeated over Dunkirk the following day, the situation would be serious'.

Duff Cooper once more stressed the urgency 'for a frank statement of the desperate situation of the British Expeditionary Force', outlining fears that 'unless this was given out, public confidence would be badly shaken and the civil population would not be ready to accept the assurances of the Government of the chances of our ultimate victory'. He suggested he make a 'short statement' on the BBC news at 1 p.m. Churchill agreed to this, and confirmed that he too would make a statement to the House of Commons on the same subject that afternoon.

Though not broadcast live, Churchill's statement to the House was also a statement to the nation, so he needed it to both prepare the public yet also rally their spirits. His speech was brief but hopeful, and suggested that a thinly veiled answer to the question of a negotiated peace that had so troubled select members of the War Cabinet was beginning to form in his mind:

> The situation of the British and French Armies now engaged in a most severe battle and beset on three sides and from the air, is evidently extremely grave. The surrender of the Belgian Army in this manner adds appreciably to their grievous peril. But the troops are in good heart, and are fighting with the utmost discipline and tenacity . . . I expect to make a statement to the House on the general position when the result of the intense struggle now going on can be known and measured . . . Meanwhile, the House should prepare itself for hard and heavy tidings. I have only to add that nothing which may happen in this battle can in any way relieve us

of our duty to defend the world cause to which we have vowed ourselves; nor should it destroy our confidence in our power to make our way, as on former occasions in our history, through disaster and through grief to the ultimate defeat of our enemies.

The House responded positively to Churchill's note of defiance, with MPs standing to congratulate him and saying, '[W]e have not yet touched the fringe of the resolution of this country', and that 'the dignified statement of the Prime Minister reflects not only the feeling of the whole House but the feeling of the whole nation'. Galvanized by this reception, Churchill departed the Chamber and proceeded to his room in the House of Commons for a 4 p.m. meeting with the War Cabinet.

The same select group who had witnessed the previous day's fiery standoff between the Prime Minister and the Foreign Secretary convened once more to discuss the issue of Italy, in what Roberts describes as 'an atmosphere pregnant with the sense of impending doom'.

Lord Halifax spoke first. During the morning meeting, he had informed the Cabinet of the 'wholly negative reply' that President Roosevelt had received from Mussolini. Since then, another message had been received from the French Government requesting that a direct approach be made to Italy by Britain and France. Now he repeated his proposal that 'we should give a clear indication that we should like to see mediation by Italy', but Churchill, still buoyed from his speech to the Commons, said he felt it was 'clear that the

French purpose was to see Signor Mussolini acting as intermediary between ourselves and Herr Hitler' and that 'he was determined not to get into this position'. Halifax – surely thinking 'here we go again!' at yet another row-back from Churchill – disagreed strongly with this suggestion, saying that Reynaud's proposal was 'that we should say that we were prepared to fight to the death for our independence, but that, provided this could be secured, there were certain concessions that we were prepared to make to Italy'. This was true in respect of Reynaud's proposal, but Halifax failed to mention that he was in fact referring to a wider European Settlement via Italy. Further than that, he also omitted to mention that the genesis of this idea came from his meeting with the Italian Ambassador, Giuseppe Bastianini, on 25 May, not from the French, who purely wanted to keep Italy from also attacking them.

Churchill continued, stating that he believed 'the French were trying to get us on to the slippery slope'. Here again the use of that term, 'slippery slope', one almost patented to irritate Halifax. And then, the revelation of an all new position: 'The position would be entirely different when Germany had made an unsuccessful attempt to invade this country.'

Was Winston, having agreed to consider a peace deal, now adding the caveat that it should be pursued only *after* a failed German attempt to invade Britain?

The idea that Britain, without an army (as it now looked), was equipped to repel a German invasion (which looked likely) was a notion that Halifax did not even want his name linked to.

He spoke again, happy to dismiss the French proposal, saying there was little prospect that anything would come of it, but focusing on his key concern: his idea of a European settlement or 'wider aspect' talks. Hammering this main theme, he felt there was a 'larger issue' involved: 'Assuming that Signor Mussolini wished to play the part of mediator, and that he could produce terms which would not affect our independence, he thought that we ought to be prepared to consider such terms.' Halifax rejected Churchill's assertion that Britain would get better terms in several months' time, after Germany had attempted a failed invasion. He believed quite the opposite, and stated that 'we must not ignore the fact that we might get better terms before France went out of the war and our aircraft factories were bombed, than we might get in three months' time'.

The argument continued, with Churchill adding that:

Signor Mussolini, if he came in as mediator, would take his whack out of us. It was impossible to imagine that Herr Hitler would be so foolish as to let us continue our re-armament. In effect, his terms would put us completely at his mercy. We should get no worse terms if we went on fighting, even if we were beaten, than were open to us now.

Halifax was understandably infuriated. He could not fathom what Churchill felt was 'so wrong' in the proposed idea of mediation. Chamberlain, sensing this frustration, came in on Halifax's side, saying, 'It was clear to the world that we were in a tight corner, and he did not see what we should lose if we said openly that, while we would fight to the end to preserve our independence, we were ready to consider decent terms if such were offered to us.'

Faced with losing Chamberlain's support to Halifax, Churchill returned to his rhetorical roots and stated, '[T]he nations which went down fighting rose again, but those which surrendered tamely were finished.' Greenwood agreed, and said that 'he did not feel that this was a time for ultimate capitulation'. This too incensed Halifax, who – surely feeling that his every word was being deliberately misconstrued – replied, 'Nothing in his suggestion could even remotely be described as ultimate capitulation.'

Attlee was worried about public reaction to any word of Anglo-French talks with Germany, and cautioned that 'it was necessary to pay regard to public opinion in this country . . . when the public realised the true position, they would sustain a severe shock. They would have to make a great effort to maintain their morale, and there was grave danger that, if we did what France wanted, we should find it impossible to rally the morale of the people.'

In a final attempt to diffuse the tension in the room, and broker some consensus, Chamberlain tried to keep alive the peace process while accepting that the French would be of little use in advancing it. He agreed with the Foreign Secretary's view on both points: that if Britain could succeed in negotiating terms which 'although grievous, would not threaten our independence, we should be right to consider such terms', and then added that the

French approach to Mussolini would not achieve this 'at this present time'.

At 6.15 p.m. the meeting adjourned. Halifax, with Chamberlain's help, had kept alive the prospect of peace talks, at least for now. And it was Halifax and Chamberlain whom Winston asked to remain to draft a letter to the French, saying, in effect, thanks but no thanks.

Churchill had an appointment to keep. And he needed to prepare himself for what his biographer Martin Gilbert describes as 'one of the most extraordinary scenes of the war'.

Earlier that day, Churchill had requested a meeting of the twenty-five Cabinet ministers outside the War Cabinet to brief them in detail on the current situation faced by Britain. He had not had the chance to speak to them since becoming PM, and this was overdue, but by 6.15 p.m., at least, he had changed his mind about the purpose of this address.

Having ridden out the storm of Halifax's resignation threats, Churchill knew that whatever course he finally decided to take – towards peace if the BEF were smashed on the beaches of Dunkirk, or to fight it out if he retained a fighting force – he would need either the support of his Foreign Secretary or, in the event of his resignation, the support of the full Cabinet.

It was the Cabinet's confidence he now wished to secure. This was his aim.

The Cabinet ministers, as we know, were not among his most ardent admirers. His dicey CV and punchy style, his flip to the Liberal Party and flop back to the Conservatives, his botched military schemes with their massive loss of life had left him a figure more tolerated than valued, more feared than loved. But come they did, filing into Winston's offices, afraid of what they might hear. What kind of tomorrow were they looking at? Was the Army truly lost? Was the invasion of Britain now unavoidable? Were they now powerless to avoid the destruction of their homes, their families, their way of life?

We have no record of how he made his way to his office at the House of Commons, where one of the most decisive moments of the war would take place, but being only a brisk walk of ten minutes, and with much mental work to do, one can suppose he walked it, strange as ever in his Edwardian clothes of black waistcoat and gold fob-chain, puffing on his Longfellow cigar, striking out with his cane, one of his innumerable hats on his smallish head, a head that was a cyclotron of thoughts and arguments and positions and possible outcomes. A leader lives and dies by such moments. The power of their argument can just as easily condemn millions to sorrow and suffering as bring salvation. What to tell his peers, then? Should he listen to them or instruct them? And how much persuasion to apply when the price his listeners might pay, if persuaded, is their own blood?

It is not certain that he knew full well what he would tell them. But as he walked he began to form an idea. He must reveal that a peace deal with Hitler has its advocates and has indeed been under consideration. It was even possible that Hitler was behind the Italians' overtures, sending out a subtle signal of readiness to talk. Out of all this, he must discern the mood of his ministers, before publicly disclosing his own. If he sensed that these men – and behind them the British people – were up for a fight, then he would conclude his address one way; if he sensed fatigue and a desire to quit, then he could modify it and finish it another way.

Entering the Commons he made for the stairs. On the first floor he pushed down the corridor that led to his offices. His colleagues were waiting. The oak-panelled room was full; the air gauzy with cigar smoke. Winston faced them, as a hush fell, looking squarely into the eyes of the men without whom he barely had a viable premiership. After days of uncertainty and personal doubt, of torturous vacillation, of heartache and torment, it was time to take stock, to test out a new vision in a synthesis of all he had absorbed in the three weeks since coming to power. It was not a speech he had prepared for. But his future would depend on its outcome.

What Winston said was not officially documented by any secretariat, but the diary of Hugh Dalton, Labour's Minister for Economic Warfare, paints a truly vivid account of his words that day:

In the afternoon all ministers are asked to meet the P.M. He is quite magnificent. The man, and the only man we have, for this hour. He gives a full, frank and completely calm account of the events in France . . .

He was determined to prepare the public opinion for bad tidings, and it would of course be said, and with some truth, that what was now happening in Northern France would be the greatest British military defeat for many centuries. We must now be prepared for the sudden turning of the war against this island, and prepared also for other events of great gravity in Europe. No countenance should be given publicly to the view that France might soon collapse, but we must not allow ourselves to be taken by surprise by any events. It might indeed be said that it would be easier to defend this island alone than to defend this island plus France, and if it was seen throughout the world that it was the former, there would be an immense wave of feeling, not least in the U.S.A. which, having done nothing much to help us so far, might even enter the war. But all this was speculative. Attempts to invade us would no doubt be made, but they would be beset with immense difficulty. We should mine all round our coast; our Navy was immensely strong; our air defences were much more easily organised from this island than across the Channel; our supplies of food, oil, etc., were ample; we had good troops in this island, others were on the way by sea, both British army units coming from remote garrisons and excellent Dominion troops, and, as to aircraft, we were now more than making good our current losses, and the Germans were not. I have thought carefully in these last days whether it was part of my duty to consider entering into negotiations with That Man [Hitler]. But it was idle to think that, if we tried to make peace now, we should get better terms from Germany than if we went on and fought it out. The Germans would demand our fleet –

that would be called 'disarmament' – our naval bases, and much else. We should become a slave state, though a British Government which would be Hitler's puppet would be set up – 'under Mosley [Sir Oswald Mosley, British fascist] or some such person'. And where should we be at the end of all that? On the other side, we had immense reserves and advantages. And I am convinced that every one of you would rise up and tear me down from my place if I were for one moment to contemplate parley or surrender. Therefore, he said, 'We shall go on and we shall fight it out, here or elsewhere, and if this long island story of ours is to end at last, let it end only when each one of us lies choking in his own blood upon the ground.'

Once more, when on the brink of defeat, Churchill – speaking from the heart – summoned all the skills in his arsenal and produced a masterful display of rhetoric, one that we must assume took its shape in the orator's head in the fleeting moments before expression, too late to edit it.

What it meant was this. He had decided. Decided no longer to sit on the fence. Decided to pre-emptively quash any campaign of support Halifax might be attempting for his 'European Settlement'. Decided to risk the Foreign Secretary's resignation, and, with it, a no-confidence vote against him. Decided, on balance, that it was better – despite all the valid and powerful arguments against – to fight on, returning to his original position, but now with a full sense of the poor odds, the dangers, the costs and possible sacrifices that lay ahead. His countrymen and countrywomen must risk death, be ready to choke in their own blood.

He did not have to wait long to find out if his words had hit their mark. The reaction came right away.

In his memoirs of the Second World War, *Their Finest Hour*, Churchill recalled the Cabinet's response with a touch more gusto than the other diary accounts of the meeting:

> There occurred a demonstration which, considering the character of the gathering – twenty-five experienced politicians and Parliament men, who represented all the different points of view, whether right to wrong, before the war – surprised me. Quite a number seemed to jump up from the table and come running to my chair, shouting and patting me on the back. There is no doubt that had I at this juncture faltered at all in the leading of the nation I should have been hurled out of office. I was sure that every Minister was ready to be killed quite soon, and have all his family and possessions destroyed, rather than give in. In this they represented the House of Commons and almost all the people.

When the War Cabinet reassembled at 7 p.m., Churchill recounted the events of this meeting with what must have been a profound sense of relief and satisfaction. And it was an account that was definitely directed at Halifax: 'They had not expressed alarm at the position in France, but had expressed the greatest satisfaction when he had told them that there was no chance of our giving up the struggle. He did not remember having ever before heard a gathering of persons occupying high places in political life express themselves so emphatically.'

Halifax and Chamberlain could see the writing on the wall. Not even their combined resignation now could shake the Churchill leadership, not after this victory with ministers, whose collective mood to fight on they had not anticipated.

Churchill had outflanked his opponents, won game, set and match, and no record can be found that these men – not Halifax, not Chamberlain – ever raised the matter of a negotiated peace between London and Berlin again.

Lord Halifax, a proud man, acknowledged his defeat silently. The events of these meetings were not mentioned in his diary, which most historians believe were written for the benefit of others rather than as an accurate record. He wrote quite a different account: 'Another Cabinet at 4 to discuss a further French appeal to us to ask Mussolini to be more reasonable. We thought this perfectly futile after all that has been attempted, and following his flat refusal to listen to Roosevelt's last approach.'

Churchill had survived. He had seen out his own period of uncertainty. There would be no vote in the house about his leadership. Against the most vigorous of attempts to back him into a corner, he had foiled, with a speech, the threat to use his weakness within the party against him. The power of his words and the conviction with which he delivered them once more bore him through. As he recalled in his memoirs of that day, 'There was a white glow, overpowering, sublime, which ran through our Island from end to end.' And while the country's trials were only beginning, he knew now that he had the support of his colleagues and of the public to continue the struggle together.

Before retiring to bed, he telephoned Paul Reynaud to confirm that Britain would not seek terms and would carry on the fight alone, if need be, but he urged the French to fight alongside him.

WEDNESDAY, 29 MAY 1940

**THE EVACUATION RATE AT DUNKIRK IS
UP TO 2,000 MEN PER HOUR AND MORE THAN
40,000 TROOPS HAVE SAFELY LANDED IN BRITAIN**

———

**THE LUFTWAFFE LAUNCHES 'MAXIMUM
EFFORT' OVER DUNKIRK,
SINKING TWENTY-FIVE VESSELS**

———

**CHURCHILL'S FIRM REPLY TO FRANCE HAS
GALVANIZED REYNAUD TO CONTINUE THE
STRUGGLE AND FIGHT ON AS LONG AS POSSIBLE**

———

10. 'Fight on the beaches'

What a difference is made by having a settled mind. On the morning of 29 May, Churchill awoke revitalized, something of a new man.

From his bed he received word that the previous night's message to Reynaud that Britain would not be seeking terms via Italy was reported by Major-General Sir Edward Spears, personal liaison officer between Reynaud and Churchill, to have had a 'magical' effect on the French leader and 'evidently reinforced [Churchill's] own inner conviction that this was the right course to pursue, and he straightaway vetoed any further communications being sent to Rome'. The stoic and positive language that Churchill had used not only in this message but also in his meeting with the Cabinet was proving to be crucial in fighting the defeatist attitude that had crept in over recent days. He knew now that the strongest weapon he had to save Britain was hope.

With that in mind, he sent a 'Strictly Confidential' memo to Cabinet ministers and senior officials:

In these dark days the Prime Minister would be grateful if all his colleagues in the Government, as well as high officials, would maintain a high morale in their circles; not minimising the gravity of events, but showing confidence in our ability and inflexible resolve to continue the war till we have broken the will of the enemy to bring all Europe under his domination.

No tolerance should be given to the idea that France will make a separate peace; but whatever may happen on the Continent, we cannot doubt our duty and we shall certainly use all our power to defend the Island, the Empire and our Cause.

Following this almost Shakespearean rallying cry, the War Cabinet met at 11.30 a.m. This time Lord Halifax did not even attempt to change the minds of Churchill or other ministers, but he did alert them to a telegram the Foreign Office had received from the British Ambassador in Rome. Confirming what many had been expecting, it stated that 'Italy's entry into the war was now a certainty; there remained only doubt about the date. It might be within a week, it might be later, but the delay could no longer be reckoned in months.' In response, the Ambassador had made clear that 'if Italy made war, war would be met with war. The responsibility would be Signor Mussolini's and his alone.'

This was not the only 'unpleasant' news presented to them. Forty thousand troops had already reached England from France, but the military advice was that it was now doubtful whether very many more men could be rescued. The Luftwaffe had completely destroyed Dunkirk harbour in continuous bombing raids and sunk several ships that were now blocking others from entering.

Lord Gort had sent a telegram requesting 'definite

guidance as to the action he should take in the last resort'. Churchill confirmed to the meeting that the General had been ordered 'to continue the struggle with the object of gaining time for the evacuation of as many troops as possible, and of inflicting the maximum amount of damage on the Germans', but Halifax – still determined to save as many lives as possible – voiced his concerns:

> [He] was not altogether happy over the very definite instructions that had been given. He agreed that the grim struggle must continue, but he would like a message sent to Lord Gort expressing the implicit trust that the Government placed in him and on any action that he would see fit to take in the last resort. It would not be dishonourable to relinquish the struggle in order to save a handful of men from massacre.

The previous days' arguments seem to have created an irreparable rift between the Prime Minister and the Foreign Secretary, and the subtext of new disagreements could easily be aligned to the now buried matter of peace talks. Lord Halifax resumed his moral argument that there was nothing heroic in dying fighting and no dishonour in saving lives through strategy or retreats, if it were possible. Churchill reacted to this by effectively saying that Halifax was stating the bloody obvious, and of course '[i]n a desperate situation any brave man was entitled, in the absence of precise order to the contrary, to use his own discretion, and that therefore he would prefer not to modify the instructions to Lord Gort'. It did not need spelling out: 'A Commander, in circumstances as desperate and distressing as those in which Lord Gort now found himself, should not be offered the difficult choice between resistance and capitulation.'

Chamberlain stepped in to mediate, as he had done so often over the past few days, and said that there was a chance that 'Lord Gort might well interpret the instructions sent him to mean that he was to resist to the last man, no matter in what circumstances he might find himself', and if the communication lines between the BEF and the Government were cut then he would be unable to request final instructions. As a compromise, Chamberlain suggested that they clarify the existing order, adding that Gort should 'continue the struggle as long as he remained in touch with His Majesty's Government . . . if communications were interrupted, then he was free to use his own judgment as to the degree of resistance he should continue to offer'. Clement Attlee thought this caveat gave insufficient credit to the well-respected general, who would know to do this already: 'Lord Gort could surely be allowed to use his own judgment if communications were severed and he found himself cut off from the sea and in circumstances in which further resistance would inflict no appreciable damage to the Germans.' Anthony Eden agreed. Churchill concluded this exasperating meeting by saying, 'The instructions sent to Lord Gort had not been intended to convey the impression that troops which were cut off from hope of relief and were without food or without water or without ammunition should attempt to continue the struggle. He would consider sending a telegram containing modified instructions on the lines suggested by [Attlee].'

Cadogan wrote in his diary that the Cabinet meeting had been '[a] horrible discussion of what instructions to send to Gort. WSC [Churchill] rather theatrically bulldoggish. Opposed by NC [Chamberlain] and H [Halifax] and yelled to a reasonable extent. Fear relations will become rather strained. That is Winston's fault – theatricality.'

It is clear that Churchill was an untested leader no longer. His fears of not having the support of his own party were behind him, and he now believed he had the confidence of the nation too. He was fully formed and free from doubts about the path that lay ahead, and he emanated a new confidence that he could lead his country safely through the danger. Hence, where others saw the numbers arriving back from Dunkirk as likely to be the best that could be achieved, Winston – with his brainchild, Operation Dynamo, barely launched – believed that more were yet to come. Where others feared the French were about to surrender, he believed he could keep them going with resolve and hope.

As soon as he came out of the meeting, Churchill set about contacting his inner circle, using positive and encouraging words to ensure they felt supported. He messaged Eden, Ismay and General Sir John Dill (who had replaced Ironside as Chief of the Imperial General Staff) to say it was 'essential that the French should share in such evacuations from Dunkirk as may be possible. Arrangements must be concerted at once with the French Missions in this country, or if necessary with the

French Government, so that no reproaches, or as few as possible, arise.' Next he telegrammed Major-General Spears: 'Your reports most interesting, and Ambassador strongly praises your work. Continue report constantly. Meanwhile reiterate our inflexible resolve to continue whatever they do . . . ' And, finally, he telegrammed Lord Gort as per the War Cabinet's conclusions:

> If you are cut from all communication with us, and all evacuation from Dunkirk and beaches had in your judgement been finally prevented, after every attempt to re-open it had failed, you would become the sole judge of when it was impossible to inflict further damage upon the enemy. His Majesty's Government are sure that the repute of the British Army is safe in your hands.

That night, Churchill dined with General Ironside and Clementine at Admiralty House and was described as being 'in great form'. The evacuation of the BEF was proceeding at a good rate, and Jock Colville's diary noted that 'Winston's ceaseless industry is impressive.' After dinner, at 11.45 p.m. Churchill telegrammed Reynaud, repeating that he wished 'French troops to share in evacuation' as much as they could, and that 'as soon as we have reorganised our evacuated troops, and prepared forces necessary to safeguard our life against threatened and perhaps imminent invasion we shall build up a new BEF'. He also informed the French leader that the British were removing army equipment from France but that 'this is only to get into order and meet impending shock, and we shall shortly send you a new scheme for reinforcement of our troops in France'; he added that he was sending this information 'in all comradeship' and 'do not hesitate to speak frankly to me'.

As Churchill was retiring to bed, an officer on duty in the War Cabinet took the opportunity to request four days' leave so he could go and help with the Dunkirk evacuations, to which the Prime Minister replied, 'God bless you; I wish I were going with you myself.'

Mist and bad weather on the morning of 30 May brought a respite from the Luftwaffe's campaign of maximum effort, but the harbour at Dunkirk was now near-impassable for anything but tiny craft. Two messengers were despatched to London to inform the Prime Minister of the latest situation. Churchill was surprised to discover that standing at the door, alongside Lord Munster (aide-de-camp to Lord Gort), was his nephew, John Spencer-Churchill, who, in his own words, arrived at his uncle's door 'still soaking wet, and in full battle kit'. He informed his uncle that 'the most urgent need is for small boats to get the troops off the beaches and out to the bigger ships', and Munster added that Lord Gort believed 'the small boats can be our salvation'.

By the afternoon's 5.30 War Cabinet meeting, Churchill was pleased to announce that over 100,000 troops had landed on the English coast, but the 'fog was now seriously interfering with the evacuation'. General Spears had sent a message to the War Cabinet updating them on the situation in France. There were fears that the battle still raging near the Somme might soon be lost: 'General Weygand had given the odds as three to one against the French. Time had never been so precious, and he [Weygand] had begged that the British should send every possible soldier . . . One British Division would make all the difference.'

Churchill felt that the list of requests from the French was becoming worryingly long and that when, inevitably, Britain refused any of them, 'as we must', they would use it as the excuse they'd been looking for to give up the struggle. The meeting discussed the options and agreed with Churchill when he suggested that Britain tell the French, once more, that they had to hold out just a little longer, that Britain would send help as soon as it could, but that 'we should make it quite clear that we had no forces that we could send at the present moment'.

As General Ismay wrote in his memoirs, Churchill 'always preferred to see things for himself and learn what was happening at first hand'. He therefore suggested that a meeting of the Supreme War Council be called the following day so he could travel to Paris and explain the situation in person to the French. Churchill was extremely anxious that as many French troops as possible were shipped out of Dunkirk alongside the BEF. In the 11 p.m. Defence Committee meeting, the Prime Minister stressed that '[t]he British Army would have to stick it out as long as possible so that the evacuation of the French could continue'. If they failed to do so, it was likely to cause 'irreparable harm' to relations between Britain and France.

At 8.30 on the morning of 31 May the party left London in two Flamingoes for Paris. Churchill's protection officer, Detective Inspector W. H. Thompson, remembers flying over 'straggling masses of refugees. With what possessions they could gather in carts, prams and even on their backs, they hurried away from the fighting line as fast as they were able.' Also in the delegation were General Ismay and, more unusually, Clement Attlee. It was the Lord Privy Seal's first time at the conference table, and Ismay recalled in his memoirs that '[h]e was brave, wise, decisive, and completely loyal to Churchill. His integrity was absolute, and no thought of personal ambition seemed to enter his mind.'

When the Supreme War Council convened, Churchill's main focus was the Dunkirk evacuation. He explained that 'up to noon on that day, 165,000 men had been evacuated by sea', to which Reynaud 'drew attention to the disparity in numbers . . . [O]f 220,000 British troops in the Low Countries, 150,000 had been evacuated, whereas of 200,000 French troops only 15,000 had been taken off. He [Reynaud] was most anxious, from the point of view of French public opinion, that the French should be withdrawn in greater numbers; otherwise the public might draw unfortunate conclusions.' Churchill tried to explain that 'the chief reason why the British had got a lot of their people off first was because there had been many Line-of-Communication troops and other rear units in the back area [of Dunkirk] who were available for immediate evacuation. The proportion of fighting troops evacuated was much smaller.' As the French troops had not yet been given an official order to evacuate as the BEF had, Churchill stressed that this was 'one of the chief reasons why he had come to Paris . . . to make sure that the same orders were now given to the French troops as had been given to the British'.

The War Council thought that 'Dunkirk could not be held for more than another 48 hours at the most, if only on the account of the growing shortage of water, food and ammunition' and Churchill confessed that 'the British Government had found itself compelled to order Lord Gort to evacuate the fighting troops before the wounded, of which there were many thousands within the perimeter. It was only the dire circumstances of the war that had made such an order necessary for the sake of the future.' The British had not got off easily, despite their expectation that 200,000 able-bodied troops could be evacuated, for they had lost all of their equipment with the exception of small arms and personal equipment. Reynaud thanked and praised the British armed forces for their wonderful work in connection with the evacuation, but was convinced that 'once the situation on the North-Eastern front had been liquidated, Germany would at once . . . undertake an attack southwards against the line of the Somme and the Aisne . . . [and asked] that as soon as the operation in the north was ended, the full strength of the Royal Air Force should be made available on the new front, together with such troops as Great Britain could spare.' Churchill, his focus now more on the defence of Britain, replied that it was 'impossible to determine what British land forces could be sent out until a clear picture had been obtained of what total forces had been retrieved from the North'.

For every hopeful or positive assessment of the situation, Reynaud retained a defeatist and pessimistic outlook. Churchill made one last attempt to put steel in Reynaud's spine as the meeting drew to a close:

He could not believe that the German Army was as good as the French. If the Allies could hold out through the summer, Britain would emerge as a most important factor ... The Allies must maintain an unflinching front against all their enemies ... England did not fear invasion, and would resist it most fiercely in every village and hamlet. To put up a stout resistance she must have troops, and it was only after her essential and urgent needs had been met that the balance of her armed forces could be put at the disposal of her French ally.

In the present emergency, it was vital that England and France should remain in the closest accord. By doing so, they could best ensure that their spirits remained high. He was absolutely convinced that they had only to carry on the fight to conquer. Even if one of them should be struck down, the other must not abandon the struggle. The British Government were prepared to wage war from the New World if, through some disaster, England herself was laid waste. It must be realised that if Germany defeated either Ally, or both, she would give no quarter: they would be reduced to the status of vassals and slaves for ever. It would be better far [sic] that the civilisation of Western Europe, with all its achievements, should come to a tragic but splendid end, than that the two great Democracies should linger on, stripped of all that made life worth living. That, he knew, was the deep conviction of the whole British people, and he would himself be proclaiming it in the British Parliament within a few days.

Though no one knew it, Churchill – for the benefit of France – had just trialled a rough version of the speech that would forever define him.

Attlee, moved by what he heard, added that 'he entirely agreed with everything Mr. Churchill had said. The British people now realised the danger with which they were faced, and knew that in the event of a German victory everything they had built up would be destroyed: for the Germans killed not only men, but ideas. Our people were resolved as never before in their history.'

There was little Reynaud could say, but he thanked Churchill and Attlee for their inspiring words, grateful for the former's assurance that if France went under Britain would not abandon the struggle. In saying that their two countries had never been closer, he adjourned the meeting.

One man who was keenly awaiting news of how the meeting had gone was Lord Halifax. Sir Ronald Campbell, the British Ambassador to France, wrote immediately to tell him that Churchill had come 'at a psychological moment and his visit was of supreme value':

He handled the French magnificently. He will give you a much better account of it than I could do by letter. All I need say is that at the end of the Supreme War Council meeting he made the most magnificent peroration on the implacable will of the British people to fight on to the bitter end, and to go down fighting rather than succumb to bondage.

This must have been the last thing Halifax wanted to read. Only the previous day he had written in his diary following the 5.30 p.m. War Cabinet meeting that he had never seen such a 'disorderly' mind as Winston's, and that he was 'coming to the conclusion that his process of thought is one that has to operate through speech. As this is exactly the reverse of my own it is irritating.'

Halifax was correct in his assessment of Churchill's thought process operating through speech, but he could not have been more wrong in describing his mind as 'disorderly', for since his speech to the House of Commons on 28 May, when he had promised to speak again in a week, his mind had done nothing but begin to create order – an order of words. It is Ambassador Campbell's observation rather than Halifax's that is the most astute, and it brings us back into the company of Churchill's old friend, Cicero.

In his book *De Inventione*, Cicero wrote of the natural order of a speech, breaking it down into six divisions, the last of which is known as the peroration and is defined as an emotional conclusion of a speech 'typically intended to inspire enthusiasm in the audience'. The 'magnificent peroration' Churchill had spoken to the Supreme War Council showed that, as before, he was already testing out the final part of a speech that would go down in history as one of the greatest ever delivered.

Back in London, word was already circulating about Churchill's masterful efforts with the French. Hugh Dalton noted in his diary: 'The King says he has had to remind Winston that he is only P.M. in England and not in France as well!' Churchill returned home in the early hours of Saturday, 1 June.

At that morning's War Cabinet meeting, members were delighted to find that 'Operation Dynamo was prospering beyond all hope and expectation', and almost 225,000 troops had now been evacuated. Lord Halifax had the previous day met with the American Ambassador, Joseph Kennedy, who had told him that 'Dunkirk was worth forty appeals from the Allies to the United States'; the prospects of Britain obtaining the destroyers it had ordered were now looking better, as 'events were moving fast in the United States', so Churchill should take this opportunity to speak directly to the President to speed things along.

Back at the Admiralty, Colville presented the Prime Minister with a suggestion that had come in 'about sending the National Gallery pictures to Canada', to which Churchill replied, 'No, bury them in caves and cellars. None must go. We are going to beat them.' A similar response was also issued regarding the removal of the Royal Family, the Crown Jewels and even the Government to an Empire territory overseas: 'I believe we shall make them rue the day they try to invade our island. No such discussion can be permitted.'

Meanwhile, clear skies over Dunkirk meant the Luft-waffe could resume its terrifying assault on the harbour and provide air-cover for German ground troops. The evacuation was continuing at the same rate, but the day had seen heavy losses: seventeen ships, among them four precious destroyers, plus ten more seriously damaged. In the Chiefs of Staff Committee meeting at 3.30 p.m., Churchill 'emphasised the importance of holding on as long as possible. The Germans might now break through, and it might be possible to continue for another night. The success or failure of our efforts to rescue the rem-nants of the French Army might have great results on the Alliance. As long as the front is held, the evacuation should be continued – even at the cost of naval losses.'

A 'Most Immediate' telegram was sent to General Weygand at 6.45 p.m., warning him that the situation was reaching boiling point, and while they would hold out as long as they could, it was quite probable that the Germans would break through and the evacuation would have to be abandoned.

Concern now shifted to the citizens of Britain, whose morale was low and among whom a general panic was growing. The newspapers were reporting on Hitler's plans to invade Britain. The War Cabinet agreed that in an attempt to boost public spirits, Duff Cooper should make a radio broadcast on the evening of 2 June to announce that 276,030 troops had been successfully evacuated. But it was not just the people who were in need of hope; concerns were still rife among Government ministers, and the diary entries of the MPs Harold

Nicolson, Hugh Dalton and Chips Channon, respectively, express these keenly:

> There are few grounds for enthusiasm really, except moral grounds. We have lost all our equipment. The French have lost 80% of their forces and feel that we deserted them. It will constitute a real problem to recreate good relations between the forces.

> What will Europe look like after six months? Famine, starvation and revolt, most of all in the slave lands which Germany has overrun.

> Everything is conspiring against us ... We are in an appalling position ...
>
> I wonder as I gaze out upon the grey and green Horse Guards Parade with the blue sky, the huge silver balloons like bowing elephants, the barbed-wire entanglements and soldiers about, is this really the end of England? Are we witnessing, as for so long I have feared, the decline, the decay and perhaps extinction, of this great island people?

By midday on 3 June the miracle evacuation of the BEF was almost complete, with 292,380 troops rescued. Churchill's Private Secretary, John Martin, wrote in his memoirs:

> Through all those terrible days the Prime Minister remained utterly steadfast; but it was easy to feel the intensity of the responsibility that weighed upon him;

and the imagination and emotion with which he watched the agony of France, eager to bring any support and comfort he could, yet steeling himself in face of desperate entreaties and his own generous instincts to hold back that bare minimum of aircraft strength on which our hope of continuing the struggle in Britain depended.

Winston was due to speak to the House of Commons in less than twenty-four hours and was yet to finish writing his speech. Throughout the day, while dashing between meetings, he stole chances to sit at his desk in Downing Street to add and delete lines to ensure the gravity of the situation was conveyed as clearly as possible. He knew the basic thrust of his message. It was more or less the same message he'd delivered to the French at the Supreme War Council meeting, but this one called for a language that would resound especially deeply in the core of the British people – a simple language, anchored in short Anglo-Saxon words, phrases falling in triplets like hammers ringing on the same anvil.

He circulated the first draft of the speech to his inner circle. Initial thoughts were that it was 'a little rough on the French High Command', given the fragility of the current situation and their request for extra British military support. He crossed out the line stating, 'Even though the United States continues to watch with a strange detachment, the growth and advance of dangers which menace them ever more darkly.' Perhaps on reflection he remembered that this speech should entice the Americans to join the war effort and not turn them off it. Wonderfully, he wrote stage directions to himself in the margins, such as 'express sympathy!' next to the line 'Our losses in men have exceeded 30,000 – killed, wounded and missing.'

Winston's method of speech-writing was painstaking and took many days. In 1973, John Martin, Winston's Private Secretary, was interviewed about his boss's process and recalled that he took 'tremendous care' over this secret art form. A typist would be called in, then Churchill would begin to 'very slowly dictate what he was going to say . . . once he saw his very careful selection of words and phrases . . . he would try out a number of words in a sort of whisper, so you could just hear a string of about half a dozen words . . . he would say them with his tongue and try them out' before finally selecting what he felt sounded the best. The next step was to have the speech typed up into 'draft form'. Once this was done, he would go through it with a red pencil and make changes before it was typed again into a 'semi-draft' form. This would then be sent out to the various 'experts for vetting' to ensure the facts and figures were correct. Finally, it would be typed into 'psalm form'. This was his own unique format – with the lines laid out like the stanzas of a poem, each new line indented a bit more than the last – that he would then begin to practise with, over and over again, pacing around the room, grabbing his lapels, trying out the full range of intonations, from bombast to whisper.

At 3.40 p.m. on 4 June 1940, the time for practice was over. The evacuation of Dunkirk was complete, and 330,000 troops had been brought miraculously to safety.

In a packed House of Commons, the Prime Minister stood up. He took four paces to the despatch box.

In all he would speak for thirty-four minutes, beginning with a detailed account of the situation in France over the past weeks and moving on to the evacuation of Dunkirk. There was no softening of the truth now, and his language was frank, vivid and shocking. The power of the Nazis was outlined in detail, as were the brave exploits of those who had lost their lives defending the port. He called the evacuation campaign '[a] miracle of deliverance, achieved by valour, by perseverance, by perfect discipline, by faultless service, by resource, by skill, by unconquered fidelity', but stressed: 'Wars are not won by evacuations.'

As Churchill began to warm up, he ratcheted ever higher the techniques of rhetoric he knew so well. He started with a question to his audience: 'Could there have been an objective of greater military importance and significance for the whole purpose of the war than this?' And he followed it with another: 'May it not also be that the cause of civilisation itself will be defended by the skill and devotion of a few thousand airmen?' He juxtaposed vivid accounts of the conflict with poetic history:

There had never been, I suppose, in all the world, in all the history of war, such an opportunity for youth. The Knights of the Round Table, the Crusaders, all fall back into the prosaic past . . . these young men, going forth every morn to guard their native land and all that we stand for . . . of whom it may be said that 'When every morning brought a noble chance . . . And every chance brought out a noble knight.'

He spoke of Hitler's plans to invade, but reminded the people that throughout the centuries Napoleon and other 'Continental tyrants' had planned similarly but never succeeded, before finally moving into the peroration he had been working on intensely:

> I have, myself, full confidence that if all do their duty, if nothing is neglected, and if the best arrangements are made, as they are being made, we shall prove ourselves once again able to defend our island home, to ride out the storm of war, and to outlive the menace of tyranny, if necessary for years, if necessary alone. At any rate, that is what we are going to try to do. That is the resolve of His Majesty's Government – every man of them. That is the will of Parliament and the nation. The British Empire and the French Republic, linked together in their cause and in their need, will defend to the death their native soil, aiding each other like good comrades to the utmost of their strength. Even though large tracts of Europe and many old and famous States have fallen or may fall into the grip of the Gestapo and all the odious apparatus of Nazi rule, we shall not flag or fail. We shall go on to the end. We shall fight in France, we shall fight on the seas and oceans, we shall fight with growing confidence and growing strength in the air, we shall defend our island, whatever the cost may be. We shall fight on the beaches, we shall fight on the landing grounds, we

shall fight in the fields and in the streets, we shall fight in
the hills; we shall never surrender, and even if, which I
do not for a moment believe, this island or a large part of
it were subjugated and starving, then our Empire beyond
the seas, armed and guarded by the British Fleet, would
carry on the struggle, until, in God's good time, the new
world, with all its power and might, steps forth to the
rescue and the liberation of the old.

The speech was a direct hit. Its power was undeniable and
the response rapturous; several Labour MPs were in tears.
Churchill later said of the great task that had fallen upon
him, namely to give voice to the people of Britain, that it
was they 'who had the lion heart' and he merely 'had the
luck to be called upon to give the roar'. At this moment,
in their darkest hour, the roar had never been louder.

The defining phrase, 'fight them on the beaches', was
actually a homage to his friend, the former French leader
Georges Clemenceau. Having written several essays on
the great man and spent time with him at the Paris Peace
Conference, Churchill had adapted a line from a November 1918 speech in which Clemenceau said, 'I will fight in
front of Paris; I will fight in Paris; I will fight behind
Paris.' It is a short hop of invention indeed to arrive at
Winston's own 'we shall fight . . . ' Again, as he did in his
'Blood, toil, tears and sweat' speech, he powerfully
employed repetition at the beginning of successive sentences. By saying '*we* shall fight', he emphasized that he
would be with the people, at their side, every step of the
way.

In his essay 'The Scaffolding of Rhetoric', Churchill stated that 'the orator is the embodiment of the passions of the multitude' and at this hour he was speaking loudly, confident that the people of Britain would fight on with him to the end. The historian David Cannadine writes that Churchill chose his language because it 'vividly and directly reflected the kind of person he himself actually was . . . a character at once simple, ardent, innocent and incapable of deception or intrigue, yet also a character larger than life, romantic, chivalrous, heroic, great-hearted and highly coloured'. All of these qualities shine through in this speech. It is filled with emotion and courage, but most of all it is filled with hope. He is offering the people his hand to guide them through the troubles ahead.

Churchill had been Prime Minister for just twenty-five days. He had faced the indomitable pressures of war, as well as the distrust of his own Cabinet, but most of all he had faced his own fears and doubts, and moved forward into a more broad and sunlit upland of confidence and leadership.

Forty-two years earlier, at the age of twenty-three, Churchill had written:

Of all the talents bestowed upon men, none is so precious as the gift of oratory. He who enjoys it wields a power more durable than that of a great king. He is an independent force in the world. Abandoned by his party, betrayed by his friends, stripped of his offices, whoever can command this power is still formidable. Many have watched its effects. A meeting of grave citizens, protected by all the cynicism of these prosaic days, is unable to resist its influence. From unresponsive silence they advance to grudging approval and thence to complete agreement with the speaker. The cheers become louder and more frequent; the enthusiasm momentarily increases, until they are convulsed by emotions they are unable to control and shaken by passions of which they have resigned the direction.

With this speech Winston met these conditions – became an 'independent force in the world', formidable, with power greater than a king – and in so doing set the direction for the passions of his people.

Epilogue: If the Truth be Told

What Winston Churchill did, what he said, and what he eventually decided in the terrifying days of May 1940 changed the fate of Britain and of Europe, as well as his own place in world history. But how he made the right decision – after a period of fiery argument, of doubt and soul searching, of fear, despair and vacillation – and how he soon after found the perfect words to explain his thinking and beliefs and feelings to the nation, has never, to my mind, been satisfactorily told. In setting out to tell this story, my aim was to show a bigger, more precarious, more psychologically tenable, and altogether more human story than has previously been allowed.

My own research, conducted while preparing the film *Darkest Hour*, and for this book, has convinced me that Winston Churchill seriously entertained the prospect of a peace deal with Hitler in May 1940, as utterly repugnant as that idea might now seem.

I am aware that this is an unpopular view, and one that puts me at odds with almost all the historians, commentators and academics far more immersed in this period of history than I can claim to be.

But in concluding this book I would like to lay out the bare facts of the case as I see them, and also to put the prevailing rival argument of those who tell us that

Churchill never seriously considered the path of negotiated peace.

First, the generally accepted argument. It essentially holds that Churchill didn't mean it when he said, on record, that he'd be 'thankful' to receive a peace offer, or when he agreed to 'consider' one. He was only stalling for time, playing a sophisticated game, wasn't serious, never wavered or wobbled. If he *seemed* to his War Cabinet colleagues to be serious – so this prevailing wisdom runs – it was only to cleverly dupe Halifax, keep him onside at a crucial moment when Halifax's resignation would probably have brought down the Government. It was also a gambit that had to be convincingly played to persuade such shrewd and wily men as Halifax and Chamberlain.

But there are several weaknesses to this reading.

The first is that there is no evidence for it, other than scholarly surmise. As Christopher Hitchens observed, what can be asserted without evidence can also be dismissed without evidence.

Winston never disclosed that he was playing a grand game of deception. He neither did so then, nor after the war, when there was ample time to do so, with much to be gained in reputation. The idea that Winston modestly hid from history so crucial an event as a brilliant outmanoeuvring of his rival Halifax strains our understanding of his personality, which, by any definition, rates rather high on the narcissistic spectrum. Rather than damage his mythic image by revealing such a story, it would enhance it. And if we doubt his desire to curate his legacy, remember, as he once quipped: 'It will be found much better by all

Parties to leave the past to history, especially as I propose to write that history.'

The second argument against the stalling scenario is that it ignores a proper consideration of the pressures – personal and political and military – that Churchill was under during that supreme crisis: how close invasion was believed to be (a matter of some days, his military advisers thought); how unprotected the British people were; how vastly outnumbered was their army in France (ten to one if the troops could be rescued in full at Dunkirk, and a hundred to one if it could not); how catastrophically rapid the collapse of Europe had been under the German assault; and how rational, moral and sane the arguments advanced by Halifax, supported by Chamberlain and others, were.

On top of all this was Halifax's threat to resign, which can only have given Winston pause to rethink his own position. A man like Halifax would never have threatened to bring down the new Government unless he was absolutely sure he was right and that Winston was wrong; and one did not easily dismiss the convictions of such a man.

Under this mass of such unholy pressures, and with so few choices, what sane person would *not* seriously consider peace talks in preference to almost certain annihilation?

It strikes me that any opponent of the 'waver' or 'wobble' argument, if we can call it that, must posit a near-unhinged Churchill, a man utterly immune to the terrifying facts on the ground and amnesiac about his own tragic miscalculations at Gallipoli or, a mere few weeks previously, Norway. The dark lessons Winston learned about himself from Gallipoli never left him (though he did try to airbrush them away, denying he felt any guilt, and later saying he 'gloried' in the bravery of the men who died there).

But history has many authors, and one afternoon in August 1915, while painting a picture of a landscape, his defences down, he told the poet and diplomat Wilfrid Scawen Blunt: 'There is more blood than paint upon these hands.' It was a rare glimpse of psychological frailty, and an even rarer insight into his own scarred humanity. The inevitable child of guilt is self-doubt, and self-doubt surely took a grip on Churchill in late May 1940. When you have been so badly wrong in the past, you cannot be quite so confident, under similar circumstances, again.

As previously noted, the historian David Cannadine said of Churchill's character that he was 'at once simple, ardent, innocent and incapable of deception or intrigue'. If so, then why foist upon him days and days of deception and intrigue when there is no record, either before or after this event, of his being so deceptive or intriguing?

The general impulse here seems to be to deny the great man his normal due of self-doubt. But it is no sin to suffer doubts. Rather, I would argue that the *ability* to have doubts, and then to be able to move on from them to synthesize opposing ideas, before reaching a balanced decision, forms the very definition of a real leader and of true leadership.

This book therefore argues for a greater and more complex portrait of Churchill, not a lesser one.

Let us assume, then, that Winston actually *meant* what

he said when debating these critical issues, when he knew full well that every word was being recorded in the minutes, without irony and for posterity.

The records of those War Cabinet meetings of late May leave me in no doubt that for a time, when it was looking like Britain might lose 90 per cent of its soldiers, Winston was gradually persuaded that, so long as British independence was assured, it made sense to seriously explore peace with Nazi Germany, as unwelcome as that prospect seemed. He knew Hitler's demands would be terrible: the surrender of Central Europe and France to Nazi rule in perpetuity; in addition, the return of certain German colonies taken after the First World War. It was a monstrous price tag, but a negotiated peace clearly began to seem an option more favourable than a Nazi invasion and possible occupation that would see the Swastika flying over Buckingham Palace and Westminster.

Any close reading of the words that Winston reportedly used during these May debates presents a vivid picture of the steady fragmentation of his previous fight-at-all-costs position, and a warming towards the idea of peace talks. Recall that in those days he went on record saying, variously, that he would 'consider' a peace deal; was happy to 'discuss' one; would be 'thankful' to get out of the current mess by way of talks if essential conditions were met, even at 'the cost of some cession of [British] territory [Malta and some African colonies]', and (as he told the War Cabinet) even if it meant granting Hitler 'Overlordship of Central Europe'. Indeed (as he advised the Defence Committee), he told France to 'accept' a peace deal should one be offered it, so long as France was not used as a staging post for an attack on Britain. Chamberlain's diary recounts, in language surely more colourful and realistic than the Cabinet Secretary's dry, tone-deaf minute book, that Churchill was ready to 'jump at' a deal if conditions were met. To prove that he was ready to 'jump', he permitted a secret Anglo-Italian meeting to take place in London between Halifax and Ambassador Bastianini on 25 May, provided it was not made public – a meeting that made explicit the matter of a peace deal with Hitler, with Mussolini acting as the intermediary in the negotiation. Subsequent to this meeting, Churchill granted Halifax formal permission to draft a memorandum to the Italian Ambassador to discuss further the terms of a peace deal that might involve both Britain and France.

These are considerable concessions from someone who never seriously thought peace talks an option.

I contend that by 27 May the essential disagreement was not *if* a deal should be sought, but *when*. Winston's belief was that his government could get the best terms after a Nazi invasion of Britain had been successfully repelled; Halifax and Chamberlain thought there was no better moment than the present, while Britain still possessed an army. For a few agonizing and uncertain hours, it was upon this dispute that the fate of the world hung.

All leaders need luck – and the luck they need is this: times commensurate with their talents.

Winston had no aptitude for peace. His was a gift for crisis and its expression, for courage and its evocation, often for risk and its underestimation. Where more reasonable men rightly feared the consequences of their decisions, he had no great feeling for the contemplation of negative outcomes – he had been this way his entire life – and he did not readily understand it in others. Audacity is a quality found in many great leaders, but it is as likely to result in ignominy as distinction. What makes the difference, finally, is whether the leader is right.

Churchill, in late May, after a great deal of vacillating, of hemming and hawing, of all-night pacing, of mental disorderliness, saying one thing and then the other, of an infuriating overuse of the *volte face*, of soul-searching, of heedfulness, of listening, of reconsideration, of option-weighing, of reckoning, of black-dog speechlessness, was able to confront the nation and offer words toughened in the fires of an intense doubt, and come down on the right side of history.

He got it right.

The events of May 1940 proved to be the making of the man. In these first fragile weeks of his premiership – when he was tested as few new leaders have been – he essentially found within himself the undiscovered lineaments of leadership that would serve him for the rest of the war, ensuring him a permanent seat in the pavilion of the truly great.

That May, Winston Churchill became Winston Churchill.

Acknowledgements

This book is dedicated to my father, who fought in the Second World War, in both the Pacific and Italian theatres. He was always a deep fan of Churchill, though as a child I never fully understood why. I hope he would approve of this book.

The Churchill Estate has been most generous in lending its blessing to this project, especially the Churchill family. The Churchill Archives have helped hugely by making available to me their extraordinary collection.

My steadfast and loyal first editor, Jane Parkin, cracked her grammatical whip and helped polish the prose to ensure clarity and order, as did this book's fine phalanx of editors: Joel Rickett and Daniel Crewe at Viking, and Jonathan Jao and Roger Labrie at HarperCollins.

I wish to thank, also, my literary agent, Jennifer Joel at ICM Partners, and also Working Title Films, Universal Pictures and Focus Features for their support.

But lastly, my deepest thanks and deepest debt is owed to Rebecca Cronshey, my heroic researcher, whose sleepless nights and archival sleuthing helped make this book what it is.

References

1. A House Divided

p. 2: You have sat . . . go!: Leo Amery's speech at Norway Debate: Hansard, Conduct of the War, HC Deb Series 5, 7 May 1940, vol. 360, cc.1140–51.

p. 3: heart-broken and shrivelled: R. R. James (ed.), *Chips: The Diaries of Sir Henry Channon* (Weidenfeld & Nicolson, London, 1993), p. 245.

p. 4: Its heart is troubled . . . apprehensive: Arthur Greenwood: Hansard, Conduct of the War, HC Deb Series 5, 7 May 1940, vol. 360, cc.1171–2.

p. 4: shocking story of ineptitude: Admiral Sir Roger Keyes: ibid., cc.1127–8.

pp. 4–5: It is not Norway . . . attack Norway: Clement Attlee: ibid., cc.1093–4.

p. 5: The P.M. is very depressed . . . ever since: John Colville, *The Fringes of Power: Downing Street Diaries 1939–1955* (Hodder and Stoughton, London, 1985), 6 May 1940, p. 91.

p. 5: indicate whether . . . conduct of affairs: Herbert Morrison: Hansard, Conduct of the War, HC Deb Series 5, 8 May 1940, vol. 360, cc.1265.

p. 6: all talking about . . . the leadership: Colville, *Fringes of Power*, p. 93: Sir Samuel Hoare (Minister for Air), Sir John Simon (Chancellor), Sir Kingsley Wood (Lord Privy Seal).

p. 7: jumped up '. . . in the Lobby': Hugh Dalton, *The Fateful Years: Memoirs 1931–1945* (Frederick Muller, London, 1957), p. 305.

p. 7: the worst strategic . . . seals of office: David Lloyd George: Hansard, Conduct of the War, HC Deb Series 5, 8 May 1940, vol. 360, c.1283.

p. 8: I am so glad . . . eye opener: National Library of Wales, Lady Olwen Carey-Evans Papers 122/14a, MLG to Mrs PHG, 15 May 1940.

p. 8: considerable pain: Neville Chamberlain diary, 16 June 1940 (Neville Chamberlain Papers, University of Birmingham).

p. 9: I take complete . . . of the burden: Winston S. Churchill: Hansard, Conduct of the War, HC Deb Series 5, 8 May 1940, vol. 360, cc.1251–1366.

p. 9: The right hon. . . . his colleagues: Lloyd George, HC Deb Series 5, 8 May 1940, vol. 360, c.1283.

pp. 10–11: We watched . . . best for England: James (ed.), *Chips*, pp. 246–7.

p. 11: you utterly . . . last night: Roy Jenkins, *Churchill: A Biography* (Macmillan, London, 2001).

p. 11: disgusting . . . Hitler's next move: Colville, *Fringes of Power*, p. 93.

p. 12: rumour and intrigue, plot and counter-plot: James (ed.), *Chips*, p. 248.

p. 12: made it clear . . . take over: Andrew Roberts, *The Holy Fox: A Biography of Lord Halifax* (Weidenfeld & Nicolson, London, 1991), p. 245, based on 'private information'.

p. 13: he thought . . . in the Government: Lord Halifax, diary, 9 May 1940, Halifax Papers (Borthwick Institute, York), A7/8/4, p. 113.

p. 13: if it were . . . House of Commons: Ibid.

p. 13: The conversation . . . to do it: Ibid., p. 114.

pp. 13–14: He [Halifax] told me . . . Prime Minister: R. A. Butler, *The Art of the Possible: The Memoirs of Lord Butler, K.G., C.H.* (Hamish Hamilton, London, 1971), p. 84.

p. 16: Naturally the only . . . to an end: Colonel Roderick Macleod, DSO, MC, and Denis Kelly (eds.), *The Ironside Diaries: 1937–1940* (Constable, London, 1962), p. 293.

p. 16: an attack . . . the question: Roberts, *Holy Fox*, p. 274.

p. 17: In March 1939 . . . at this juncture: D. R. Thorpe, *Eden: The Life and Times of Anthony Eden, First Earl of Avon, 1897–1977* (Pimlico, London, 2004), p. 237.

p. 17: rehearsed to me . . . must be formed: The Rt Hon. The Earl of Avon, KG, PC, MC, *The Eden Memoirs*, vol. 2: *The Reckoning* (Cassell, London, 1965), p. 96.

p. 17: I will serve . . . the War: A. J. P. Taylor, *Beaverbrook* (Hamish Hamilton, London, 1972), p. 409.

pp. 17–18: that if asked . . . I seconded it: Avon, *Reckoning*, pp. 96–7.

p. 18: he would happily . . . either man: Lord Halifax, diary, p. 114.

p. 19: stomach ache continued . . . really mattered: Lord Halifax, diary, p. 115

p. 19: suitable expression . . . my view: Ibid.

p. 19: 'Can you see' . . . Armistice Day: Winston S. Churchill, *The Second World War*, vol. 1: *The Gathering Storm* (The Folio Society, London, 2000), pp. 522–3.

p. 20: Chief Whip . . . steady Winston: David Dilks (ed.), *The Diaries of Sir Alexander Cadogan, O.M.* (Cassell, London, 1971), 9 May 1940, p. 280; Roberts, *Holy Fox*.

p. 20: **nothing in particular:** Churchill, *Gathering Storm*, p. 522.

p. 20: **hoped NC . . . of [the] party:** Avon, *Eden Memoirs*, p. 97.

p. 21: **I felt as if . . . not fail:** Churchill, *Gathering Storm*, pp. 525–6.

2. *The Social Wastrel*

p. 25: **fell in love with her at first sight:** Winston S. Churchill, *My Early Life* (Eland, London, 2000), author's preface.

p. 25: **My mother . . . at a distance:** Ibid., p. 13.

p. 26: **My father died . . . his memory:** Churchill, *My Early Life*, p. 70.

p. 27: **After all . . . all lessons:** Ibid., pp. 17–18.

p. 27: **a most delightful man . . . into [his] bones:** Ibid., p. 24.

pp. 28–9: **9 August 1893 . . . Randolph S.C.:** Randolph S. Churchill (ed.), *The Churchill Documents*, vol. 1: *Youth 1874–1896* (Heinemann, London, 1967), pp. 390–91.

p. 30: **I am all . . . there again:** Churchill, *My Early Life*, p. 47.

p. 30: **exceeded in severity . . . military equitation:** Ibid., p. 71

p. 30: **She still knew . . . I had lived:** Ibid., p. 80.

p. 31: **the closing decade . . . live my life:** Ibid., p. 83.

p. 32: **When first . . . Treasure Island:** Ibid., p. 85.

p. 32: **keenest realization . . . our own:** Ibid., p. 110.

p. 33: **resolved to read . . . standard works:** Ibid., p. 117.

p. 33: embarked on that . . . strong wind: Ibid., p. 118.

p. 34: know rest only . . . resist it: Winston S. Churchill, *Savrola: A Tale of the Revolution in Laurania* (George Newnes, London, 1908), p. 32.

p. 36: believed in . . . over Oldham: Roy Jenkins, *Churchill: A Biography* (Macmillan, London, 2001), p. 65.

p. 36: who was for . . . swore his fealty: Ibid., p. 71.

p. 37: I was all . . . retrenchment and reform: Churchill, *My Early Life*, p. 374.

pp. 37–8: put in an appearance . . . the Liberals: Violet Bonham-Carter, *Winston Churchill: An Intimate Portrait* (Harcourt, Brace & World, New York, 1965), p. 89.

pp. 42–3: I thought of the peril . . . next day: Winston S. Churchill, *The World Crisis, 1911–1918* (Macmillan, London, 1931), p. 46.

p. 43: the Germans that . . . build more: Jenkins, *Churchill*, p. 220.

p. 44: foremost enemy: Ibid., p. 232.

p. 44: For many in Britain . . . unthinkable: Michael Shelden, *Young Titan: The Making of Winston Churchill* (Simon & Schuster, New York, 2013), p. 296.

p. 44: The lamps . . . in our lifetime: Viscount Grey of Falloden, *Twenty-Five Years 1892–1916*, vol. II (Hodder and Stoughton, London, 1925), p. 223.

p. 45: and undertake command . . . Antwerp: Winston S. Churchill to Herbert Asquith, 5 October 1914, cited in Martin Gilbert, *Winston S. Churchill*, vol. III: *The Challenge of War, 1914–1916* (Minerva, London, 1971), p. 163.

p. 46: evolving army-based plan: Timothy Travers, *Gallipoli 1915* (Tempus, Stroud, 2001), p. 23.

p. 46: **seething cauldron:** Jenkins, *Churchill*, p. 260.

p. 48: **I am finished! . . . Germans:** Gilbert, *Challenge of War*, p. 457.

p. 48: **thought he would die of grief:** Ibid., p. 473.

p. 48: **If you throw Winston . . . Government:** Ibid., p. 459.

p. 49: **the German shell-fire . . . constant hazard:** Martin Gilbert, *Churchill: A Life* (Heinemann, London, 1991), p. 346.

pp. 49–50: **To be great . . . requires explanation:** Mary Soames (ed.), *Winston and Clementine: The Personal Letters of the Churchills* (Houghton Mifflin, Boston, p. 198), p. 198.

p. 50: **belief that will . . . task envisaged:** Jenkins, *Churchill*, p. 351.

p. 51: **I'm forever blowing . . . mortal pain:** Mary Soames, *Clementine Churchill* (Doubleday, London, 2002), p. 202.

pp. 51–2: **did not indulge . . . with life:** Ibid.

p. 52: **His 'life seat' . . . in his hands:** Jenkins, *Churchill*, p. 375.

p. 53: **This fulfils . . . splendid Office:** Gilbert, *Churchill: A Life*, p. 465.

p. 56: **The Indian issue . . . three years:** Jenkins, *Churchill*, p. 440.

p. 57: **[a]ll these bands . . . the Fatherland:** Winston S. Churchill, speech to House of Commons, Hansard, HC Deb Series 5, 23 November 1932, vol. 272, cc.73–92.

p. 57: **Germany got off lightly . . . Great War:** Ibid., 13 April 1933, vol. 276, cc.2786–800.

pp. 57–8: **that she [Germany] . . . their birth:** Ibid.

p. 58: **Hitler himself claimed . . . communism:** Martin Gilbert, *The Roots of Appeasement* (Weidenfeld & Nicolson, London, 1966), p. 143.

p. 61: My heart sank . . . vision of Death: Winston S. Churchill, *The Second World War*, vol. 1: *The Gathering Storm* (The Folio Society, London, 2000), p. 231.

p. 61: I predict that . . . stand alone: Winston S. Churchill, speech to House of Commons, Hansard, HC Deb Series 5, 22 February 1938, vol. 332, cc.235–48.

p. 62: Hitler angry that . . . the proposal: Gilbert, *Roots of Appeasement*, p. 175.

p. 62: tell Germany . . . war with her: Lord Halifax, referring to a conversation between himself, Churchill and Neville Chamberlain, CAB 23/95/5.

p. 62: symbolic of the desire . . . war again: Chamberlain returns from Munich with Anglo-German agreement, 30 September 1938, BBC National Programme 1938-09-30 (BBC Archive Recording, Feston Airport, Hounslow, West London).

pp. 63–4: I will . . . begin . . . olden time: Winston S. Churchill, speech to House of Commons, Hansard, HC Deb Series 5, 5 October 1938, vol. 339, cc.359–74.

3. A Leader Falls

p. 67: I think I shall . . . tomorrow: Randolph S. Churchill recollection, dictated at Stour, East Bergholt, 13 February 1963, cited in Martin Gilbert, *The Churchill War Papers*, vol. 1: *At the Admiralty: September 1939–May 1940* (Heinemann, London, 1993), p. 1266.

p. 67: Boxes with telegrams . . . Foreign Office: Winston S. Churchill, *The Second World War*, vol. I, *The Gathering Storm* (The Folio Society, London, 2000), p. 523.

pp. 67–8: spirit, so far from . . . morning ride: Samuel Hoare, *Nine Troubled Years* (Collins, London, 1954), pp. 431–2.

p. 68: could not get out . . . for security: Colonel Roderick Macleod, DSO, MC, and Denis Kelly (eds.), *The Ironside Diaries: 1937–1940* (Constable, London, 1962), 10 May 1940, p. 301.

p. 68: It is reported . . . invaded Holland: BBC Home Service, 7 a.m. bulletin, Friday, 10 May 1940.

p. 69: the German hordes . . . beating the enemy: Randolph S. Churchill, in Gilbert, *At the Admiralty*, pp. 1269–70.

p. 70: the whole plan . . . move quickly: CAB 65/7/9.

p. 70: withhold his resignation . . . was finished: Hoare, *Nine Troubled Years*, p. 432; Churchill, *Gathering Storm*, p. 523.

p. 70: Newspaper headlines, 10 May 1940: *Daily Express*, *Daily Mirror*, *Daily Mail*, *Daily Telegraph*.

p. 73: on the contrary . . . confront it: Churchill, *Gathering Storm*, p. 523.

p. 73: Ironside informed . . . Albert Canal: CAB 65/7/10.

pp. 73–4: along the Meuse . . . airmen in trouble: Philip Warner, *The Battle of France, 10 May–22 June 1940: Six Weeks Which Changed the World* (Cassell, London, 1990), pp. 50–52.

p. 74: open towns in Belgium: CAB 69/1.

p. 74: in the event . . . speed into Belgium: Lionel Hastings, Baron Ismay, *The Memoirs of General the Lord Ismay K.G., P.C., G.C.B., C.H., D.S.O.* (Heinemann, London, 1960), p. 123.

p. 74: that if the accumulated . . . in Germany: CAB 83/3/12.

p. 75: psychological effect of . . . 24 hours: CAB 65/7/11.

pp. 75–6: The Labour Party . . . the nation: Ibid.

p. 76: in the light . . . that evening: Ibid.

p. 76: Although [he] . . . last-minute approaches: Andrew Roberts, *The Holy Fox: A Biography of Lord Halifax* (Weidenfeld & Nicolson, London, 1991), p. 280.

pp. 76–7: How grossly unfairly . . . to send for: Sir John Wheeler-Bennett, *King George VI: His Life and Reign* (Macmillan, London, 1958), p. 444.

p. 77: It is a terrible risk . . . the prospect: John Colville, *The Fringes of Power: Downing Street Diaries 1939–1955* (Hodder and Stoughton, London, 1985), p. 96.

p. 78: During these tense . . . as possible: Mary Soames, *Clementine Churchill* (Cassell, London, 1979), ch. 19.

p. 78: the public had not . . . Palace gates: Churchill, *Gathering Storm*, p. 525.

pp. 78–9: His majesty received . . . certainly do so: Ibid.

p. 79: full of fire . . . Prime Minister: Wheeler-Bennett, *King George VI*, p. 444.

p. 79: God alone knows . . . do our best: Ex-Detective Inspector W. H. Thompson, *I was Churchill's Shadow* (Christopher Johnson, London, 1951), p. 37.

p. 80: [T]his sudden coup . . . half-breed American: Colville, *Fringes of Power*, pp. 96–7.

p. 80: My dear Neville . . . Winston S. Churchill: Winston S. Churchill to Neville Chamberlain, 19 February, cited in Gilbert, *At the Admiralty*, p. 1285.

p. 81: It gives me so much . . . the master: Churchill to Lord Halifax, cited in Gilbert, *At the Admiralty*, p. 1285.

p. 82: had known both . . . Liberal Oppositions: Churchill, *Gathering Storm*, p. 526.

p. 82: Minister of Defence . . . scope and powers: Ibid.

pp. 83–4: Early this morning . . . and overthrown: Neville Chamberlain, resignation speech, 10 May 1940. BBC broadcast on the British Library's Sound Server.

pp. 84–5: During these last . . . than dreams: Churchill, *Gathering Storm*, pp. 526–7.

4. The Holy Fox

p. 87: I don't understand . . . 'noblesse oblige': R. R. James (ed.), *Chips: The Diaries of Sir Henry Channon* (Weidenfeld & Nicolson, London, 1993), p. 249.

p. 88: a paragon amongst women: Andrew Roberts, *The Holy Fox: A Biography of Lord Halifax* (Weidenfeld & Nicolson, London, 1991), p. 12.

pp. 88–9: I have no desire . . . a gentleman: Ben Pimlott (ed.), *The Second World War Diary of Hugh Dalton* (Jonathan Cape, London, 1985), 14 November 1940, p. 101.

p. 89: aloof, serious, devout, . . . 'Holy Fox': Andrew Muldoon, *Empire, Politics and the Creation of the 1935 India Act: Last Act of the Raj* (Routledge, London, 2016), p. 44. Also cited in Roberts, *Holy Fox*, p. 6.

p. 90: to affect your judgement: Roberts, *Holy Fox*, p. 51.

p. 90: catalogue of errors and disasters: Ibid., p. 53.

p. 90: carried himself . . . wasn't one: Ibid., p. 63.

p. 91: that our policy . . . of acceptance: CAB 23/83, 10 March 1936.

p. 92: improve our contacts . . . criticism of Germany: CAB 23/87/3, 13 January 1937.

p. 93: confine himself ... and Czechoslovakia: The Rt Hon. The Earl of Avon KG, PC, MC, *The Eden Memoirs*, vol. 1: *Facing the Dictators* (Cassell, London, 1965), p. 509.

p. 93: possible alterations ... and Czechoslovakia: Ibid., p. 515. Also cited in Halifax Papers (Borthwick Institute, York), A4 410 3 3.

p. 94: both personally and ... feel the same!: Halifax to Baldwin, 15 November 1937, Baldwin Papers, 173/61.

p. 94: there was much ... fully informed: Halifax Papers, A4 410 3 3.

p. 95: struck me as ... everything he said: Ibid.

p. 95: His personality ... at Chatsworth: Ibid.

p. 95: The Germans had ... their country: CAB 23/90/43, 24 November 1937.

p. 96: the British people ... to merge: Alan Bullock (ed.), *The Ribbentrop Memoirs* (Weidenfeld & Nicolson, London, 1954), p. 84.

p. 96: a man of uncertain ... opinions: Martin Gilbert, *The Roots of Appeasement* (Weidenfeld & Nicolson, London, 1966), p. 182.

p. 97: in the possibility ... been swept: Ibid.

pp. 97–8: [Halifax] made the ... catastrophic: Roberts, *Holy Fox*, p. 66.

pp. 98–9: I spent an hour ... for himself: Ambassador Joseph Kennedy to Cordell Hull, US Secretary of State, FRUS, 1938, 1:722, 12 October 1938.

p. 99: The happenings in ... very difficult: CAB 27/624/32, 14 November 1938.

p. 99: ultimate end ... be uncertain: CAB 23/96/59 (38), 15 December 1938.

p. 100: for some time: Keir Papers, cited in Roberts, *Holy Fox*, p. 191.

pp. 100–101: On our way home . . . being raped: The Earl of Halifax, *Fulness of Days* (Collins, London, 1957), p. 215.

p. 101: that there was a rational . . . solutions: Roberts, *Holy Fox*, p. 157.

5. The Great 'Dictator'

p. 105: you and Edward . . . directing the war: Winston S. Churchill to Neville Chamberlain, 11 May 1940, Churchill Papers, 20/11, and Chamberlain's reply. Cited in Martin Gilbert, *The Churchill War Papers*, vol. 2: *Never Surrender: May 1940–December 1940* (William Heinemann, London, 1993).

pp. 105–6: long interview. . . Winston considerably: Kevin Jefferys, *War and Reform: British Politics during the Second World War* (Manchester University Press, Manchester, 1994), p. 42.

p. 107: the Labour People . . . House of Commons: Lord Halifax, diary, 11 May 1940, Halifax Papers (Borthwick Institute, York), A7/8/4, p. 119.

p. 107: About one o'clock . . . were announced: R. R. James (ed.), *Chips: The Diaries of Sir Henry Channon* (Weidenfeld & Nicolson, London, 1993), 11 May 1940, p. 251.

pp. 107–8: always [being] particularly . . . indiscretions: Ruth Ive, *The Woman Who Censored Churchill* (History Press, Stroud, 2008), p 56.

p. 108: **[w]e want all . . . pull us through:** Colonel Roderick Macleod, DSO, MC, and Denis Kelly (eds.), *The Ironside Diaries: 1937–1940* (Constable, London, 1962), 11 May 1940, p. 303.

p. 108: **Attlee and Greenwood . . . on intellect:** Lord Halifax, diary, 11 May 1940, p. 119.

p. 108: **[i]t is the personalities . . . much else:** Neville Chamberlain to Winston S. Churchill, 11 May 1940, Churchill Papers, 20/11, cited in Gilbert, *Never Surrender.*

p. 109: **The Queen spoke . . . administrative methods:** Lord Halifax, diary, 11 May 1940, pp. 119–20.

p. 109: **War Cabinet announced . . . Awful:** Charles Stuart (ed.), *The Reith Diaries* (Collins, London, 1975), 11 May 1940, p. 250.

p. 110: **By the time . . . possible delay:** Winston S. Churchill to Sir John Reith, Churchill Papers, 2/398, 12 May 1940, cited in Gilbert, *Never Surrender.*

p. 110: **this night-life is no good to me:** Lord Halifax, diary, 11 May 1940, p. 120.

p. 110: **The meeting Winston . . . subject:** Ibid., p. 121.

p. 111: **certain air of 'malaise' . . . is depressing:** John Colville, *The Fringes of Power: Downing Street Diaries 1939–1955* (Hodder and Stoughton, London, 1985), 14 May 1940, p. 103.

pp. 111–12: **stomach queasy . . . line of the Dyle:** Sir John Sinclair: recollection, 12 May 1940, Davy Papers, cited in Gilbert, *Never Surrender.*

p. 112: **two-thirds full . . . cloakroom below:** Sonia Purnell, *First Lady: The Life and Wars of Clementine Churchill* (Aurum Press, London, 2015), p. 149.

p. 112: 'Don't come in!' . . . wanted to say: Chips Gemmell, TV interview, in Martin Gilbert, *The Complete Churchill*, part 4: *Never Despair* (A & E Home Video, 1992).

pp. 112–13: porpoise-like quality . . . lukewarm seawater: Roy Jenkins, *Churchill: A Biography* (Macmillan, London, 2001), p. 712.

p. 113: robed like a Roman . . . his bedroom: Mary Soames, *Clementine Churchill* (Cassell, London, 1979), p. 293.

p. 113: [f]ollowing his ablutions . . . 'don't look!': Purnell, *First Lady*, p. 149.

p. 113: I am coming out . . . watch it!: Elizabeth Gilliatt, TV interview, in Gilbert, *Never Despair*.

p. 113: just like a rather nice pig: Colville, *Fringes of Power*, 16 June 1940.

p. 114: A book on Churchill . . . hugely amusing: Joseph Goebbels, diary, cited in Michael Paterson, *Winston Churchill: Personal Accounts of the Great Leader at War* (David & Charles, 2005), 3 May 1941, p. 26.

p. 115: raffish worlds: David Cannadine, *Aspects of Aristocracy: Grandeur and Decline in Modern Britain* (New Haven, Conn./London, Yale University Press, 1994), p. 147.

p. 115: I found complete chaos . . . I doubt: Lord Hankey to Sir Samuel Hoare, 12 May 1940, Beaverbrook Papers, cited in Gilbert, *Never Surrender*.

p. 116: two or three days . . . '. . . a long time': Lionel Hastings, Baron Ismay, *The Memoirs of General the Lord Ismay K.G., P.C., G.C.B., C.H., D.S.O.* (Heinemann, London, 1960), p. 116.

6. Blood, Toil, Tears and Sweat

p. 120: Absurdly dramatic . . . regular ovation: R. R. James (ed.), *Chips: The Diaries of Sir Henry Channon* (Weidenfeld & Nicolson, London, 1993), 13 May 1940, p. 252.

pp. 121–3: I beg to move . . . united strength: Winston S. Churchill, speech to the House of Commons, Hansard, HC Deb Series 5, 13 May 1940, vol. 360, cc. 1501–3.

p. 124: was not well received: James (ed.), *Chips*, p. 252.

p. 124: I congratulate the country . . . all time: David Lloyd George, Hansard, Conduct of the War, HC Deb Series 5, 8 May 1940, vol. 360, cc.1510–12.

p. 124: mop[ped] his eyes: Harold Nicolson, *Diaries and Letters 1930–1964*, ed. Stanley Olson (Penguin Books, Harmondsworth, 1980), p. 183.

p. 124: only references . . . raised enthusiasm: James (ed.), *Chips*, p. 252.

p. 124: [v]ery short . . . but to the point: Nicolson, *Diaries and Letters*, p. 183.

p. 124: brilliant little speech: John Colville, *The Fringes of Power: Downing Street Diaries 1939–1955* (Hodder and Stoughton, London, 1985), p. 102.

p. 124: The new PM spoke . . . dramatically: James (ed.), *Chips*, p. 252.

pp. 125–6: I entered the presence . . . this afternoon: The Rt Hon. Malcolm MacDonald, *Titans and Others* (Collins, London, 1982), pp. 94–5.

p. 126: the composition . . . or to hurry: John Colville, in *Action This Day: Working With Churchill*, ed. Sir John Wheeler-Bennett (Macmillan, London, 1968), p. 69.

p. 126: Rhetorical power . . . by practice: Winston S. Churchill, 'The Scaffolding of Rhetoric', Churchill Papers, CHAR 8/13.

p. 126: sudor et sanguis: Livy, *The fifth, sixth and seventh Books of Livy's History of Rome. A literal translation from the text of Madvig, with historical introduction, summary to each book and . . . notes, by a First-classman* (J. Thornton, Oxford, 1879), pp. 157, 283.

p. 127: That 'tis in vain . . . or blood: John Donne, *An Anatomy of the World. A facsimile of the first edition, 1611. With a postscript by Geoffrey Keynes* (Cambridge, Cambridge University Press, 1951).

p. 127: Year after year . . . why? for rent!: Lord Byron, *Age of Bronze*, IV: 'Satiric – The Landed Interest' (London, 1823).

p. 127: Tears, sweat, blood . . . glorified now: Robert Browning, 'Ixion', in *Jocoseria* (1883).

p. 127: I offer neither pay . . . and death: 'Offro fame, sete, marce forzate, battaglie e morte', speech by Giuseppe Garibaldi, St Peter's Square, Rome, 2 July 1849.

p. 127: Because of the blood . . . to triumph: Theodore Roosevelt, *American Ideals, and Other Essays, Social and Political* (G. P. Putnam's Sons, New York, 1897), p. 260.

p. 127: only a question . . . blood and tears: Winston S. Churchill, *London to Ladysmith via Pretoria* (Longmans, Green, London, 1900), p. 96.

pp. 127–8: It will all seem . . . war comes: Winston S. Churchill, *Saturday Evening Post*, vol. 173, Issue 1, p. 29.

p. 128: **[r]ecord the toils ... endless plain:** Winston S. Churchill, 'The Eastern Front', in *The World Crisis, 1911–1918* (Macmillan, London, 1931), p. 17.

p. 128: follies in blood and toil: Winston S. Churchill, *Marlborough: His Life and Times* (Harrap, London, 1933), vol. 1, p. 217.

p. 128: new structures ... being united: Winston S. Churchill, 'Hope in Spain, 23 February 1939', in Winston S. Churchill, *Step by Step: Political Writings, 1936–1939* (Butterworth, London, 1939).

p. 128: the orator is ... himself believe: Churchill, 'Scaffolding of Rhetoric'.

p. 129: the repetition ... sense of optimism: Richard Toye, *The Roar of the Lion: The Untold Story of Churchill's World War II Speeches* (OUP, Oxford, 2013), p. 42.

p. 131: a series of vivid ... be assailed: Churchill, 'Scaffolding of Rhetoric'.

p. 131: [Mr. Fox] defies me ... much energy: Winston S. Churchill, *A History of the English-Speaking Peoples*, vol 3: *The Age of Revolution* (Cassell, London, 1957), p. 296.

p. 132: the unreflecting ... understandings: Churchill, 'Scaffolding of Rhetoric'.

pp. 132–3: the art of working ... delicate touch: Plutarch, *Life of Pericles*, citing Plato, *Phaedrus*, 271c, cited in Algis Valiunas, *Churchill's Military Histories: A Rhetorical Study* (Oxford, Rowman & Littlefield, 2002).

p. 133: loudly cheered: *Daily Telegraph*, 14 May 1940, *Evening Standard*, 13 May 1940.

p. 133: he felt an air attack ... the situation: CAB 65/7/15 and CAB 65/13/7, 13 May 1940.

7. The Worsening Situation

pp. 137–8: one lived with the battle . . . be done: Winston S. Churchill, *The Second World War*, vol. II: *Their Finest Hour* (Cassell, London, 1949), p. 11.

p. 139: we should not regard . . . in or not: CAB 65/7/16, 14 May 1940.

pp. 139–40: Germany intends to . . . not fail us: CAB 65/7/17, 14 May 1940.

p. 140: amphibious tanks . . . intentions of the French: Ibid.

p. 140: merchant vessels . . . being laid: Ibid.

p. 140: highest Fascist standing . . . go to war: Ibid.

p. 140: the most prudent course . . . that light: Ibid.

pp. 140–41: curious ugly dolphin . . . pills and powders: John Colville, *Action This Day: Working With Churchill*, ed. Sir John Wheeler-Bennett (Macmillan, London, 1968), p. 49; John Colville, *The Fringes of Power: Downing Street Diaries 1939–1955* (Hodder and Stoughton, London, 1985), p. 103.

p. 141: motley gathering appeared . . . Mr Kennedy: Colville, *Fringes of Power*, p. 104.

p. 141: very excited mood: Churchill: telephone conversation with Paul Reynaud, Premier Papers, 3/188/1, cited in Martin Gilbert, *The Churchill War Papers*, vol. 2, *Never Surrender: May 1940–December 1940* (William Heinemann, London, 1993).

p. 142: the road to Paris . . . giving up: Ibid.

p. 142: He [Reynaud] must not . . . after 9 a.m.: Ibid.

p. 142: the situation was . . . now plugged: CAB 65/7/18, 15 May 1940.

p. 143: announcing the surrender . . . loss of life: Ibid.

p. 143: it should be made . . . particular area: Ibid.

p. 143: the situation had . . . the Netherlands: Ibid.

p. 144: The war is coming . . . economic means: Colonel Roderick Macleod, DSO, MC, and Denis Kelly (eds.), *The Ironside Diaries: 1937–1940* (Constable, London, 1962), 15 May 1940, p. 310.

p. 144: might be of some . . . Signor Mussolini: CAB 65/7/18.

p. 144: particulars of the . . . the situation: Ibid.

p. 145: a good deal shaken . . . was off him: Lord Halifax, diary, 11 May 1940, Halifax Papers (Borthwick Institute, York), A7/8/4, p. 127.

pp. 145–6: Although I have . . . armed forces: Churchill to President Roosevelt, Churchill Papers, 20/14, cited in Gilbert, *Never Surrender*.

p. 146: latest types of aircraft . . . all the same: Ibid.

p. 146: the visit of a United States . . . wishes and respect: Ibid.

p. 147: being built in and for the United States: Martin Gilbert, *Winston S. Churchill*, vol. 6: *Finest Hour, 1939–1941* (Heinemann, London, 1983), p. 344.

p. 147: we [America] could . . . Botwood [Newfoundland]: Ibid.

pp. 148–9: Now that I have . . . given by us: Churchill to Benito Mussolini, Churchill Papers, 20/14, cited in Gilbert, *Never Surrender*.

p. 149: I reply to the . . . event whatsoever: Benito Mussolini to Churchill, Churchill Papers, 20/14, cited in Gilbert, *Never Surrender*.

p. 150: there was no doubt . . . to launch: CAB 65/7/19, 16 May 1940.

p. 151: From the moment . . . the flames: Lionel Hastings, Baron Ismay, *The Memoirs of General the Lord Ismay K.G., P.C., G.C.B., C.H., D.S.O.* (Heinemann, London, 1960), p. 127.

p. 151: again emphasise . . . (i.e. six more) tomorrow: Churchill to the War Cabinet, Churchill Papers, 4/149, cited in Gilbert, *Never Surrender*.

p. 152: [Churchill was] delighted . . . received it: Ismay, *Memoirs*, pp. 128–9.

p. 153: had been faced . . . considerable degree: CAB 65/7/21, 17 May 1940.

p. 153: the life of the country . . . only 150 left: CAB 99/3, 16 May 1940.

pp. 153–4: we had bombarded . . . ground action: Ibid.

p. 154: of course giving every . . . take time: CAB 65/7/21, 17 May 1940.

p. 154: supreme emergency . . . the following day: CAB 65/13/11, 18 May 1940.

p. 154: You ought to have cried. . . with lies!: Colville, *Fringes of Power*, 19 May 1940, p. 108.

p. 154: a gruelling week . . . (. . . eaten by foxes): John Colville, *Man of Valour: The Life of Field-Marshal the Viscount Gort, VC, GCB, DSO, MVO, MC* (Collins, London, 1972), p. 204.

p. 155: would be closely . . . our own Army: CAB 65/13/12, 19 May 1940.

pp. 155–6: After forty years . . . a small room: William Manchester, *The Last Lion: Winston Spencer Churchill, Defender of the Realm, 1940–1965* (Michael Joseph, London, 1983), Kindle edn, Loc. 1549.

pp. 156–60: I speak to you ... '... even so let it be': Churchill, broadcast to the nation, 19 May 1940, Churchill Archives Centre, CHAR 9/176A-B.

p. 161: You have never ... thank God for you: Anthony Eden to Churchill, Churchill Papers, 2/394, cited in Gilbert, *Never Surrender*.

p. 161: The PM gave a ... everybody here: Captain Berkley, diary, Berkley Papers, 20 May 1940, cited in Gilbert, *Never Surrender*.

p. 161: I listened to your ... lies on you: Earl Baldwin of Bewdley to Churchill, Churchill Papers, 20/1, cited in Gilbert, *Never Surrender*.

8. Fear, Doubts and Pressures from Within

p. 165: It is always ... enormous front: Lionel Hastings, Baron Ismay, *The Memoirs of General the Lord Ismay K.G., P.C., G.C.B., C.H., D.S.O.* (Heinemann, London, 1960), p. 129.

p. 166: already reached ... continue the war: CAB 66/7/262, 18 May 1940.

p. 166: may give up the struggle: CAB 66/7/263, 18 May 1940.

p. 166: a telegram for those bloody Yankees: John Colville, *The Fringes of Power: Downing Street Diaries 1939–1955* (Hodder and Stoughton, London, 1985), 19 May 1940, p. 109.

p. 166: soothing words: Ibid.

pp. 166–7: In no conceivable ... German will: Churchill to President Roosevelt, 20 May 1940, Churchill Papers, 20/14, cited in Martin Gilbert, *The Churchill War Papers*, vol. 2: *Never Surrender: May 1940–December 1940* (William Heinemann, London, 1993).

p. 167: in a state of indecision: CAB 65/7/27, 21 May 1940.

p. 167: lost his temper ... completely beaten: Colonel Roderick Macleod, DSO, MC, and Denis Kelly (eds.), *The Ironside Diaries: 1937–1940* (Constable, London, 1962), 20 May 1940, p. 321.

p. 167: hundreds of thousands ... French towns: CAB 65/7/27, 21 May 1940.

p. 168: In all the history ... such mismanagement: Colville, *Fringes of Power*, p. 110.

p. 168: not seen Winston so depressed: Ibid.

p. 168: in spite of his ... his plan of war: Martin Gilbert, *Winston S. Churchill*, vol. 6: *Finest Hour, 1939–1941* (Heinemann, London, 1983), p. 57.

pp. 168–9: there were at Calais ... the town: Supreme War Council minutes, CAB 99/3, 22 May 1940.

p. 169: there could be no ... certain disaster: Ibid.

p. 169: not entirely satisfactory: Ibid.

p. 169: on a note of restrained optimism: Ismay, *Memoirs*, p. 130.

p. 169: almost in buoyant ... by Weygand: Macleod and Kelly (eds.), *Ironside Diaries*, p. 328.

p. 169: lost a chance ... and ammunition: Colville, *Fringes of Power*, p. 111.

pp. 169–70: really worried ... to that extent: Ibid.

p. 170: observed that ... time to mount: CAB 65/13/15, 22 May 1940.

p. 170: were not prepared ... doing so: Ibid.

p. 170: seemed to me ... means to mount it: The Rt Hon. The Earl of Avon KG, PC, MC, *The Eden Memoirs*, vol. 2: *The Reckoning* (Cassell, London, 1965), p. 108.

p. 170: **very much larger . . . become so critical:** CAB 65/7/3, 23 May 1940.

p. 171: **the whole success . . . of doing so:** Ibid.

p. 171: **seething mass . . . completely demoralised:** Ibid.

p. 171: **in danger of falling . . . Channel Ports:** Ibid.

pp. 171–2: **Signor Mussolini . . . declare war:** Ibid.

p. 172: **renews and reiterates . . . 'Yes, Sir':** Mr Gurney Braithwaite to Churchill, Hansard, HC Deb Series 5, 23 May 1940, vol. 361, c330W.

p. 173: **the Germans were . . . yet begun:** Gilbert, *Finest Hour*, pp. 384–5.

p. 173: **there was no reason . . . way to elation:** John Colville, *Man of Valour: The Life of Field-Marshal the Viscount Gort, VC, GCB, DSO, MVO, MC* (Collins, London, 1972), p. 213.

p. 173: **[T]he reason for . . . '. . . if *they* did':** Jock Colville in conversation with Martin Gilbert, 21 January 1981: Gilbert, *Finest Hour*, p. 385.

pp. 173–4: **been giving further . . . General Weygand's plan:** CAB 65/7/31, 23 May 1940.

p. 174: **The Prime Minister . . . probably be immense:** King George VI, diary, 23 May 1940, cited in John Wheeler-Bennett, *King George VI: His Life and Reign* (Macmillan, London, 1958), p. 456.

pp. 174–5: **War is usually . . . received no directive:** Telegram from Churchill to General Weygand, 24 May 1940, Churchill Papers, 20/14, cited in Gilbert, *Never Surrender*.

p. 175: **no (repeat no) . . . serious attack:** Ibid.

p. 175: **We have not here . . . at earliest?:** Ibid.

p. 175: **time is vital as supplies are short:** Telegram from Churchill to Reynaud, Churchill Papers, 20/14, cited in Gilbert, *Never Surrender*.

p. 176: **President Roosevelt ... opposite sides:** CAB 65/7/32, 24 May 1940.

p. 176: **that a reply ... on these lines:** Ibid.

p. 177: **The only effect of ... on its front:** Churchill to General Ismay, Churchill Papers, 4/150, cited in Gilbert, *Never Surrender*.

p. 177: **German tanks ... town and the sea:** CAB 69/1–24 May 1940.

p. 178: **Reinforcements urgent ... not overwhelmed:** 'Narrative of operations conducted from Dover May 21–26, 1940: Calais' (the Calais war diary), in NA/PRO ADM 199/795, cited in Hugh Sebag-Montefiore, *Dunkirk* (Viking, London, 2006), p. 228.

p. 178: **You must comply ... and fight on:** Calais war diary, NA/PRO WO 106/1693 and 1750, cited in Sebag-Montefiore, *Dunkirk*, p. 3.

p. 178: **all regular troops, and I need not say more:** Ibid., NA/PRO WO 106/1697.

p. 178: **Pray find out ... fight to the end:** Churchill to Anthony Eden and General Ironside, 25 May 1940, Churchill Papers, 4/150, cited in Gilbert, *Never Surrender*.

pp. 178–9: **To Brigadier Nicholson ... British name:** Calais war diary, NA/PRO WO 106/1750, 25 May 1940, cited in Sebag-Montefiore, *Dunkirk*, p. 230.

p. 180: **[an] Italian diplomat ... with a rebuff:** CAB 65/7/33, 25 May 1940.

p. 180: **very likely nothing ... their own policy:** Ibid.

p. 180: If it was to honour ... event whatsoever: Benito Mussolini to Churchill, 18 May 1940, cited in Winston S. Churchill, *The Second World War,* vol. II, *Their Finest Hour* (Cassell, London, 1949), pp. 107–8.

pp. 180–81: to an approach ... of weakness: CAB 65/7/33.

p. 181: it was very ... bargaining position: Ibid.

p. 181: the public don't grasp the situation at all: David Dilks (ed.), *The Diaries of Sir Alexander Cadogan O.M., 1938–1945* (Cassell, London, 1971), 23 May 1940, p. 288.

p. 181: STAY IN PARIS ... ALLIED FORCES: *Manchester Guardian,* 25 May 1940.

p. 181: ALLIES POUNDING ... STRONGLY DEFENDED: *News of the World,* 26 May 1940.

p. 182: FRANCE SACKS ... '... THE ENEMY': *Sunday Express,* 26 May 1940.

p. 182: NAZIS CLAIM ALLIED ... ENEMY LOSSES: *People,* 26 May 1940.

p. 182: NAVY GOES INTO ACTION ... SHELLS ENEMY: *Daily Mail,* 27 May 1940.

p. 182: 'ENORMOUS' GERMAN ... HELD TO-DAY: *Evening Standard,* 27 May 1940.

p. 182: FIGHTING IN THE ... ARMOURED DIVISIONS: *Daily Express,* 27 May 1940.

p. 183: the march to the sea: Churchill, *Their Finest Hour,* p. 66.

p. 183: be prepared ... Expeditionary Force: CAB 63/13/20, 26 May 1940.

p. 183: we had to face ... our own Empire: Ibid.

p. 184: Mussolini's principal ... peace in Europe: Ibid.

p. 184: we should naturally . . . were assured: Ibid.

p. 184: [P]eace and security . . . rights and power: Ibid.

pp. 184–5: a powerful lever . . . separate peace: Ibid.

p. 185: the Germans would . . . with England: Ibid.

p. 185: our ability to carry . . . out of gear: Ibid.

p. 186: while he would obey . . . in the Mediterranean: CAB 65/13/21, 26 May 1940.

p. 186: we were not prepared . . . in the war: Ibid.

p. 187: stick things out . . . entirely different: Ibid.

p. 187: the last thing that . . . have to consider: Ibid.

p. 188: too rambling and . . . and temperamental: Dilks (ed.), *Diaries of Sir Alexander Cadogan*, 23 May 1940, p. 288.

p. 188: it was incredible . . . jump at it: Neville Chamberlain, diary, 26 May 1940, cited in David Reynolds, 'Churchill and the British "Decision" to Fight on in 1940: Right Policy, Wrong Reasons', in Richard Langhorne (ed.), *Diplomacy and Intelligence during the Second World War* (Cambridge and New York, CUP, 2003), p. 152.

pp. 188–9: In the discussion . . . cession of territory: CAB 65/13/23, 27 May 1940.

p. 189: there was no limit . . . had her way: CAB 63/13/21, 26 May 1940.

p. 190: at the same time . . . serious fighting: Ibid.

p. 190: perhaps rather more . . . harm in trying: Ibid.

p. 191: take a line independent . . . point of view: Ibid.

p. 191: thought it was best . . . of the Force: Ibid.

p. 192: no such option . . . must part company: Ibid.

p. 192: At the same time . . . Signor Mussolini: Ibid.

p. 193: **if Paris was likely . . . serve any purpose?:** Ibid.

p. 193: **found that we could . . . not accept them:** Ibid.

p. 194: **He has a hundred . . . downright dangerous:** Cited in Nassir Ghaemi, *A First-Rate Madness: Uncovering the Links between Leadership and Mental Illness,* Penguin Books, London, 2011, p. 61.

p. 195: **The Prime Minister . . . French coast:** CAB 65/7/26, 20 May 1940.

p. 196: **hurling himself about . . . never give in:** Captain Berkley, diary, Berkley Papers, 26 May 1940, cited in Gilbert, *Never Surrender.*

p. 196: **Operation Dynamo is to commence:** Signal sent from the Admiralty, cited in L. F. Ellis, *The War in France and Flanders, 1939–1940* (London, HMSO, 1953), p. 182; Gilbert, *Never Surrender.*

p. 196: **fight it out until the bitter end:** Ismay, *Memoirs,* p. 131.

p. 197: **one of the most painful of the war:** The Rt Hon. The Earl of Avon, KG, PC, MC, *The Eden Memoirs,* vol. 2: *The Reckoning* (Cassell, London, 1965), p. 109.

p. 197: **unusually silent during . . . evident distaste:** Ismay, *Memoirs,* p. 131.

p. 197: **I feel physically sick:** Ibid.

9. Cabinet Crisis and Leadership

p. 201: **a bad situation . . . approaching Dunkirk:** Vice-Admiral Somerville to Churchill, 7.15 a.m., 27 May 1940, Premier Papers, 3/175, cited in Martin Gilbert,

The Churchill War Papers, vol. 2: *Never Surrender: May 1940–December 1940* (William Heinemann, London, 1993).

p. 201: **the King of the Belgians . . . with Germany:** CAB 65/7/36, 27 May 1940.

p. 201: **transferred themselves . . . the struggle:** Ibid.

p. 201: **considered that the . . . Hitler's protection:** Ibid.

p. 202: **impress on him . . . present choice:** Churchill to Roger Keyes, 27 May 1940, Churchill Papers, 20/14, cited in Gilbert, *Never Surrender*.

p. 202: **'[W]e are asking . . . themselves for us:** Churchill to Lord Gort, 27 May 1940, Churchill Papers, 20/14, cited in Gilbert, *Never Surrender*.

p. 202: **we should cede . . . our war debt:** CAB 65/7/36, 27 May 1940.

p. 202: **an offer of this kind . . . our security:** Ibid.

p. 202: **The United States . . . own defence:** Ibid.

pp. 202–3: **issue a general . . . of defeat:** CAB 65/13/22, 27 May 1940.

p. 203: **what are the . . . next meeting:** Churchill to Ismay, 27 May 1940, Churchill Papers, 20/13, cited in Gilbert, *Never Surrender*.

p. 203: **Cadogan:** The Hon. Sir Alexander Cadogan, Permanent Under-Secretary of State for Foreign Affairs.

p. 203: **Sinclair:** The Right Hon. Sir Archibald Sinclair, Bt, MP, Secretary of State for Air.

p. 203: **Bridges:** The Cabinet Secretary, Sir Edward Bridges.

p. 204: **If Signor Mussolini . . . these wishes:** CAB 66/7/50, 26 May 1940, 'Suggested Approach to Signor Mussolini'.

p. 204: **President Roosevelt . . . the Memorandum:** CAB 65/13/23, 27 May 1940.

p. 204: nothing would come . . . failing ally: Ibid.

pp. 204–5: would encourage the . . . terms for us: Ibid.

p. 205: If it got out that . . . those approaches: Ibid.

pp. 205–6: He was increasingly . . . Nazi tyranny: Ibid.

p. 207: while he agreed . . . complete refusal: Ibid.

p. 207: it was generally . . . course to take: Ibid.

p. 207: it does drive one . . . and reason: Lord Halifax, diary, 27 May 1940, Halifax Papers (Borthwick Institute, York), A7/8/3/, p. 142.

p. 208: profound differences of points of view: CAB 65/13/23, 27 May 1940.

p. 208: He could not . . . to disaster: Ibid.

pp. 208–9: On the present . . . avoidable disaster: Ibid.

p. 209: he would be . . . Cabinet Ministers: CAB 65/13/21, 26 May 1940.

p. 209: WC [Churchill] said . . . be content: Neville Chamberlain, diary, 26 May 1940, Neville Chamberlain Papers (University of Birmingham), 2/24A.

p. 210: Wars fought for ideas . . . much the better: Andrew Roberts, *The Holy Fox: A Biography of Lord Halifax* (Weidenfeld & Nicolson, London, 1991), p. 289.

p. 211: If Herr Hitler was . . . was one thing: CAB 65/13/23, 27 May 1940.

p. 211: It was quite . . . such offer: Ibid.

p. 212: The Foreign Secretary . . . discuss them?: Ibid.

p. 212: I thought Winston . . . would separate: Lord Halifax, diary, 27 May 1940, p. 142.

p. 214: surprised and mellowed: Ibid.

p. 214: that he would not . . . consider them: CAB 65/13/23, 27 May 1940.

p. 214: in good temper... on our own: Ibid.

p. 214: I can't work with Winston any longer: David Dilks (ed.), *The Diaries of Sir Alexander Cadogan O.M., 1938–1945* (Cassell, London, 1971), p. 291.

p. 214: Nonsense: his rodomontades ... stress of that: Ibid.

p. 215: the hyperbole which ... been avoidable: Roberts, *Holy Fox*, p. 298.

p. 215: full of apologies and affection: Lord Halifax, diary, 27 May 1940, p. 142.

p. 215: hoped he really ... hasty decisions: Dilks (ed.), *Diaries of Sir Alexander Cadogan*, p. 291.

p. 215: The Cabinet are ... and independence: John Colville, *The Fringes of Power: Downing Street Diaries 1939–1955* (Hodder and Stoughton, London, 1985), 19 May 1940, p. 109.

p. 216: even more desperate... on the way: CAB 69/1, 27 May 1940.

p. 216: were now paying ... was now faced: Ibid.

p. 216: telegraphed to his ... 27th–28th May: Telephone conversation between Major-General Sir Edward Spears and Churchill, 27 May 1940, Cabinet Papers, 65/7, cited in Gilbert, *Never Surrender*.

p. 216: The Defence Committee ... Belgian armistice: CAB 69/1, 27 May 1940.

pp. 216–17: importance of ensuring ... through to Dunkirk: Ibid.

pp. 217–18: a statement should be issued ... to do so: CAB 65/7/38, 27 May 1940.

p. 218: at midnight ... went up to bed: Colville, *Fringes of Power*, p. 109.

p. 218: a very black day: Lord Halifax, diary, 28 May 1940, p. 143.

p. 218: Belgian Government . . . cracked at once: CAB 65/7/39, 28 May 1940.

p. 219: All Belgian troops . . . will be overcome: Ibid.

p. 219: Considerable numbers . . . would be serious: Ibid.

p. 220: for a frank . . . short statement: Ibid.

pp. 220–21: The situation of the . . . our enemies: Churchill, Hansard, HC Deb Series 5, 28 May 1940, vol. 361, cc.421–2.

p. 221: [W]e have not yet . . . this country: Mr Lees-Smith, in ibid.

p. 221: the dignified statement . . . whole nation: Sir Percy Harris, in ibid.

p. 221: an atmosphere . . . impending doom: Roberts, *The Holy Fox*, p. 300.

p. 221: wholly negative reply: CAB 65/13/24, 28 May 1940.

p. 221: we should give a . . . mediation by Italy: Ibid.

pp. 221–2: clear that the French . . . this position: Ibid.

p. 222: that we should say . . . make to Italy: Ibid.

p. 222: the French were trying . . . this country: Ibid.

p. 223: wider aspect . . . consider such terms: Ibid.

p. 223: we must not ignore . . . months' time: Ibid.

p. 223: Signor Mussolini . . . to us now: Ibid.

pp. 223–4: so wrong . . . offered to us: Ibid.

p. 224: [T]he nations which . . . as ultimate capitulation: Ibid.

p. 224: it was necessary . . . of the people: Ibid.

pp. 224–5: although grievous . . . present time: Ibid.

p. 225: one of the most . . . scenes of the war: Martin Gilbert, *Winston S. Churchill*, vol. 6: *Finest Hour, 1939–1941* (Heinemann, London, 1983), p. 419.

pp. 227–9: In the afternoon . . . upon the ground: Ben Pimlott (ed.), *The Second World War Diary of Hugh Dalton* (Jonathan Cape, London, 1985), pp. 27–8.

p. 230: There occurred . . . all the people: Winston S. Churchill, *The Second World War*, vol. II, *Their Finest Hour* (Cassell, London, 1949), p. 88.

pp. 230–31: They had not expressed . . . so emphatically: CAB 65/13/24, 28 May 1940.

p. 231: Another Cabinet at 4 . . . last approach: Lord Halifax, diary, 28 May 1940, p. 144.

pp. 231–2: There was a white . . . end to end: Churchill, *Their Finest Hour*, p. 88.

10. 'Fight on the beaches'

p. 233: THE LUFTWAFFE . . . TWENTY-FIVE VESSELS: Douglas C. Dildy, *Dunkirk 1940: Operation Dynamo* (Osprey, Oxford, 2010), p. 9.

p. 235: magical . . . being sent to Rome: General Sir Edward Spears, *Assignment to Catastrophe*, 2 vols. (William Heinemann, London, 1954), vol. 1, p. 255.

pp. 235–6: In these dark days . . . and our Cause: Churchill to Cabinet ministers and senior officials, 29 May 1940, Premier Papers, 4/68/9, cited in Martin Gilbert, *The Churchill War Papers*, vol. 2: *Never Surrender: May 1940 –December 1940* (William Heinemann, London, 1993).

p. 236: Italy's entry into . . . and his alone: CAB 65/7/41, 29 May 1940.

p. **236: unpleasant:** David Dilks (ed.), *The Diaries of Sir Alexander Cadogan O.M., 1938–1945* (Cassell, London, 1971), p. 292.

pp. **236–7: definite guidance ... the last resort:** CAB 65/13/25, 29 May 1940.

p. **237: to continue the struggle ... the Germans:** Ibid.

p. **237: [He] was not altogether ... from massacre:** Ibid.

p. **237: [i]n a desperate situation ... to Lord Gort:** Ibid.

p. **238: A Commander ... resistance and capitulation:** Ibid.

pp. **238–9: Lord Gort might well ... suggested by [Attlee]:** Ibid.

p. **239: [a] horrible discussion ... theatricality:** Dilks (ed.), *The Diaries of Sir Alexander Cadogan*, p. 292.

pp. **239–40: essential that the ... possible, arise:** Churchill to Anthony Eden, General Ismay and General Dill, 29 May 1940, Premier Papers, 3/175, cited in Gilbert, *Never Surrender*.

p. **240: Your reports most ... whatever they do:** Churchill to General Spears, 29 May 1940, FO Papers, 800/312, cited in Gilbert, *Never Surrender*, p. 000.

p. **240: If you are cut ... in your hands:** Churchill to Lord Gort, 29 May 1940, Premier Papers, 3/175, cited in Gilbert, *Never Surrender*, p. 000.

p. **240: in great form:** Colonel Roderick Macleod, DSO, MC, and Denis Kelly (eds.), *The Ironside Diaries: 1937–1940* (Constable, London, 1962), p. 344.

p. **240: Winston's ceaseless industry is impressive:** John Colville, *The Fringes of Power: Downing Street Diaries 1939–1955* (Hodder and Stoughton, London, 1985), p. 115.

p. 240: French troops to share ... new BEF: Churchill to Reyanud , 29 May 1940, Premier Papers, 3/175, cited in Gilbert, *Never Surrender.*

pp. 240–41: this is only ... troops in France: Ibid.

p. 241: in all comradeship ... frankly to me: Ibid.

p. 241: God bless you ... with you myself: Captain Pim, recollection, 29 May 1940, Pim Papers, cited in Gilbert, *Never Surrender.*

p. 241: still soaking wet ... our salvation: John Spencer-Churchill, *Crowded Canvas* (Odhams Press, London, 1961), pp. 162–3.

p. 241: fog was now ... with the evacuation: CAB 65/7/43, 30 May 1940.

p. 242: General Weygand ... all the difference: CAB 65/13/26, 30 May 1940.

p. 242: as we must ... the present moment: Ibid.

p. 242: always preferred to see ... at first hand: Lionel Hastings, Baron Ismay, *The Memoirs of General the Lord Ismay K.G., P.C., G.C.B., C.H., D.S.O.* (Heinemann, London, 1960); p. 136.

p. 242: [t]he British Army ... could continue: CAB 69/1, 30 May 1940.

p. 242: irreparable harm: Ibid.

p. 243: straggling masses ... they were able: Ex-Detective Inspector W. H. Thompson, *I was Churchill's Shadow* (Christopher Johnson, London, 1951), p. 41.

p. 243: [h]e was brave ... enter his mind: Ismay, *Memoirs*, p. 133.

pp. 243–4: up to noon on that day ... to the British: CAB 99/3, 31 May 1940.

pp. 244–5: Dunkirk could not . . . from the North: Ibid.

pp. 245–6: He could not believe . . . a few days: Ibid.

p. 246: he entirely agreed . . . their history: Ibid.

p. 246: at a psychological . . . supreme value: Sir Ronald Campbell to Lord Halifax, 31 May 1940, Foreign Office Papers, 800/212, cited in Gilbert, *Never Surrender*.

pp. 246–7: He handled the French . . . to bondage: Ibid.

p. 247: disorderly . . . it is irritating: Lord Halifax, diary, 30 May 1940, Halifax Papers (Borthwick Institute, York), A7/8/4, p. 146.

p. 247: typically intended . . . in the audience: definition of peroration, *Oxford English Dictionary* (Oxford University Press, Oxford, 2017).

p. 248: The King says . . . France as well!: Ben Pimlott (ed.), *The Second World War Diary of Hugh Dalton* (Jonathan Cape, London, 1985), 31 May 1940, p. 31.

p. 248: Operation Dynamo . . . and expectation: Ismay, *Memoirs*, p. 135.

p. 248: Dunkirk was worth . . . United States: Lord Halifax, diary, 30 May 1940, p. 147.

p. 248: events were moving . . . United States: CAB 65/7/46, 1 June 1940.

p. 248: about sending the . . . to beat them: Colville, *Fringes of Power*, p. 115.

p. 248: I believe we shall . . . can be permitted: Churchill to Desmond Morton, Premier Papers, 7/2, cited in Gilbert, *Never Surrender*.

p. 249: emphasised the importance . . . naval losses: CAB 79/4, 1 June 1940.

p. 250: **There are few grounds . . . the forces:** Harold Nicolson, *Diaries and Letters 1930–1964*, ed. Stanley Olson (Penguin Books, Harmondsworth, 1984), 1 June 1940, p. 186.

p. 250: **What will Europe . . . has overrun:** Pimlott (ed.), *Second World War Diary of Hugh Dalton*, 3 June 1940, p. 34.

p. 250: **Everything is conspiring . . . island people:** R. R. James (ed.), *Chips: The Diaries of Sir Henry Channon* (Weidenfeld & Nicolson, London, 1993), 2 June 1940, p. 255.

pp. 250–51: **Through all those terrible . . . Britain depended:** Sir John Martin, *Downing Street: The War Years* (Bloomsbury, London, 1991), p. 5.

p. 251: **a little rough on the French High Command:** Anthony Eden to Churchill, 3 June 1940, Churchill Papers, CHAR 9/172/104.

p. 251: **Even though the . . . more darkly:** Churchill, speech notes for 4 June 1940, Churchill Papers, CHAR 9/172/23.

p. 252: **express sympathy! . . . and missing:** Ibid., CHAR 9/172/16.

p. 252: **tremendous care . . . psalm form:** Interview with Sir John Martin in 1973, BBC Archives, 'Remembering Winston Churchill', http://www.bbc.co.uk/archive/churchill/11021.shtml.

p. 253: **[a] miracle of deliverance . . . by evacuations:** Churchill, Hansard, War Situation, HC Deb Series 4, 4 June 1940, vol. 361, cc.787–98.

p. 253: **Could there have . . . thousand airmen:** Ibid.

pp. 253–4: **There had never . . . noble knight:** Ibid.

p. 254: **Continental tyrants:** Ibid.

pp. 254–5: **I have, myself . . . liberation of the old:** Ibid.

p. 255: **The speech was . . . were in tears:** James (ed.), *Chips*, 2 June 1940, p. 255.

p. 255: who had the lion … give the roar: Churchill, speech to Westminster Hall, 30 November 1954, for his eightieth birthday, Churchill Papers, CHAR 5/56B/235.

p. 255: fight them on … behind Paris: Georges Clemenceau, speech in Paris, November 1918, cited in Donald McCormick, *The Mask of Merlin: A Critical Study of David Lloyd George* (Macdonald, London, 1963), p. 143.

p. 256: the orator is … the multitude: Winston S. Churchill 'The Scaffolding of Rhetoric', Churchill Papers, CHAR 8/13/1–13.

p. 256: vividly and directly … highly coloured: Winston S. Churchill, *Blood, Toil, Tears and Sweat: The Great Speeches*, ed. David Cannadine (Penguin Books, London/New York, 2007), Introduction, p. xxii.

pp. 256–7: Of all the talents … the direction: Churchill 'Scaffolding of Rhetoric'.

Epilogue: If the Truth be Told

pp. 260–61: It will be found … write that history: Churchill, Hansard, Commons Sitting, HC Deb, 23 January 1948, vol. 446, cc.556–62.

p. 262: There is more … these hands: See e.g. Nigel Jones, 'Churchill and Hitler: At Arms, at Easels', *History Today*, vol. 64, Issue 5, May 2014.

p. 262: at once simple … deception or intrigue: Winston S. Churchill, *Blood, Toil, Tears and Sweat: The Great Speeches*, ed. David Cannadine (Penguin Books, London/New York, 2007), Introduction, p. xxii.

Index

He just wanted a decent book to read ...

Not too much to ask, is it? It was in 1935 when Allen Lane, Managing Director of Bodley Head Publishers, stood on a platform at Exeter railway station looking for something good to read on his journey back to London. His choice was limited to popular magazines and poor-quality paperbacks – the same choice faced every day by the vast majority of readers, few of whom could afford hardbacks. Lane's disappointment and subsequent anger at the range of books generally available led him to found a company – and change the world.

'We believed in the existence in this country of a vast reading public for intelligent books at a low price, and staked everything on it'
Sir Allen Lane, 1902–1970, founder of Penguin Books

The quality paperback had arrived – and not just in bookshops. Lane was adamant that his Penguins should appear in chain stores and tobacconists, and should cost no more than a packet of cigarettes.

Reading habits (and cigarette prices) have changed since 1935, but Penguin still believes in publishing the best books for everybody to enjoy. We still believe that good design costs no more than bad design, and we still believe that quality books published passionately and responsibly make the world a better place.

So wherever you see the little bird – whether it's on a piece of prize-winning literary fiction or a celebrity autobiography, political tour de force or historical masterpiece, a serial-killer thriller, reference book, world classic or a piece of pure escapism – you can bet that it represents the very best that the genre has to offer.

Whatever you like to read – trust Penguin.